Lecture Notes in Computer Science 15559

Founding Editors

Gerhard Goos
Juris Hartmanis

W0193278

The series Lecture Notes in Computer Science (LNCS), including its subseries Lecture Notes in Artificial Intelligence (LNAI) and Lecture Notes in Bioinformatics (LNBI), has established itself as a medium for the publication of new developments in computer science and information technology research, teaching, and education.

LNCS enjoys close cooperation with the computer science R & D community, the series counts many renowned academics among its volume editors and paper authors, and collaborates with prestigious societies. Its mission is to serve this international community by providing an invaluable service, mainly focused on the publication of conference and workshop proceedings and postproceedings. LNCS commenced publication in 1973.

Xianhui Lu · Chris J. Mitchell
Editors

Security Standardisation Research

9th International Conference, SSR 2024
Kunming, China, December 16, 2024
Proceedings

 Springer

Editors
Xianhui Lu 🆔
Institute of Information Engineering
Beijing, China

Chris J. Mitchell 🆔
University of London
Egham, Surrey, UK

ISSN 0302-9743   ISSN 1611-3349 (electronic)
Lecture Notes in Computer Science
ISBN 978-3-031-87540-3   ISBN 978-3-031-87541-0 (eBook)
https://doi.org/10.1007/978-3-031-87541-0

This Springer imprint is published by the registered company Springer Nature Switzerland AG
The registered company address is: Gewerbestrasse 11, 6330 Cham, Switzerland

If disposing of this product, please recycle the paper.

Preface

The Security Standardization Research (SSR) Conference 2024 was the 9th iteration of the SSR conference series, launched in 2014. SSR 2024 was co-located with Inscrypt 2024 in Kunming, China, and took place on December 16th, 2024.

In the past two decades, cybersecurity standards have advanced significantly and many of them have become very widely used. Despite their widespread use, it is essential to continually revise existing standards and develop new standards to cover emerging domains, such as post-quantum cryptography, fully homomorphic encryption, 6G and artificial intelligence. The purpose of the 2024 SSR conference was to discuss the numerous research challenges arising from studies of existing standards, the development of revisions to these standards, and the exploration of entirely new areas of standardization. Many security standards bodies are only beginning to address the issue of transparency, ensuring that the process of selecting security techniques for standardization is as scientific and unbiased as possible.

The SSR conference series covers the full spectrum of research on security standardization, including, but not restricted to, work on cryptographic techniques, security management, security evaluation criteria, security policy, network security, privacy and identity management, smart cards and RFID tags, biometrics, security modules, and industry-specific security standards (e.g. those produced by the payments, telecommunications and computing industries for such things as payment protocols, mobile telephony and trusted computing). Through these discussions and research presentations, the conference series aims to advance the field of security standardization, fostering a collaborative environment for both revising existing standards and developing new ones to address the evolving challenges in cybersecurity. We are pleased to say that the SSR 2024 programme reflected our goal of achieving a broad coverage of the area.

We received a total of 19 high-quality submissions to SSR 2024 via the EasyChair conference management system, a pleasing increase on numbers submitted to recent iterations of the event. Each submission was reviewed by at least three members of the program committee in a mutually anonymous way. After a period of discussion, we chose to accept only 7 (i.e. 37%) of the submissions for presentation at the conference. We are very grateful to the 26 excellent members of the programme committee for proving detailed reviews in a prompt way.

As has recently become established practice for this conference series, we again explicitly solicited submissions beyond regular research papers. More specifically, we invited papers providing a systematization of knowledge (SoK) of areas related to security standardization; we also encouraged the submission of vision papers relating to security standardization, with an emphasis on sparking discussions on work in progress or concrete ideas for work that has yet to begin. We were very happy to see those ideas reflected in the final program, which was made up of five research papers, one SoK paper, and one vision paper.

We were delighted to have two distinguished invited (keynote) speakers who contributed their expertise and perspectives from both academia and the standardization community to the SSR 2024 program.

- Lily Chen from NIST in the USA;
- Liqun Chen from the University of Surrey in the UK.

We would like to sincerely thank everyone who contributed to the success of SSR 2024. First and foremost, we must thank all the authors for submitting their work to the conference, and the speakers at the conference for making such a valuable contribution to the conference program. We are, of course, heavily indebted to the program committee, which, as we already mentioned, did a great job in the interactive discussion and by providing thorough reviews — it was a pleasure to work with you. We would like to offer our gratitude and thanks to the general chair Guilin Wang, and the organizing and publicity chair Limin Liu; without their hard work and dedication the conference could never have happened. The generous sponsorship of Huawei is acknowledged with our grateful thanks. Finally, we must thank all attendees of SSR 2024.

December 2024   Xianhui Lu
                                                                     Chris J. Mitchell

Organization

General Chair

Guilin Wang   Huawei International Pte Ltd, Singapore

Program Committee Chairs

Xianhui Lu   Chinese Academy of Sciences, China
Chris J. Mitchell   Royal Holloway, University of London, UK

Steering Committee

Liqun Chen   University of Surrey, UK
Shin'Ichiro Matsuo   Georgetown University, USA
Bart Preneel   Katholieke Universiteit Leuven, Belgium

Organizing and Publicity Chair

Limin Liu   Institute of Information Engineering, CAS, China

Program Committee

Aysajan Abidin   Katholieke Universiteit Leuven, Belgium
Sofía Celi   Brave, Portugal
Lily Chen   NIST, USA
Yu Chen   Shandong University, China
Zhaohui Cheng   Olym Info Sec Inc, China
Benjamin Curtis   Zama, UK
Benjamin Dowling   University of Sheffield, UK
Huijing Gong   Intel Labs, USA
Matt Henricksen   Huawei International Pte Ltd, Singapore
Stephan Krenn   AIT Austrian Institute of Technology, Austria
Thalia Laing   HP Security Lab, UK
Shin'Ichiro Matsuo   Georgetown University, USA

Yanbin Pan	Academy of Mathematics and Systems Science, CAS, China
Christopher Patton	Cloudflare, USA
Bertram Poettering	IBM Research Zurich, Switzerland
Gaëtan Pradel	Incert, Luxembourg
Kazue Sako	Waseda Universaity, Japan
Alan Sherman	University of Maryland, Baltimore County, USA
Christoph Striecks	AIT Austrian Institute of Technology, Austria
Jacques Traore	Orange Labs, France
Mathy Vanhoef	Katholieke Universiteit Leuven, Belgium
Guilin Wang	Huawei International Pte Ltd, Singapore
Gaven J. Watson	Meta, USA
Christian Weinert	Royal Holloway, University of London, UK
Kazuki Yoneyama	Ibaraki University, Japan
Yu Yu	Shanghai Jiao Tong University, China

Additional Reviewers

Keita Xagawa
Jing Xu

NIST Post-Quantum Cryptography Standardization — What did we learn? (Extended Abstract)

Lily Lidong Chen

National Institute of Technology and Standards, Gaithersburg, MD, 20899-8930 USA

NIST published the first set of Post-Quantum Cryptography (PQC) Standards on August 13, 2024, after a journey of eight years. This presentation shares NIST's experience in developing PQC Standards. It reviews the progress made in the past eight years and provides an update on the status. The presentation highlights challenges and explores strategies for the migration to PQC standards.

NIST announced a call for proposals for PQC candidates in 2016. Before the announcement, NIST had surveyed the state-of-the-art research on PQC and explored requirements and criteria for the candidates. Even though PQC has been a very active research area in the past two decades, it takes extensive effort to develop standards. To make standards applicable, it is necessary to balance theoretical security and practical useability. Furthermore, it is rather challenging to gain confidence in PQC algorithms in a matter of five to six years. The first lesson we learned is that community engagement is the key. Without such a huge community effort, NIST could not achieve its milestones in such a short period of time. This presentation will demonstrate the community effort and communications during the PQC standardization process through pqc-forum discussions, NIST reports, workshops, and public feedback on draft standards.

Today, public-key cryptography has been deployed everywhere. Before NIST started the PQC standardization process, we had very much hoped that we could find drop-in replacements for the well-deployed public-key cryptosystems such as RSA and ECC to make the minimum impact on applications. But it turned out that the PQC standards are not exact drop-in replacements. Applications have been dealing with the larger keys and signatures for PQC. It shows industry's capability in adapting the new algorithms for existing protocols and applications. The presentation shares our pathway in understanding the challenges of the PQC transition.

The NIST PQC standardization process has promoted extensive research. The attacks on some candidates and finalists have shown great breakthroughs in cryptanalysis of PQC algorithms. The process has accelerated our learning about PQC designs and their implications in security. The extensive research is critical for gaining confidence in PQC standards. In this presentation, we highlight how the extensive research has advanced techniques for designing PQC algorithms.

The transition to PQC is more than just from quantum vulnerable to quantum resistant. It is a transition to cryptographic standards with advanced security concepts in mind. It has reflected the research in the past few decades and included state-of-the-art cryptographic algorithm design ideas. PQC is a starting point for a new age of cryptographic standards. The presentation lays out a plan for NIST's next steps after publishing the first set of PQC standards. It includes developing guidance for using PQC standards in different applications and updating the existing standards to coordinate with the newly introduced PQC standards. It also introduces NIST's collaborations with industry through the "Migration to PQC" project at the National Cybersecurity Center of Excellence.

In summary, the presentation shares NIST's journey in developing PQC standards with security standards researchers.

Contents

Invited Keynote Talks

Standardisation of and Migration to Post-Quantum Cryptography

Liqun Chen[✉]

University of Surrey, Guildford, UK
liqun.chen@surrey.ac.uk

Abstract. Recent reports on the timeline of quantum threats suggest that large, scalable quantum computers will likely become a reality in the near future. This impending technological advancement has increased the urgency for standardisation of and migration to Post-Quantum Cryptography (PQC), making it a critical focus for information and cybersecurity experts. In this document, we will provide an overview of the current state of standardisation efforts in the field of PQC and explore its implications across various sectors, including industry, academic research, open-source development, and government agencies. Additionally, we will address some future work that remains unaddressed within existing standardisation initiatives, offering insights into the areas that require further attention and development.

1 Introduction

When I came across claims from some online data backup services stating that they can preserve data backups for 100 years, I began to wonder whether their data protection relies on cryptography. If that is the case, what types of cryptographic algorithms could possibly remain secure for 100 years? From my understanding, any widely used and effective cryptographic algorithm tends to have a limited lifespan. History has shown us this: many elegant algorithms, such as DES, MD5, RC2 and SHA-1, have been compromised over time.

Now, we face an even greater risk: the rise of quantum computers, which makes Post-Quantum Cryptography (PQC) increasingly important. Is migrating to PQC necessary? Following Shor's algorithm and Grover's algorithm, many experts believe the answer is a resounding yes. Peter Shor's algorithm [23] demonstrates that quantum computers are capable of solving mathematical problems that are difficult or intractable for conventional computers (e.g. the factorisation problem and the discrete logarithm problem). Current public-key cryptographic solutions rely on these computationally hard problems to make them secure. If large-scale quantum computers are built they will be able to break most of the cryptographic asymmetric-key algorithms currently in use. Therefore, these public-key cryptography algorithms need to be changed to protect against a potential future quantum computer. Lov Grover's algorithm [8] could brute-force an n-bit symmetric cryptographic key in roughly $2^{n/2}$ iterations. While Grover's algorithm may not pose a significantly increased risk to encryption over existing

© The Author(s), under exclusive license to Springer Nature Switzerland AG 2025
X. Lu and C. J. Mitchell (Eds.): SSR 2024, LNCS 15559, pp. 3–13, 2025.
https://doi.org/10.1007/978-3-031-87541-0_1

classical symmetric cryptographic algorithms, updating security parameters for those algorithms will need to be considered in the future.

How urgent is this migration? Opinions vary on this issue. While some still doubt that large-scale quantum computers will be developed in the near future, many scientists, governments, and industrial researchers argue that building a functional quantum computer is primarily an engineering challenge. For example, predictions [16] suggest that within the next 10 to 15 years, quantum computers will be capable of breaking the RSA-2048 scheme, which is currently widely used. According to the Global Risk Institute,s quantum threat timeline report [10], the 2024 estimates indicate a cumulative 10% probability of a digital quantum computer being able to break RSA-2048 in just 5 years, escalating to 85% in 30 years. This all demonstrates that research on how to move smoothly from the existing public-key cryptographic infrastructures to new quantum-resistant ones is necessary and urgent.

2   Standardisation of Migrating to PQC

Who determines when and how we should migrate? It's the standards bodies! Many people are awaiting recommendations from these organizations. For migration to be effective, we need a consensus on algorithms, which are provided by cryptographic standards.

Interestingly, although cryptography has been in existence for thousands of years - dating back to the Scytale used by the Spartans around 500 BC - established cryptographic standards have only emerged in the past 50 years. An old cipher algorithm acts like a black box, remaining secure only if its inner workings are not disclosed. In contrast, for modern cryptography to be widely utilized, it impractical to keep algorithms secret. This highlights the need for standardised cryptographic algorithms.

To secure global communications, it is essential to have universal standards that ensure interoperability. A global standard can be embraced internationally and is not subject to the control of any single country or agency. Maintaining international standards is crucial for industries as it offers a degree of legal protection. According to the World Trade Organization (WTO), a country that adheres to international standards is less likely to face legal challenges within the WTO than a country that establishes its own standards [20].

There are many standards bodies for cryptographic algorithms, protocols and services. For example:

- ISO/IEC JTC 1/SC 27/WG 2 is a working group of the International Organization for Standardization/International Electrotechnical Commission (ISO/IEC) Joint Technical Committee 1 Subcommittee 27. This subcommittee has developed and standardised methods, technologies, and guidelines for information security, cybersecurity, and privacy protection. Specifically, Working Group 2 (WG 2) focuses on developing and standardising cryptographic and other security mechanisms.

- The National Institute of Standards and Technology (NIST) issues specifications and guidelines for cryptography as the USA Federal Information Processing standards.
- The American National Standards Institute (ANSI) Data and Information Security Subcommittee (X9F) generates cryptographic mechanisms standards for the financial services industry.
- The Security Experts Group of the European Telecommunications Standards Institute (ETSI SAGE) reports in the area of cryptographic algorithms and protocols specific to public/private telecommunications networks. Their remarkable work includes GSM, 3GPP, TETRA, TIPHON, SPAN, TISPAN, etc.
- The Institute of Electrical and Electronics Engineers (IEEE) has many remarkable Standard Projects, which have specified many well-known cryptographic and security mechanisms, such as 802.11i, 802.1X, etc. A standardisation project for public-key cryptography (IEEE P1363) provides standard specifications for public-key cryptography.
- The Internet Engineering Task Force (IETF) creates voluntary standards, e.g., Request For Comments (RFC) for cryptographic solutions, such as IP Security Protocols, Transport Layer Security, Public-Key Infrastructure (X.509), S/MIME Mail Security, etc.
- The Trusted Computing Group (TCG) develops and specifies Trusted Platform Modules (TPM) and their various services and applications.
- The International Telecommunication Union Telecommunication Standardization Sector (ITU-T) develops standards for telecommunications and Information Communication Technology (ICT), including cryptographic mechanisms, such as X509, Public-key and attribute certification.

Algorithm	Version (category)	Function	Specification
ML-KEM	ML-KEM-512 (1) ML-KEM-768 (3) ML-KEM-1024 (5)	Module-Lattice-based Key-Encapsulation Mechanism	NIST FIPS 203
ML-DSA	ML-DSA-44 (2) ML-DSA-65 (3) ML-DSA-87 (5)	Module-Lattice-Based Digital Signature Algorithm	NIST FIPS 204
SLH-DSA	4 versions (1) 4 versions (3) 4 versions (5)	Stateless Hash-Based Digital Signature Algorithm	NIST FIPS 205
LMS	Multiple versions	Stateful Hash-Based Digital Signature Algorithm	NIST SP 800-208
XMSS	Multiple versions	Stateful Hash-Based Digital Signature Algorithm	NIST SP 800-208
Falcon		Digital signature algorithm	Available later

Fig. 1. NIST PQC (draft) standards.

As for standardisation of post-quantum cryptography, all of these standards bodies have been actively involved. Particularly NIST, who have played a leading role, selected and specified one Key Encapsulation Mechanism (KEM) and several digital signature schemes, as shown in Fig. 1. The security categories include levels from 1 to 5 [18]. In addition, NIST currently has two more ongoing standardisation activities, the 4th round public-key encryption and key-establishment algorithms, and additional digital signature schemes [19].

The PQC standardisation activities of ISO/IEC JTC 1/SC 27/WG 2 is summarised in Fig. 2. Four KEMs have been selected and their specifications are under development. Note that currently ISO/IEC does not include ML-KEM-512 or any other security level 1 mechanisms. The standard for two stateful hash-based signature schemes has recently been published as ISO/IEC 14888-4 [11].

Algorithm	Version (category)	Function	Specification
Classic McEliece KEM	16 versions	Code-based KEM	ISO/IEC 18033-2/ WD Amendment
FrodoKEM	4 versions	LWE-based KEM	ISO/IEC 18033-2/ WD Amendment
ML-KEM*	ML-KEM-768 (3) ML-KEM-1024 (5)	Module-Lattice-based KEM	ISO/IEC 18033-2/ WD Amendment
LMS	Multiple versions	Stateful Hash-Based Signature	ISO/IEC 14888-4
XMSS	Multiple versions	Stateful Hash-Based Signature	ISO/IEC 14888-4
NTRU		Module-Lattice-based KEM	ISO/IEC PWI 29192-4

* Currently ISO/IEC does not include ML-KEM-512 or any other security level 1 mechanisms.

Fig. 2. ISO/IEC PQC (draft) standards.

The IETF has begun specifying lattice-based KEMs and digital signatures, as well as stateful hash-based signature schemes, as outlined in Fig. 3.

The IETF also focuses on standardising post-quantum protocols, e.g.

– Use of SLH-DSA in the Cryptographic Message Syntax (CMS);
– Internet X.509 PKI: Algorithm identifiers for ML-KEM;
– Internet X.509 PKI: Algorithm identifiers for ML-DSA;
– IPSec maintenance and extensions (ipsecme);
– Mixing preshared keys in the Internet Key Exchange Protocol Version 2 (IKEv2) for Post-quantum Security;
– Intermediate Exchange in IKEv2;
– Multiple Key Exchanges in IKEv2;

Algorithm	Function	Specification
XMSS	Stateful Hash-Based Signature	RFC 8391
LMS	Stateful Hash-Based Signature	RFC 8554
Kyber	Module-Lattice-based KEM	RFC under development, https://www.ietf.org/archive/id/draft–cfrg–schwabe–kyber–04.html
FALCON	Lattice-based Signature	RFC under development, https://datatracker.ietf.org/doc/draft–uni–qsckeys–falcon/

Fig. 3. IETF (draft) standards for PQC algorithms.

– Hybrid key exchange in TLS 1.3;
– TLS 1.3 extension for certificate-based authentication with an external pre-shared key;
– JOSE and COSE encoding for post-quantum signatures;
– Terminology for post-quantum traditional hybrid schemes.

The ETSI has published migration strategies and recommendations for PQC schemes, along with the technical specification ETSI TS 103 744 V1.1.1 (2020) [4], which focuses on quantum-safe hybrid key exchanges by using CYBER.

ITU-T published a technical report [13], which provides an overview of the standardisation activities related to hybrid key exchange approaches for transitioning to quantum-safe algorithms or protocols. Hybrid key exchange involves creating a key exchange functionality by combining at least two different key exchange methods. The report examines how to integrate quantum key distribution protocols within the framework of these hybrid key exchange approaches.

The TCG is preparing for TPMs to support PQC [24,25].

IEEE P1363 standardised several lattice-based schemes in IEEE 1363.1-2008 [9], including mathematical primitives for secret value (key) derivation, public-key encryption, identification and digital signatures, and cryptographic schemes based on those primitives. However, this standard was withdrawn in 2019.

3 Approaches for Migrating to PQC

Migrating to Post-Quantum Cryptography (PQC) can be approached in two main ways, similar to how one would transition between cryptographic algorithms. The first approach is known as "algorithm renewal", which involves moving from a weaker algorithm to a stronger one. The second approach is referred to as "algorithm agility", which allows for the use of multiple algorithms simultaneously.

Both ISO/IEC 18014 time-stamping services [12] and ANSI X9.95 time stamp management and security [2] have outlined processes for algorithm renewal. Regarding algorithm agility, the Trusted Computing Group (TCG) has established an algorithm registry to facilitate this flexibility within Trusted Platform Modules (TPM) [7]. Current standardisation efforts in PQC by organisations like NIST and ISO/IEC serve as examples of promoting algorithm agility.

To decide how to migrate to PQC, we need to consider two key requirements:

- data confidentiality, and
- data authenticity and integrity.

For data confidentiality, we must prepare for the "harvest now, decrypt later" threat. The duration for which we need to maintain data confidentiality depends on the lifespan of the cryptographic algorithms used to protect the data. If any single algorithm is not entirely trustworthy, it is advisable to use a hybrid solution or combine multiple algorithms. Overall, ensuring long-term data confidentiality provides a significant challenge.

Regarding data authenticity and integrity, we can establish long-term solutions using short-term cryptographic algorithms. This approach is particularly suitable for digital signatures. It is based on the premise that while individual cryptographic mechanisms may only be secure for a short time, cryptography as a whole can provide long-term security. In this context, a long-term solution can be defined as one that is not limited by the lifetimes of the underlying cryptographic algorithms. A common example of this idea is time-stamping. If someone wishes to prove the existence of their data through a time-stamping service over an extended period, this can be accomplished effectively.

Fig. 4. Timeline of cryptographic algorithm lifetime and renewal

Meng and Chen [15] present a timeline of cryptographic algorithm lifetime and renewal, as shown in Fig. 4. For $i \in [1, n]$ with an integer n, let c_i be a single cryptographic algorithm or a set of algorithms, which have a secure lifetime covering the interval between t_i and t_i' and which are used in the time period between t_i and t_{i+1}, where $t_i' \geq t_{i+1}$. At time t_i, c_{i-1} and c_i are both secure, but c_i is stronger than c_{i-1}, so this is the right time to renew c_{i-1} to c_i.

4   Many Other Bodies Play Their Roles

Cryptography is not exclusively the domain of cryptographers; it involves a variety of stakeholders and regulatory bodies. Many groups contribute to the transition to Post-Quantum Cryptography (PQC), including governments, open-source developers, and industry players. Below are some examples of their activities, although this is not an exhaustive list.

4.1   Actions from Governments

Governments have taken various actions to facilitate the transition towards post-quantum cryptography. The following are a few examples:

- European Commission published recommendation on post-quantum cryptography [3].
- The Dutch government published the PQC migration handbook [1].
- The UK National Cyber Security Centre (NCSC) released a whitepaper providing guidance for system and risk owners to plan their migration to PQC [17].
- The US government has provided recommendations around migrating to quantum-resistant cryptographic algorithms, recommending that, for sensitive systems, quantum-resistant cryptography be used from 2025 and be required from 2030 [18].
- Singapore has issued an advisory for Financial Institutions (FIs) to mitigate quantum computing risks [14] and suggests developing crypto agility to tackle vulnerable algorithms. Particularly, they warn banks to prepare for any quantum computing cyber threat [5].
- The French embassy in Washington transmitted the first diplomatic letter encrypted to withstand future quantum computers, according to President Emmanuel Macron [22]. The transmission was part of Macron's Quantum Plan, unveiled in January 2021. In the plan, President Macron presented the National Strategy on Quantum Technologies. With a budget of 1.8 billion Euros, the aim of this plan is to set up an ecosystem capable of propelling France into the top tier of nations mastering these technologies [21].

4.2   Actions from Implementation Developers

Reliable and secure implementations are essential for the transition to post-quantum cryptography. We must integrate PQC implementations into actual applications, protocols, and products.

As an example, Linux foundations PQC alliance has been working on the following open-source projects [6]:

- Open quantum safe (OQS) project aims to support the transition to PQC.
- Post-quantum crypto VPN is a fork of OpenVPN integrated with PQC to enable testing and experimentation with these algorithms.
- Post-quantum TLS is a PQ Crypto enlightened fork of OpenSSL.
- Post-quantum SSH is a fork of OpenSSH 7.7 that adds PQ key exchange and signature algorithms.

4.3   Actions from Industry

Figure 5 is a list of examples of PQC products or plans. Again, this is not a complete list.

Company	PQC products
Google	hybrid X25519Kyber768 for Chrome and Google Servers
AWS	hybrid PQ TLS (ECDHE+Kyber)
Cloudflare	hybrid PQ TLS (X25519Kyber512 and X25519Kyber768)
IBM	PQ tape drive
CISCO	preshared keys (manually configure keys or QKD)
Apple	iMessage with PQ3: PQC key establishment + ongoing PQC rekeying, using hybrid with Kyber
HP	a PQ security chip uses both RSA and LMS signatures
Intel	aims to make products quantum-resistant by 2030
Infineon	world's first TPM with a PQC-protected firmware update mechanism
Huawei	Introduce quantum-safe algorithms into its products at an early date

Fig. 5. Examples of PQC products or industrial plans.

5   Future Work and Conclusion

Are we ready to welcome large, scalable quantum computers? Not yet. As Lily Chen from NIST mentioned, "We have just started." There is still a long way to go. In my opinion, future work should include the following items:

– We need to focus on all necessary replacements for post-quantum cryptography (PQC). While we have started selecting and standardising quantum-resistant key encapsulation mechanisms (KEMs) and digital signatures, much work is still needed before we can provide real-world implementations of all the required PQC solutions. Figure 6 shows that most ISO/IEC cryptographic standards are relevant to the transition to PQC and are pending migration. A question mark indicates that although a standard may not require immediate replacement, it might need further evaluation in the future.
– Trust in cryptographic algorithms varies among individuals, and there is no universal consensus on which algorithms are the most reliable and secure. People often have their preferred algorithms. The ISO/IEC has adopted numerous cryptographic algorithms from various national standards. The TCG also supports algorithm agility for Trusted Platform Modules (TPM). While NIST has begun the standardisation process for post-quantum KEMs and digital signatures, there is a strong need for a broader range of options in PQC standardisation to meet the diverse preferences of individuals from different countries and regions.

standard number	content	PQC relevant	standard number	content	PQC relevant
4922	secure multiparty computation	?	18032	prime number generation	?
9796	message recovery signatures	yes	18033	encryption algorithms	yes
9797	message authentication codes	?	18370	blind digital signatures	yes
9798	entity authentication	yes	19772	authenticated encryption	?
10116	modes of operation	?	19592	secret sharing	yes
10118	hash-functions	yes	20008	anonymous signatures	yes
11770	key management	yes	20009	anonymous authentication	yes
13888	non-repudiation	yes	23264	redaction of authentic data	yes
14888	signatures with appendix	yes	28033	fully homomorphic encryption	yes
15946	elliptic curve techniques	yes	29150	signcryption	yes
18014	time-stamping services	yes	29192	lightweight cryptography	yes
18031	random bit generation	?			

Fig. 6. ISO/IEC cryptographic standards review

– Cryptography is becoming increasingly complex, and PQC is more intricate than traditional cryptography. Can we switch to PQC as we do with a standard software update? For many applications, the answer is YES. Users of standard IT tools, such as common browsers or operating systems, will see the transition to PQC implemented through a software update. This process is designed to be seamless, ideally occurring without end-users even noticing it. We are accustomed to frequently updating our operating systems, Microsoft Office, mobile phone software, and more. However, updates to cryptographic algorithms are rare, but this situation may change. Updating hardware implementations presents more challenges. Embedded systems, like Trusted Platform Modules (TPM), have limited computing power, energy, and memory, which can complicate the integration of PQC without sacrificing efficiency. PQC standards should provide guidance on selecting the appropriate algorithms and managing the migration process for both software and hardware updates.

In conclusion, transitioning to post-quantum cryptography (PQC) should be both smooth and collaborative. This requires cooperation among the cryptographic community, standards organizations, industry stakeholders, open-source developers, and government entities. While there are many barriers and challenges to migrating to PQC, we have at least begun this lengthy and demanding journey.

Acknowledgments. This work is supported by the European Union,s Horizon research and innovation program under grant agreement numbers: 779391 (FutureTPM), 952697 (ASSURED), 101019645 (SECANT),101069688 (CONNECT), 101070627 (REWIRE), 101095634 (ENTRUST) and 101167904 (CASTOR). These projects are funded by the UK government Horizon Europe guarantee and administered by UKRI. The author would like to thank Christopher Newton for providing valuable comments.

References

1. Netherlands national communications security agency. The PQC migration handbook (2023). https://english.aivd.nl/publications/publications/2023/04/04/the-pqc-migration-handbook
2. ANSI. ANSI X9.95-2022: Time stamp management and security
3. European Commission. Commission publishes recommendation on post-quantum cryptography (2024). https://digital-strategy.ec.europa.eu/en/news/commission-publishes-recommendation-post-quantum-cryptography
4. ETSI. ETSI TS 103 744 v1.1.1 (2020-12), CYBER; Quantum-safe hybrid key exchanges. https://www.etsi.org/deliver/etsi_ts/103700_103799/103744/01.01.01_60/ts_103744v010101p.pdf
5. Finextra. Singapore warns banks to prepare for quantum computing cyber threat (2024). https://www.finextra.com/newsarticle/43739/singapore-warns-banks-to-prepare-for-quantum-computing-cyberthreat#:~:text=to%20our%20community.-,Singapore%20warns%20banks%20to%20prepare%20for%20quantum%20computing%20cyber%20threat,risks%20posed%20by%20quantum%20computing
6. The Linux Foundation. Post-quantum cryptography alliance launches to advance post-quantum cryptography (2024). https://www.linuxfoundation.org/press/announcing-the-post-quantum-cryptography-alliance-pqca
7. Trusted computing group. TCG algorithm registry, Family "2.0", Level 00 revision 01.34, 24 Aug 2023. https://trustedcomputinggroup.org/wp-content/uploads/TCG-Algorithm-Registry-Revision-1.34_pub-1.pdf
8. Grover, L.K.: A fast quantum mechanical algorithm for database search. In: STOC 1996: Proceedings of the Twenty-Eighth Annual ACM Symposium on Theory of Computing, pp. 212–219 (1996)
9. IEEE. IEEE standard specification for public key cryptographic techniques based on hard problems over lattices. https://standards.ieee.org/ieee/1363.1/3074/
10. Global Risk Institute. 2024 opinion-based estimates of the cumulative probability of a digital quantum computer able to break RSA-2048 in 24 hours, as function of timeframe. https://globalriskinstitute.org/publication/2024-quantum-threat-timeline-report
11. ISO/IEC. ISO/IEC 14888-4:2024 Information security – Digital signatures with appendix – Part 4: Stateful hash-based mechanisms. https://csrc.nist.gov/pqc-standardization
12. ISO/IEC. ISO/IEC 18014-1 (all parts) Information technology – Security techniques – Time-stamping services
13. ITU-T. Overview of hybrid approaches for key exchange with quantum key distribution. https://www.itu.int/dms_pub/itu-t/opb/tut/T-TUT-ICTS-2022-1-PDF-E.pdf

14. Abbinaya Kuzhanthaivel. Singapore issues an advisory for FIs to mitigate quantum computing risks (2024). https://www.itnews.asia/news/singapore-issues-advisory-for-fis-to-mitigate-quantum-computing-risks-605273

15. Meng, L., Chen, L.: A blockchain-based long-term time-stamping scheme. In: Proceedings of 27th European Symposium on Research in Computer Security (ESORICS 2022), Part 1, LNCS 13554, pp. 3–24 (2022)

16. Mosca, M.: Cybersecurity in an era with quantum computers: will we be ready? Cryptology ePrint Archive, Paper 2015/1075 (2015). https://eprint.iacr.org/2015/1075

17. NCSC. Next steps in preparing for post-quantum cryptography (2024). https://www.ncsc.gov.uk/whitepaper/next-steps-preparing-for-post-quantum-cryptography

18. NIST. Internal Report, NIST IR 8547 ipd, Transition to post-quantum cryptography standards (2024). https://nvlpubs.nist.gov/nistpubs/ir/2024/NIST.IR.8547.ipd.pdf

19. NIST. Post-quantum cryptography standardization (2024). https://csrc.nist.gov/pqc-standardization

20. World Trade Organization. Standards and safety (2024). https://www.wto.org/english/thewto_e/whatis_e/tif_e/agrm4_e.htm

21. Anne-Françoise Pelé. French president details €1.8b quantum plan (2021). https://www.eetimes.eu/french-president-details-e1-8b-quantum-plan/

22. Potter, J.: France sends first post-quantum encrypted diplomatic message (2022). https://www.iotworldtoday.com/industry/france-sends-first-post-quantum-encrypted-diplomatic-message

23. Shor, P.W.: Polynomial-time algorithms for prime factorization and discrete logarithms on a quantum computer. SIAM J. Comput. **26**(5), 1484–1509 (1997)

24. TCG. Interview with Joe Pennisi, President of TCG. https://trustedcomputinggroup.org/interview-with-joe-pennisi-president-of-tcg/

25. TCG. Trusted computing group triumph as it reaches its 20-year milestone. https://trustedcomputinggroup.org/trusted-computing-group-triumph-as-it-reaches-its-20-year-milestone/

Contributed Papers

The Vision of Secure Multi-party Computation Technical Standards

Jingqiang Lin[✉] and Zhiquan Gao

School of Cyber Science and Technology, University of Science and Technology
of China (USTC), Hefei 230026, China
linjq@ustc.edu.cn, gaozhiquan@mail.ustc.edu.cn

Abstract. Secure multi-party computation (SMPC) enables the output of an intended function to be computed, while it keeps the individual inputs confidential. Thus, SMPC will play an important role in the data industry to protect privacy, and promote data flow to produce values in privacy-sensitive scenarios. Before SMPC has been widely adopted and applied in real-world information systems, related technical standards are imperative to coordinate developers, manufacturers, service providers, and users. This paper proposes a vision of SMPC technical standards. The proposed SMPC technical framework is composed of four layers, namely, the SMPC protocol layer, the SMPC device layer, the SMPC system layer, and the layer of common supporting function (CSF). Each layer includes several standards specifying some aspects of SMPC technologies and applications: (a) the SMPC protocol layer specifies different types of protocols and also protocol components; (b) the device layer defines various SMPC devices, each of which runs independently and implements a certain set of SMPC protocol operations; (c) the system layer specifies function requirements of an SMPC system, such as computation function, configuration and coordination, and security requirements, such as authentication, privilege management, data authorization, communication security, storage security, and log; and (d) the CSF layer defines typical common supporting functions for popular applications, such as joint data aggregation, joint modeling/prediction, privacy-preserving information retrieval, and sample alignment.

Keywords: Secure multi-party computation · Technical standard · Privacy · Security

1 Introduction

Secure multiple-party computation (SMPC) [67,68] enables the output of an intended function to be computed, while it keeps the individual inputs confidential. After more than 40 years, a lot of SMPC schemes have been proposed for various intended functions in diverse application scenarios, following different threat models, at a variety of costs of communication and computation. At the same time, while data-driven information technologies (e.g., deep learning, large model, and neural network) imply unlimited possibilities in the future, more

X. Lu and C. J. Mitchell (Eds.): SSR 2024, LNCS 15559, pp. 17–30, 2025.
https://doi.org/10.1007/978-3-031-87541-0_2

and more attentions are being paid to data privacy (e.g., the General Data Protection Regulation in European Union and the Personal Information Protection Law of China). Thus, in the future SMPC will play an important role in the data industry to protect privacy, and then greatly promote data flow to produce values in privacy-sensitive scenarios.

Before SMPC has been widely adopted and applied in real-world information systems, comprehensive technical standards are imperative. Such standards may cover SMPC schemes, protocols, devices, data formats, systems, interfaces, services, testing, evaluation and other aspects. Recently, several international technical standards on SMPC have been published, e.g., IEEE P2842: Recommended practice for secure multi-party computation [26], ITU-T X.1770: Technical guidelines for secure multi-party computation [62], ISO/IEC 4922-1:2023 Information security – Secure multiparty computation Part 1: General [28], and ISO/IEC 4922-2:2024 Information security – Secure multiparty computation Part 2: Mechanisms based on secret sharing [29]. Meanwhile, National Institute of Standards and Technology (NIST) initiated the Multi-Party Threshold Cryptography (MPTC) project [49] to standardize threshold schemes of the cryptographic primitives such as signing, decryption, key generation, key exchange, and zero-knowledge proof of knowledge. In summary, there are recently more and more efforts on SMPC standardization.

These existing standards present a technical overview of SMPC, requirements of SMPC systems, and also some typical SMPC protocols, but do not cover all aspects systematically. In this paper, we propose a vision of SMPC technical standards. In this vision, in addition to the introduction of SMPC technologies, we take the following important issues into considerations, attempting to provide more guidelines for SMPC implementations and deployments in the data industry:

- *Comprehensive SMPC protocols and protocol components.* We consider different types of SMPC protocols for general-purpose computation functions, various SMPC protocols for special computation functions, basic protocol components as building blocks, and also switch mechanisms between different SMPC schemes.
- *Testing and evaluation of SMPC equipments.* An SMPC device runs independently and implements a certain set of SMPC protocol operations, and an SMPC system is composed of several SMPC devices. As they are typical cryptographic equipments, the testing and evaluation of SMPC devices and systems should be planned. These requirements of SMPC equipments are considered mainly to protect each SMPC device against the attacks exploiting software and network vulnerabilities.
- *The interfaces to access SMPC computation services.* Three suites of application programming interfaces (APIs) are considered: one to invoke basic general-purpose SMPC computation functions (e.g., arithmetic operations and bit-wise operations), one to invoke special computation functions (e.g., set operations and information retrievals), and the third one for the common supporting functions by encapsulating the native functions as above.

– *Interoperability among SMPC devices from different manufacturers.* SMPC attempts to promote data flow among organizations of different domains, so an SMPC system composed of SMPC devices from different manufacturers is rather possible in the future. For example, the data formats of internal messages for each standardized protocol will be specified.

2   The Proposed Vision of SMPC Technical Standards

In this section, we firstly present the SMPC technical framework, and then discuss the standards in each layer of this framework.

2.1   Technical Framework of SMPC

From the perspective of standards, the technical framework of SMPC is composed of four layers, namely, *the SMPC protocol layer*, *the SMPC device layer*, *the SMPC system layer*, and *the SMPC CSF layer*, as shown in Fig. 1. It is worthy noting that this vision is not restricted to only some particular types of SMPC schemes, but general principles and requirements are proposed.

In this technical framework, each layer includes several standards relevant to some aspects of SMPC: (*a*) the protocol layer specifies different types of *SMPC protocols*, *SMPC protocol components* and *switch mechanisms between SMPC schemes*; (*b*) the device layer defines *SMPC devices*, each of which runs independently and implements a certain set of protocol operations; (*c*) the system layer presents function requirements and security requirements of an *SMPC system*; and (*d*) the CSF layer defines typical supporting functions common among popular applications, which will be implemented as *SMPC middleware*.

This framework will be built as follows. SMPC protocols need to be specified firstly, and each protocol is implemented cooperatively by some SMPC devices. For example, a secret-sharing-based SMPC (SS-SMPC) protocol is implemented as SS-SMPC clients and SS-SMPC computing servers, and a garbled-circuit SMPC (GC-SMPC) protocol is implemented as GC-SMPC computing servers. Then, an SMPC system is constructed by coordinating some SMPC devices, providing the computation functions of at least one SMPC protocol. The interfaces to access the native computation functions, are ported to some SMPC devices (of an SMPC system). Finally, the native computation functions provided by SMPC systems are further encapsulated into SMPC common supporting functions as middleware, facilitating the applications to access SMPC computation services. Anyway, some applications may access SMPC services, by directly invoking the native computation functions of an SMPC system.

2.2   The Protocol Layer and Standards on SMPC Protocols

The following types of SMPC protocols and mechanisms are considered in this technical framework.

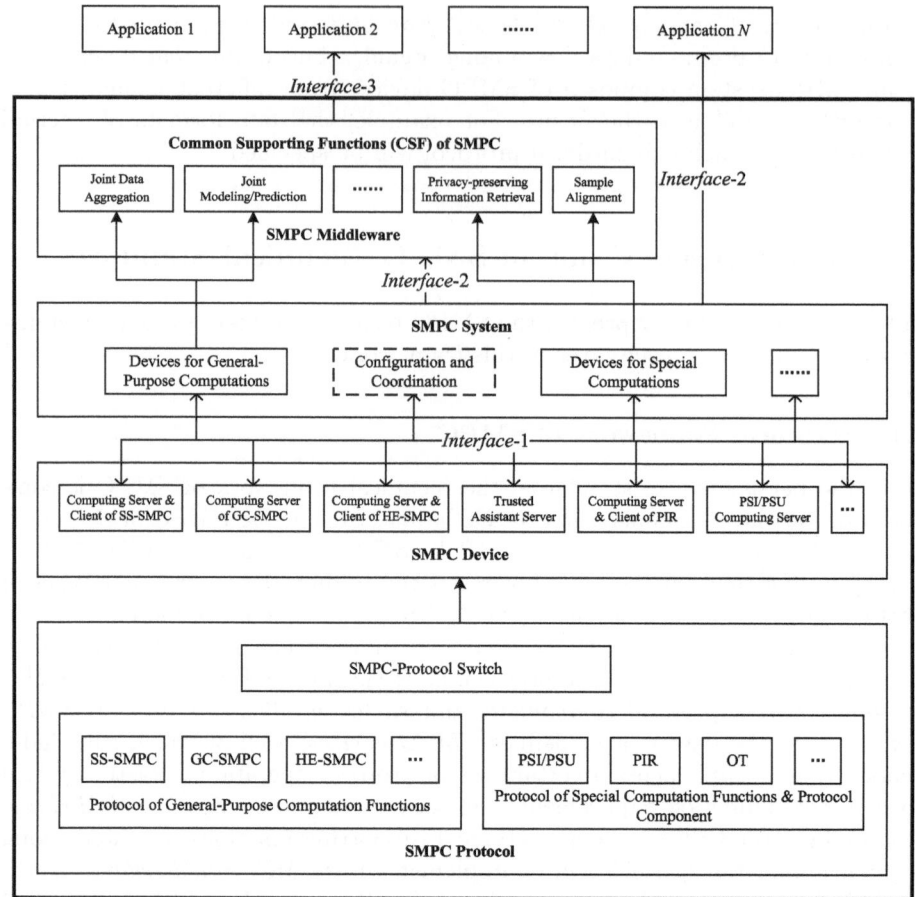

Fig. 1. The technical framework of SMPC, from the perspective of standards.

– **SMPC protocols for general-purpose computation functions**, such as SS-SMPC protocols [6,7,22,29,42,46,64], GC-SMPC protocols [18,24,39,41, 65,66,69], and homomorphic-encryption-based SMPC (HE-SMPC, especially multi-key HE) protocols [8,13–15,56,57]. Such an SMPC protocol exports *flexible user-defined intended functions*, for general purposes [29].
– **SMPC protocols for special computation functions**, such as private set intersection (PSI) [19,38,43,58,59], private set union (PSU) [40,63,70], and private information retrieval (PIR) [1,3,20,21,25]. Such a protocol exports *a fixed intended function* (i.e., special computation function).
– **SMPC protocol components**, such as oblivious transfer (OT) [4,10,36,38], oblivious pseudo-random function (OPRF) [37,48,59], and vector oblivious linear evaluation (VOLE) [9,58,59]. Some components, such as partially homomorphic encryption [55] and fully homomorphic encryption [11,16,17],

are also used in other cryptographic schemes and may be standardized somewhere. These components are used in the specified SMPC protocols as basic building blocks.

- **Switch mechanisms between different SMPC protocols**. Such a mechanism enables intermediate variables to be switched as the computations factors across different SMPC protocols [46], while the individual inputs are still kept confidential during the switching.

Schemes will be carefully selected, analyzed and standardized. In these standards, the security model of an SMPC protocol must be explicitly declaimed, e.g., the assumptions of adversaries (semi-trusted or malicious adversaries, computational security or information-theoretic security), and the maximum number (or proportion) of compromised parties. In addition to the detailed protocol schemes, recommended parameters for different levels of security strength (e.g., 128-bit, 192-bit and 256-bit) are needed. Other recommended security settings (e.g., the number of SS-SMPC computing servers and the threshold of an SS-SMPC protocol adopted in different scenarios, for various privacy data) are also needed in the protocol standards.

2.3   The Device Layer and Standards on SMPC Devices

In this layer, various SMPC devices are defined. Each SMPC device runs independently and implements some SMPC protocol operations, and multiple devices work cooperatively following some SMPC protocol. Typical SMPC devices are listed as examples, and the list of SMPC devices will become greater as more SMPC schemes are standardized.

- A *GC-SMPC computing server* implements the protocol operations of GC garbler and evaluator. A GC-SMPC computing server accepts individual data, runs together with another GC-SMPC server, and finally outputs the results.
- An *SS-SMPC client* accepts individual data, splits them into shares, and sends them to multiple *SS-SMPC computing servers*. The SS-SMPC computing servers run cooperatively to finish computations on these shares. Finally, the SS-SMPC computing servers send updated shares to some SS-SMPC client, which then combines them into the output results.
- A *HE-SMPC client* encrypts individual data, and sends encrypted data to *HE-SMPC computing servers*. HE-SMPC computing servers process the encrypted data, and finally return them to the clients, which then decrypt the results.
- A *PIR client* communicates with a remote *PIR computing server* to fetch records from the PIR computing server, without revealing to the server which records are being fetched.
- Multiple *PSI computing servers* run cooperatively to compute the intersection of their input sets, without revealing anything except the intersection. Similarly, multiple *PSU computing servers* run cooperatively to compute the union of their input sets, without revealing anything except the union.

– A *trusted assistant server* may be needed in some SMPC schemes. For example, a trusted assistant server is designed to generate Beaver triples [5] for SS-SMPC computing servers. However, different from trusted servers in other information systems, *a trusted assistant server in SMPC systems does not receive any individual data* (i.e., the inputs of the intended function) *or any variables derived from the individual data.*
– Finally, more SMPC devices will be designed, implemented and evaluated in the future, while another type of SMPC protocols is proposed and the protocols are specified in standards.

An SMPC device is considered as a cryptographic device, and may be software-based, hardware-based, firmware-based, or hybrid. The individual inputs (or factors) are protected and processed in SMPC devices. Therefore, the general security requirements of cryptographic modules [27,50] should be satisfied, while critical security parameters and sensitive security parameters must be carefully identified in each types of SMPC devices. That is, these security requirements, including (*a*) interfaces, (*b*) roles, services, and authentication, (*c*) software/firmware security, (*d*) operational environment, (*e*) physical security, (*f*) non-invasive security, (*g*) security parameter management, (*h*) self-tests, (*i*) life-cycle assurance, and (*j*) mitigation of other attacks, should be considered accordingly. Note that different levels of security requirements will be specified, for different kinds of privacy data processed in SMPC systems.

It seems that these security requirements are not related to any SMPC schemes, but they are necessary for protecting the privacy data which are processed in SMPC devices. For example, when a data item is split into several shares and each share is kept on an SS-SMPC computing server, we need to ensure that attackers are unable to easily steal any of these shares; otherwise, the attackers will collect enough shares soon and reconstruct the individual inputs. Or, even when a perfect PSI protocol is adopted, we still need to ensure that an attacker is unable to easily break into any PSI computing server to learn all elements directly from this broken server. Thus, these security requirements are necessary in SMPC devices.

These requirements will be used in the evaluation of SMPC devices and systems. Moreover, *enhanced security requirements* can be additionally proposed for some particular types of SMPC devices, for example, *trusted* assistant servers and *semi-trusted* nodes in an SMPC system, due to the stronger assumptions than the nodes which are assumed to be malicious. Such enhanced requirements may include remote attestation, secure boot, hardware-based runtime isolation, data sealing and transparency.

2.4 The System Layer and Standards on SMPC Systems

An SMPC system is composed of SMPC devices, and optional supplementary subsystems (e.g., configuration and coordination, audit and log, and so on). An SMPC system provides computation functions on privacy data using some SMPC protocols, the intended functions implemented in it may be *statically-determined* or *dynamically-configured*, and the SMPC devices are coordinated to follow the protocols as pre-determined or configured on the fly.

The security requirements of an SMPC system, such as authentication, privilege management, data authorization, communication security, storage security and log, are specified in these standards [26, 62]. These security requirements will be used in the evaluation of SMPC systems.

An application accesses the computation functions of an SMPC system with coordinated SMPC devices, by placing its input data in some devices (clients and/or computing servers). Then, the computation functions are finished by these SMPC devices, when the application launches SMPC protocol operations to finish intended functions on the input data and finally obtains the results, by invoking the native computation-function interfaces.

2.5   The CSF Layer and Standards on Common Supporting Functions of SMPC Services

The native functions provided by an SMPC system (i.e., the native interfaces ported to SMPC devices), are further encapsulated as SMPC common supporting functions of the CSF interfaces by *SMPC middleware*, facilitating the applications to access SMPC computation services, such as joint data aggregation, joint modeling/prediction, privacy-preserving information retrieval, and sample alignment. Therefore, an application can conveniently access the SMPC computation services with much fewer invocations. This layer is designed for better usability, but not for security.

In the future, the common supporting functions will be progressively extended and updated in the SMPC middleware, as more popular applications work on top of SMPC systems and more supporting functions are extracted from their common operations.

2.6   Standards on Data Formats and Interfaces

After presenting four layers of the SMPC technical framework, we describe potential standards on data formats and interfaces for better interoperability. These specifications will promote interoperability among the SMPC devices from different manufacturers.

First of all, the communications between each pair of SMPC devices are protected to ensure end-to-end confidentiality, data integrity and authenticity (e.g., using TLS [33], QUIC [35], TLCP [60], or other secure transport-layer protocols). The secure communications prevent attackers on the networks, and the underlying key exchange can be finished using (*a*) pre-shared keys, each of which is established between each pair of the SMPC devices, or (*b*) certificates issued by a certification authority (CA) with a secure distribution of trust [49]. Moreover, there should be *specifications on data formats of the SMPC protocol messages among devices*. For example, the sender, receiver, protocol ID, operation ID, algorithm ID, and variables in processing are expressed in network packets, in a standard format. Because SMPC promotes data flow among organizations of different domains, it is rather possible to construct an SMPC system by coordinating SMPC devices from different manufacturers. In this case, such data-format specifications are necessary, and are helpful for transparent monitoring and audits in an SMPC system. These specifications are shown as *Interface-1* in Fig. 1. This interface may be also used to configure and coordinate SMPC devices into an SMPC system.

Next, two suites of the following interfaces can be specified in standards, both of which are available to applications.

- *The interfaces for invoking native computation functions of an SMPC system.* These interfaces are ported to some SMPC devices of this system. The APIs for basic computation functions (e.g., arithmetic addition, arithmetic multiplication, comparison, bit-AND, bit-OR, bit-NOT, and bit-XOR) can be specified. Similarly, the APIs for invoking special computation functions (e.g., various set operations) of an SMPC system, can be also specified. These interfaces are denoted as *Interface-2* in Fig. 1.
- *The interfaces for invoking common supporting functions of an SMPC system.* These CSF interfaces will be specified by encapsulating the native computation functions, facilitating the applications to access SMPC services. The common supporting functions will be extracted from the common operations of popular applications. These APIs are denoted as *Interface-3* in the framework.

In the *ideal* state, the interfaces should be *uniform with different SMPC protocols of a given intended function* to mask the implementation differences and details, but limited differences in the interfaces for different SMPC protocols have to be allowed.

3   Discussions

In this section, we discuss some international standards on SMPC within the proposed framework, and also compare the standards in this framework and those of traditional cryptographic algorithms.

3.1   The Relationship with Existing International Standards on SMPC

Existing international SMPC standards work in only two layers of this framework. IEEE P2842 [26] is related to two layers, partially. It presents security requirements and models of general SMPC protocols (i.e., works in the system layer), and (only a little part of) the protocol layer is also covered. Most sections of IEEE P2842 are related to the system layer, including roles, deployment modes and security requirements of a general-purpose SMPC system. ITU-T X.1770 [62] works similarly to IEEE P2842, in the layers of SMPC protocol and system.

On the other hand, ISO/IEC 4922-1 and ISO/IEC 4922-2 [28,29] are typical standards in the protocol layer. ISO/IEC 4922-1 specifies security requirements and models of general SMPC protocols, and ISO/IEC 4922-2 presents several typical SMPC protocols based on secret sharing. Besides, ISO/IEC 4922-3 Information security – Secure multiparty computation Part 3: Mechanisms based on garbled circuits [30] is still in development, and obviously it will also work in the protocol layer.

3.2   Comparison with the Area of Traditional Cryptographic Algorithms

Next, we compare the technical standards of SMPC in this framework and those of traditional cryptographic algorithms, to explain our approach and also its practicability. In the area of traditional cryptographic algorithms, including symmetric algorithms such as AES, Ascon, SM4 and ZUC, traditional public-key algorithm such as RSA, ECDSA and SM2, and cryptographic hash algorithms such as SHA-3, SHA-256 and SM3, the standard family is also composed roughly of four layers as below, namely, the algorithm layer, the device layer, the system layer, and the layer of common supporting service.

The algorithm layer of traditional cryptographic technologies includes various kinds of standard cryptographic algorithms, and the most critical standard of its device layer is NIST FIPS-140: Security requirements for cryptographic modules [27,50], which roughly correspond to the layers of protocol and device in the SMPC framework, respectively. Moreover, when much higher security requirements are applied to a trusted CA [12,23,47] than regular cryptographic modules [27,50], this proposed framework also plans *higher security requirements for trusted assistant servers and semi-trusted nodes* than those nodes with malicious assumptions in an SMPC system. A trusted SMPC device should be protected better than semi-trusted nodes in an SMPC system. It is worthy noting that, even for an SMPC node with malicious assumptions, there are necessary security requirements because an SMPC system tolerates only a threshold number of malicious nodes.

While various cryptographic systems based on traditional cryptographic algorithms are deployed in the real world, e.g., CA, TLS server, IPsec gateway, cryptographic coprocessor, FIDO token, one-time password token, PCIe cryptographic accelerator, and hardware security module, various SMPC systems will be possible in the future. Thus, there will be a number of standards on SMPC systems specifying the requirements of function and security. Meanwhile, there are some de facto standards to access the functions of these traditional cryptographic equipments, such as PKCS #11 Cryptographic token interface base specification [54], OpenSSL EVP interface to cryptographic functions [52], Java cryptography extension (JCE) [53] and Windows CNG [44]. Therefore, the standard interfaces to access the native computation functions of SMPC systems will be also needed in the future.

Finally, the CSF layer (i.e., SMPC middleware) works for SMPC applications. The CSF interfaces will be developed according to the computation function requirements common among popular data-driven applications, for example, linear regression, logistic regression, and gradient boosting decision tree (GBDT). Similarly, there are a lot of standard common security services based on traditional cryptographic algorithms, such as X.509 PKI certificate services [61], key management services [2,45], trusted timestamping services [32], TLS/HTTPS secure transport services [31,33], end-to-end secure Email [34], and OpenID Connect authentication [51]. These prevailing security services can be viewed as common supporting services (or functions) of traditional cryptographic algorithms, to some extent.

4   Summary, Recent Progress and Future Work

This comprehensive vision of SMPC technical standards covers four layers, namely, the protocol layer, the SMPC device layer, the SMPC system layer, and the CSF layer. Each layer will include several specifications on some aspect of SMPC technologies, and is explained with details in this paper. This vision is not restricted to particular types of SMPC schemes. The framework considers (a) which types of SMPC protocols and mechanisms will be specified as standards, (b) how an SMPC system will be constructed using SMPC devices, evaluated, and operated with protected privacy data, and (c) how applications will access the SMPC computation services.

This proposed vision of SMPC technical standards has been submitted to Cryptography Standardization Technical Committee of China as a standard draft, but it is still in discussion until December 2024. Since 2021, this vision has been discussed within the committee and improved for several rounds. At the same time, some SMPC standard proposals in the protocol layer have been approved by Cryptography Standardization Technical Committee of China, but the standard drafting is in progress and these protocol standards are not formally published yet.

In the future, we will keep improving this technical framework, and submit more standard proposals which are planned in this framework, especially to Cryptography Standardization Technical Committee of China and/or National Technical Committee on Cybersecurity (TC260) of Standardization Administration of China. Any comments and suggestions are always welcome. Meanwhile, we hope this vision work will also contribute to international standards, interoperable equipments and large-scale deployments of SMPC.

Acknowledgements. This work was partially supported by the Standard-Research Project "The Cryptography Technical Framework of Multi-Party Computations" from Cryptography Standardization Technical Committee of China. Any opinions, findings, conclusions, and recommendations expressed in this material are those of the authors and do not necessarily reflect the view of Cryptography Standardization Technical Committee of China. Finally, the authors would like to thank all participants of this project for their efforts and comments.

References

1. Ali, A., et al.: Communication-computation trade-offs in PIR. In: 30th USENIX Security Symposium, pp. 1811–1828 (2021)
2. Amazon Web Services (AWS): AWS key management service. https://aws.amazon.com/kms/
3. Angel, S., Chen, H., Laine, K., Setty, S.: PIR with compressed queries and amortized query processing. In: 39th IEEE Symposium on Security and Privacy (S&P), pp. 962–979 (2018)
4. Asharov, G., Lindell, Y., Schneider, T., Zohner, M.: More efficient oblivious transfer extensions with security for malicious adversaries. In: Advances in Cryptology - EUROCRYPT, pp. 673–701 (2015)
5. Beaver, D.: Efficient multiparty protocols using circuit randomization. In: Advances in Cryptology - CRYPTO, pp. 420–432 (1991)
6. Ben-Or, M., Goldwasser, S., Wigderson, A.: Completeness theorems for non-cryptographic fault-tolerant distributed computation. In: 20th Annual ACM Symposium on Theory of Computing (STOC), pp. 1–10 (1988)
7. Bogdanov, D., Laur, S., Willemson, J.: Sharemind: a framework for fast privacy-preserving computations. In: 13th European Symposium on Research in Computer Security (ESORICS), pp. 192–206 (2008)
8. Boneh, D., et al.: Threshold cryptosystems from threshold fully homomorphic encryption. In: Advances in Cryptology - CRYPTO, pp. 565–596 (2018)
9. Boyle, E., Couteau, G., Gilboa, N., Ishai, Y.: Compressing vector OLE. In: 26th ACM Conference on Computer and Communications Security (CCS), pp. 896–912 (2019)
10. Boyle, E., et al.: Efficient two-round OT extension and silent non-interactive secure computation. In: 26th ACM Conference on Computer and Communications Security (CCS), pp. 291–308 (2019)
11. Brakerski, Z., Gentry, C., Vaikuntanathan, V.: (Leveled) Fully homomorphic encryption without bootstrapping. ACM Trans. Comput. Theor. **6**(3), 13:1–13:36 (2014)
12. Chartered professional accountants of Canada (CPA Canada): WebTrust principles and criteria for certification authorities (2021)
13. Chen, H., Chillotti, I., Song, Y.: Multi-key homomorphic encryption from TFHE. In: Advances in Cryptology - ASIACRYPT, pp. 446–472 (2019)
14. Chen, H., Dai, W., Kim, M., Song, Y.: Efficient multi-key homomorphic encryption with packed ciphertexts with application to oblivious neural network inference. In: 26th ACM Conference on Computer and Communications Security (CCS), pp. 395–412 (2019)
15. Chen, L., Zhang, Z., Wang, X.: Batched multi-hop multi-key FHE from Ring-LWE with compact ciphertext extension. In: 15th International Conference on Theory of Cryptography (TCC) (2017)
16. Cheon, J.H., Kim, A., Kim, M., Song, Y.S.: Homomorphic encryption for arithmetic of approximate numbers. In: Advances in Cryptology - ASIACRYPT, pp. 409–437 (2017)
17. Chillotti, I., Gama, N., Georgieva, M., Izabachene, M.: Faster fully homomorphic encryption: Bootstrapping in less than 0.1 seconds. In: Advances in Cryptology - ASIACRYPT, pp. 3–33 (2016)
18. Choi, S.G., Katz, J., Malozemoff, A., Zikas, V.: Efficient three-party computation from cut-and-Choose. In: Advances in Cryptology - CRYPTO, pp. 513–530 (2014)

19. Cong, K., et al.: Labeled PSI from homomorphic encryption with reduced computation and communication. In: 28th ACM Conference on Computer and Communications Security (CCS), pp. 1135–1150 (2021)
20. Corrigan-Gibbs, H., Henzinger, A., Kogan, D.: Single-server private information retrieval with sublinear amortized time. In: Advances in Cryptology - EUROCRYPT, pp. 3–33 (2022)
21. Corrigan-Gibbs, H., Kogan, D.: Private information retrieval with sublinear online time. In: Advances in Cryptology - EUROCRYPT, pp. 44–75 (2020)
22. Damgard, I., Pastro, V., Smart, N., Zakarias, S.: Multiparty computation from somewhat homomorphic encryption. In: Advances in Cryptology - CRYPTO, pp. 643–662 (2012)
23. European Telecommunications Standards Institute (ETSI): ETSI EN 319 401: Electronic signatures and infrastructures (ESI) – General policy requirements for trust service providers, v2.2.1 (2018)
24. Frederiksen, T., Jakobsen, T., Nielsen, J., Nordholt, P., Orlandi, C.: MiniLEGO: efficient secure two-party computation from general assumptions. In: Advances in Cryptology - EUROCRYPT, pp. 537–556 (2013)
25. Henzinger, A., Hong, M., Corrigan-Gibbs, H., Meiklejohn, S., Vaikuntanathan, V.: One server for the price of two: simple and fast single-server private information retrieval. In: 32nd USENIX Security Symposium, pp. 3889–3905 (2023)
26. Institute of Electrical and Electronics Engineers (IEEE): P2842: Recommended practice for secure multi-party computation (2021)
27. International organization for standardization (ISO): ISO/IEC 19790: information technology – security techniques – security requirements for cryptographic modules (2012)
28. International organization for standardization (ISO): ISO/IEC 4922-1:2023 information security – secure multiparty computation Part 1: General (2023)
29. International organization for standardization (ISO): ISO/IEC 4922-2:2024 information security – secure multiparty computation Part 2: mechanisms based on secret sharing (2024)
30. International organization for standardization (ISO): ISO/IEC 4922-3 information security – secure multiparty computation Part 3: mechanisms based on garbled circuits (Under development) (2024)
31. Internet engineering task force (IETF): RFC 2818: HTTP over TLS (2000)
32. Internet engineering task force (IETF): RFC 3161: Internet X.509 public key infrastructure time-stamp protocol (TSP) (2001)
33. Internet engineering task force (IETF): RFC 8446: the transport layer security (TLS) protocol version 1.3 (2018)
34. Internet engineering task force (IETF): RFC 8551: secure/multipurpose internet mail extensions (S/MIME) version 4.0 message specification (2019)
35. Internet engineering task force (IETF): RFC 9000: QUIC - a UDP-based multiplexed and secure transport (2021)
36. Ishai, Y., Kilian, J., Nissim, K., Petrank, E.: Extending oblivious transfers efficiently. In: Advances in Cryptology - CRYPTO, pp. 145–161 (2003)
37. Jarecki, S., Kiayias, A., Krawczyk, H.: Round-optimal password-protected secret sharing and T-PAKE in the password-only model. In: Advances in Cryptology - ASIACRYPT, pp. 233–253 (2014)
38. Kolesnikov, V., Kumaresan, R., Rosulek, M., Trieu, N.: Efficient batched oblivious PRF with applications to private set intersection. In: 23rd ACM Conference on Computer and Communications Security (CCS), pp. 818–829 (2016)

39. Kolesnikov, V., Mohassel, P., Rosulek, M.: FleXOR: flexible garbling for XOR gates that beats Free-XOR. In: Advances in Cryptology - CRYPTO, pp. 440–457 (2014)
40. Kolesnikov, V., Rosulek, M., Trieu, N., Wang, X.: Scalable private set union from symmetric-key techniques. In: Advances in Cryptology - ASIACRYPT, pp. 636–666 (2019)
41. Kolesnikov, V., Schneider, T.: Improved garbled circuit: free XOR gates and applications. In: 35th International Colloquium on Automata, Languages and Programming (ICALP), pp. 486–498 (2008)
42. Li, Y., Xu, W.: PrivPy: general and scalable privacy-preserving data mining. In: 25th ACM International Conference on Knowledge Discovery & Data Mining (KDD), pp. 1299–1307 (2019)
43. Meadows, C.: A more efficient cryptographic matchmaking protocol for use in the absence of a continuously available third party. In: 7th IEEE Symposium on Security and Privacy (S&P), pp. 134–137 (1986)
44. Microsoft corporate: cryptography API: next generation. https://learn.microsoft.com/en-us/windows/win32/seccng/cng-portal
45. Microsoft corporate: key management in Azure. https://learn.microsoft.com/en-us/azure/security/fundamentals/key-management
46. Mohassel, P., Rindal, P.: ABY3: a mixed protocol framework for machine learning. In: 25th ACM Conference on Computer and Communications Security (CCS), pp. 35–52 (2018)
47. Mozilla foundation: Mozilla root store policy, version 2.9 (2023)
48. Naor, M., Reingold, O.: Number-theoretic constructions of efficient pseudo-random functions. J. ACM **51**(2), 231–262 (2004)
49. National institute of standards and technology (NIST): multi-party threshold cryptography. https://csrc.nist.gov/Projects/threshold-cryptography
50. National institute of standards and technology (NIST): FIPS 140-2: security requirements for cryptographic modules (2001)
51. OpenID foundation: openID connect core 1.0 (2023)
52. OpenSSL foundation: OpenSSL documentation 3.0. https://docs.openssl.org/master/
53. Oracle corporate: java cryptography architecture (JCA) reference guide (2024)
54. Organization for the advancement of structured information standards (OASIS): PKCS #11 Cryptographic token interface base specification version 3.0 (2020)
55. Paillier, P.: Public-key cryptosystems based on composite degree residuosity classes. In: Advances in Cryptology - EUROCRYPT, pp. 223–238 (1999)
56. Pedersen, T.: A threshold cryptosystem without a trusted party. In: Advances in Cryptology - EUROCRYPT, pp. 522–526 (1991)
57. Peikert, C., Shiehian, S.: Multi-key FHE from LWE, Revisited. In: 14th International Conference on Theory of Cryptography (TCC), pp. 217–238 (2016)
58. Raghuraman, S., Rindal, P.: Blazing fast PSI from improved OKVS and subfield VOLE. In: 29th ACM Conference on Computer and Communications Security (CCS), pp. 2505–2517 (2022)
59. Rindal, P., Schoppmann, P.: VOLE-PSI: Fast OPRF and circuit-PSI from vector-OLE. In: Advances in Cryptology - EUROCRYPT, pp. 901–930 (2021)
60. Standardization administration of China: GB/T 38636-2020: information security technology – transport layer cryptography protocol (TLCP) (2020)
61. Telecommunication standardization sector of ITU (ITU-T): recommendation x.509: information technology - open systems interconnection - the directory: public-key and attribute certificate frameworks (2019)

62. Telecommunication standardization sector of ITU (ITU-T): recommendation X.1770: technical guidelines for secure multi-party computation (2021)
63. Tu, B., Chen, Y., Liu, Q., Zhang, C.: Fast unbalanced private set union from fully homomorphic encryption. In: 30th ACM Conference on Computer and Communications Security (CCS), pp. 2959–2973 (2023)
64. Wagh, S., Gupta, D., Chandran, N.: SecureNN: 3-party secure computation for neural network training. Proc. Priv. Enhancing Technol. (PETS) **2019**(3), 26–49 (2019)
65. Wang, X., Ranellucci, S., Katz, J.: Authenticated garbling and efficient maliciously secure two-party computation. In: 24th ACM Conference on Computer and Communications Security (CCS), pp. 21–37 (2017)
66. Wang, X., Ranellucci, S., Katz, J.: Global-scale secure multiparty computation. In: 24th ACM Conference on Computer and Communications Security (CCS), pp. 39–56 (2017)
67. Yao, A.: Protocols for secure computations. In: 23rd Annual Symposium on Foundations of Computer Science (FOCS), pp. 160–164 (1982)
68. Yao, A.: How to generate and exchange secrets. In: 27th Annual Symposium on Foundations of Computer Science (FOCS), pp. 162–167 (1986)
69. Zahur, S., Rosulek, M., Evans, D.: Two halves make a whole - reducing data transfer in garbled circuits using half gates. In: Advances in Cryptology - EUROCRYPT, pp. 220–250 (2015)
70. Zhang, C., Chen, Y., Liu, W., Zhang, M., Lin, D.: Linear private set union from multi-query reverse private membership test. In: 32nd USENIX Security Symposium, pp. 337–354 (2023)

Vision Paper: Do We Need Standardization of Blockchain Consensus?

Progress and Challenges to Standardizing Blockchain Consensus

Zhaoxin Yang[1], Xiao Sui[1], Mingfei Zhang[2], Rujia Li[1], and Sisi Duan[1(✉)]

[1] Tsinghua University, Beijing, China
{zhaoxin_yang,suixiao,rujia,duansisi}@tsinghua.edu.cn
[2] Shandong University, Jinan, China

Abstract. Blockchain builds a trustworthy service among parties that do not have to trust each other. In recent years, blockchain applications have exploded, ranging from financial services to governmental applications. In this article, we review blockchain consensus, the crucial building block for blockchains to achieve security goals. By selectively discussing the trade-offs made by each type of consensus protocol and conducting a review of blockchain-related standards, we discuss why we need to standardize blockchain consensus and what challenges are yet to be solved before or even after blockchain consensus is standardized.

Keywords: Byzantine consensus · standardization

1 Introduction

Blockchain is a distributed ledger that ensures the high availability of service and the integrity of data. From a technical perspective, blockchain operates among multiple parties (also called nodes, miners, validators, or replicas). Even if a fraction of the parties are Byzantine faulty (that fail arbitrarily), honest parties can still reach an agreement on the order of the blocks of transactions. The service provided by the blockchain is therefore highly available, and any data that are *finalized* on the blockchain cannot be changed. Accordingly, blockchain is also called a public *tamper-proof* ledger or distributed ledger technology (DLT). From a non-technical perspective, blockchain operates among a group of parties that do not have to trust each other [82]. It serves as a trusted service that provides a shared state and reliable data storage and processing service.

Blockchain has many forms, ranging from cryptocurrencies such as Bitcoin [68] to general-purpose platforms such as Hyperledger Fabric [2] (some cryptocurrencies are generally proposed as well, e.g., Ethereum [94]). Blockchains drive innovations in decentralized finance (DeFi) [93], Non-fungible token (NFT) [91], and decentralized exchanges [97]. Cryptocurrencies like Bitcoin [68] and Ethereum [94] have transformed traditional finance, pushing the market cap to trillions.

© The Author(s), under exclusive license to Springer Nature Switzerland AG 2025
X. Lu and C. J. Mitchell (Eds.): SSR 2024, LNCS 15559, pp. 31–56, 2025.
https://doi.org/10.1007/978-3-031-87541-0_3

The consensus algorithm is the fundamental building block of Blockchain. Informally, blockchain consensus allows honest parties to agree on the chain of blocks/transactions even in the presence of Byzantine parties. The protocol is also known as the Byzantine fault-tolerant (BFT) protocol, originating from the Byzantine general's problem [54]. Driven by the needs of the industry and concrete applications, blockchain consensus has evolved into many forms, making different assumptions about the network and the adversary. We summarize an incomplete list in Table 1.

Although so many types of protocols have been proposed and even used in the industry, designing and implementing a secure Byzantine consensus is still known to be a challenging problem [15]. Indeed, many industrial platforms are known to suffer from various vulnerabilities due to the lack of formal analysis and proof. For instance, many types of *reorganization attacks* have been proposed for the Proof-of-Stake (PoS) protocol used by Ethereum 2.0, and a provably secure *reorg-resilient* solution is yet to be found for PoS in general [70,71,80,100].

Table 1. Industrial blockchain projects and their consensus mechanism. Please refer to §2.1 for the definitions of the timing assumption and adversary models. *Fabric uses a crash-fault-tolerant protocols such a Raft [72] and Zab [51] that tolerate crash failures.

type of blockchain	platform	consensus	timing	adv
cryptocurrency	Bitcoin [68]/Ethereum1.0 [94]	PoW	sync.	CTA
	Ethereum2.0 [94]	PoS	partial sync.	TTA
	Aptos [3]	BFT	partial sync.	TA
	Algorand [39]	PoS	partial sync.	TTA
	Cardano [17]	PoS	sync.	TTA
general purposed	Hyperledger Fabric [2]	CFT*	partial sync.	TA
	Cosmos [21]	BFT	partial sync.	TA
	FISCO BCOS [55]	BFT	partial sync.	TA
	mBridge [77]	BFT	partial sync.	TA

In this paper, we review the blockchain consensus mechanism proposed by both industry and academia (§2). Due to the space limitation, we focus on discussing the models often considered by the industry. By selectively showing some recent results for each model, we discuss the trade-offs made by different consensus approaches. On top of it, in §3, we provide a survey result about the standardization of blockchain-related techniques and blockchain consensus. Based on the review of the underlying techniques and standardization, we discuss whether we need standardizing blockchain consensus and what challenges remain to be solved (§4). The organization of this paper is presented in Fig. 1.

We would like to acknowledge that several nice survey papers on the technical review and applications of blockchain and BFT have been proposed in the past [15,20,22,92]. We do not aim to provide a more comprehensive review.

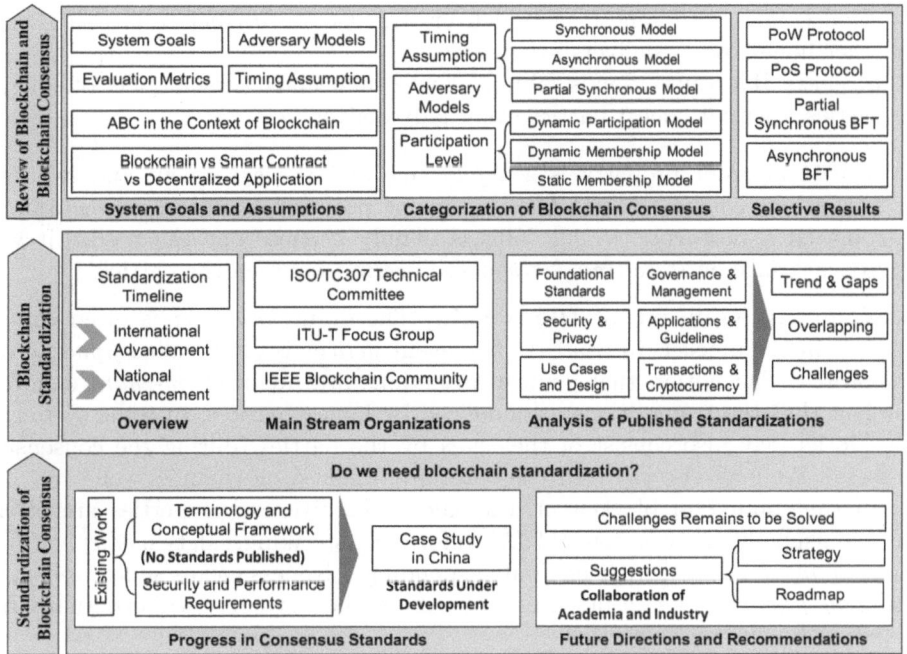

Fig. 1. Organization structure of this paper.

Instead, we focus on the consensus mechanisms used in the industry, selective new research results, and the pathway of standardization of blockchain consensus. To the best of our knowledge, our work is the first one to study the standardization of blockchain consensus.

2   Review of Blockchain and Blockchain Consensus

2.1   System Goals and Assumptions

System Goals. Following the literature of distributed computing, Blockchain consensus achieves *atomic broadcast (ABC)* in the Byzantine failure model [13]. In a system with n parties, up to f of them may fail arbitrarily, i.e., suffering from hardware errors, software bugs, and adversarial attacks. The faulty parties are called Byzantine failures. Non-faulty parties are called *honest* parties.

The ABC primitive is specified by the *broadcast* and *deliver* events. Each party may broadcast some transaction (or a batch of transactions), and honest parties deliver the transactions according to a certain order. The correctness of the ABC can be defined as follows.

- *Agreement.* If an honest party delivers a transaction m, then every honest party delivers m.

- *Total Order.* If an honest party delivers transaction m_1 before m_2, then any other honest party delivers m_1 before m_2.
- *Liveness.* If a transaction is submitted to a sufficiently large number of honest parties, then all honest parties eventually deliver m.

The total order property is a *safety* rule and the agreement and liveness properties are *liveness* rules. The agreement property is not clearly specified in some BFT protocols [18,98]. This is mainly because one can realize it via approaches such as *state transfer/synchronization* between the parties.

ABC in the Context of Blockchain. The event *broadcast* is often called *propose* in the blockchain context. The event *deliver* is often called *finalized* or *committed.* The notion that some transactions are finalized *on-chain* denotes the fact that the transactions are finalized by honest parties. In some systems, the blocks may also consist of the *votes* by the parties (during the consensus process). We may also say that the votes are finalized on-chain as well.

In the context of blockchain, the safety and liveness properties are often defined using different notions [11,37]. Informally speaking, safety means *nothing bad will happen*, i.e., there is no double-spending. Liveness means *something good eventually happens*, i.e., a block proposed by an honest party will eventually be delivered by all honest parties.

As mentioned in the introduction, each party that participates in the consensus may also be called *miners*, *validators*, *replicas*, or *nodes* in different literature. We use them interchangeably in this paper. The votes are sometimes called *attestations.*

Timing Assumption. The timing assumptions can be categorized into the three following models.

- *Synchronous model.* There exists a known upper bound Δ for message delivery and processing.
- *Asynchronous model.* There does not exist an upper bound for message delivery and processing.
- *Partially synchronous model.* There are different ways to model partially synchronous assumptions. The most commonly used one is that there exists an unknown upper bound for message delivery and processing [29]. Alternatively, one may assume the existence of a *global stabilization time* (GST), such that after GST, the network becomes synchronous, but the upper bound is still unknown. In some recent literature, it is assumed that all parties locally maintain an estimated upper bound Δ. After GST, the message transmission and processing delay is lower than or equal to Δ [60].

A reasonable assumption about the asynchronous network is that there exists a malicious *network scheduler* (which can be considered the adversary as well). The network scheduler may arbitrarily delay the messages between any two honest parties. However, if an honest sender sends a message to an honest receiver, the receiver eventually receives the message.

Adversary Models. Following the literature, the adversary models can roughly be divided into the following three types [1,92].

- *Threshold Adversary (TA) model.* In a system with n parties, the adversary controls up to f of the parties. The system remains secure as long as the number of adversarial parties does not exceed f.
- *Computational Threshold Adversary (CTA) model.* In a system with n_c computational power, the adversary controls up to f_c of the computational power.
- *Token Threshold Adversary (TTA) model.* In a system with n_t tokens (also called *stake*, the adversary controls up to f_t of the tokens.

The ratios n/f, n_c/f_c, and n_t/f_t represent the adversary's control over different types of resources: the number of parties, computational power, and tokens, respectively. These models apply to different blockchain systems.

- The model based on n/f works well in environments where all participants have equal resources or computational power. A common example is Practical Byzantine Fault Tolerance (PBFT) [18], assuming $n > 3f$. In the industrial projects, Tendermint [10] (a variant of PBFT, used by the Cosmos project [21]) and AptosBFT (a variant of HotStuff [98], used by the Aptos project [3]) also fall into this category.
- The model based on n_c/f_c reflects the scenario where the adversary can gain or lose computational power over time. Examples include proof-of-work (PoW) based systems like Bitcoin [68] and Ethereum 1.0 [12].
- The model based on n_t/f_t reflects the adversary's influence on the amount of stake. Typical examples in this category are the proof-of-stake (PoS) protocols, such as those used in Ethereum 2.0, Algorand [39], and Cardano [17]. Notably, if all parties in PoS own the same amount of the stake, PoS protocols can often be interpreted (or even proved) as conventional BFT protocols.

In the TA model, there is an important concept called **Byzantine quorum** [13]. For instance, consider the ABC problem in a partially synchronous network. The tight bound is $f \leq \lfloor \frac{n-1}{3} \rfloor$ (we use the notation $f < \frac{n}{3}$ below to simplify the notation). A Byzantine quorum is $\lceil \frac{n+f+1}{2} \rceil$. Most consensus protocols that consider the TA model require a quorum of parties to vote before an agreement can be reached. Matching votes from a quorum of parties are also called *quorum certificate* (QC), or certificate for short.

In each adversary model, different bounds exist for the relationships between n/f, n_c/f_c, and n_t/f_t. We list some of them in Table 2. For protocols in the TA model, it is well known that $f < \frac{n}{3}$ is the tight bound in the partially synchronous network or asynchronous network, and $f < \frac{n}{2}$ is the tight bound in the synchronous network. Protocols that achieve the tight bound are called to achieve *optimal resilience*. In the CTA model, it was shown that PoW can be proved in the synchronous model under the $f_c < \frac{n_c}{2}$ assumption [36]. Finally, the bounds for protocols in the TTA model largely mimic those in the TA model. Informally, this is because the two models can, in general, be reduced to each other, as mentioned above.

Table 2. Comparison of the adversary models for selective blockchain projects.

project/protocol	TA (n/f)	CTA (n_c/f_c)	TTA (n_t/f_t)
PBFT [18]/Tendermint [10]	$f < \frac{n}{3}$	N/A	N/A
Bitcoin (PoW) [68]	N/A	$f_c < \frac{n_c}{2}$	N/A
Ethereum 1.0 (PoW) [12]	N/A	$f_c < \frac{n_c}{2}$	N/A
Ethereum 2.0 (PoS)	N/A	N/A	$f_t < \frac{n_t}{3}$
Algorand (PoS) [39]	N/A	N/A	$f_t < \frac{n_t}{3}$
Cardano (PoS) [17]	N/A	N/A	$f_t < \frac{n_t}{2}$

Blockchain Consensus vs. Smart Contracts vs. Decentralized Applications. From a layered view, blockchain consists of three broad layers [1,92]: consensus, smart contracts, and decentralized applications (DApps). Smart contracts are computer programs that can be written by end users. They can be deployed on the blockchain in the form of transactions and authorized parties can execute the transactions on-chain. In some systems, smart contracts can be executed *off-chain* (e.g., also called layer 2 solutions [42]). Execution results are then submitted on-chain to validate the results. Popular smart contracts include Ethereum virtual machine (EVM) and Hyperledger Chaincode.

Blockchain consensus and smart contracts can together be modelled as Byzantine fault-tolerant state machine replication (BFT-SMR). Namely, BFT consensus allows honest parties to reach an agreement on the order of the transactions. Each party is associated with a *deterministic* state machine. Given the same initial state and the same input, the state machines always output a consistent result. Ideally, smart contracts realize the state machine at the replicas.

On top of smart contracts, various types of DApps can be built to serve different purposes in diverse domains [56,75,76,96,103]. These applications leverage the underlying blockchain infrastructure to provide decentralized, trustless solutions to real-world problems. DApps can range from decentralized finance (DeFi) platforms and non-fungible token (NFT) marketplaces to supply chain management systems and voting mechanisms.

Evaluation Metrics. There are several metrics for evaluating the performance of blockchain/blockchain consensus: latency, throughput, server scalability, and client scalability, as defined below.

- *Latency.* The time it takes for a transaction (after a transaction is submitted to the blockchain) to be finalized.
- *Throughput.* The number of transactions that can be processed per second. The notion is often called transactions per second (TPS). This indicator directly reflects the transaction processing capability of the blockchain platform.
- *Server scalability.* The number of parties the systems can have to achieve a decent throughput. A system is scalable if the performance does not degrade significantly as the number of parties grows.

- *Client scalability.* The number of concurrent *clients* that can be handled. In this particular notion, one has to differentiate the role of the *clients* who submit the transactions from the roles of the parties that participate in the consensus protocol. In practice, each party can have multiple roles.

There are also several other theoretical metrics for evaluating communication overhead/cost.

- *Message complexity.* The total number of messages parties need to exchange.
- *Communication complexity.* The total size of the messages parties need to exchange.
- *Time complexity.* The expected number of *rounds/steps* it takes for parties to reach an agreement.
- *Computational complexity.* The computation cost for computations such as cryptographic primitives may affect the performance of the system. The computational complexity is usually determined by the number of *expensive* operations such as exponentiation or pairings.

Following the notion in the literature [13], a step (mentioned above) consists of the following behavior of a party: receiving a message from another party; executing a local computation; and sending a message to some other parties. Additionally, the round is more of a concept of *iteration* in some protocols, where each iteration consists of multiple steps. In the literature, time complexity is sometimes called round complexity.

2.2   Categorization of Blockchain Consensus

Classification Based on the Participation Level. Blockchains can be generally classified into permissionless blockchains and permissioned blockchains [62]. In permissionless blockchains, any party can join the system without obtaining any particular *permission*. Most cryptocurrencies (e.g., Bitcoin and Ethereum) belong to permissionless blockchains. In contrast, permissioned blockchains require parties to obtain a *permission*, possibly from parties that are already participating in the systems, to join the system.

The concepts of permissionless and permissioned blockchains are often associated with public blockchains, private blockchains, and consortium blockchains. In public blockchains, any party can join the system. In private blockchains, only parties in a single organization can join the system. In consortium blockchains, several organizations collaboratively join the system and operate the blockchain systems. Most permissionless blockchains are public blockchains. However, some permissionless blockchains can be deployed in the private setting as well. For example, Ethereum Testnet, Sepolia [87], is maintained by a set of authorized parity for helping developers to simulate the Ethereum mainnet. Most permissioned blockchains are deployed as private blockchains and consortium blockchains.

Besides, the concept of *dynamic participation* is related to the permissionless/permissioned setting. Dynamic participation refers to the model where each honest party can join the system and determine whether it participates in the protocol. This is also called the *sleepy consensus* model, where some party unpredictably sleeps (e.g., by turning off the server) and wakes up (e.g., by turning on the server and participating in the system) [73]. In the literature, this is also called the *crash-recovery* model, where parties keep infinitely often crashing and recovering [13].

One typical feature of blockchains in the dynamic participation model is that one does not need to know the total number of parties (and their identities) that participate in the system. Bitcoin is one typical example (in fact, the motivation for defining the sleepy model [73]. In contrast, most other systems do not have such a feature. This does not mean that new parties cannot join the system, and existing parties cannot leave the system. Instead, parties can submit *transactions* (also called membership requests in some work [27]) to join and leave the system.

Accordingly, we classify the systems into the following types.

- *Dynamic participation model.* Any honest party can freely join and leave the system without notifying other parties beforehand.
- *Dynamic membership model.* Any party can join and leave the system after notifying other parties or after an agreement is reached by parties that are already in the system.
- *Static membership model.* Every honest party remains in the system ever since the beginning of the system.

Besides Bitcoin, most known blockchain systems fall into the category of the dynamic membership model or the static membership model. Supporting dynamic participation for the consensus protocols is an active research area [6,59,65,69]. Additionally, many consensus protocols are not designed particularly for the dynamic membership model or dynamic participation model. To support dynamic membership, some systems treat membership requests as normal transactions. Namely, after an agreement is reached by existing parties in the protocol, parties can join or leave the system. In this way, one does not have to modify the protocol. It was found that in a partially synchronous model or asynchronous model, such a modification may make the system suffer from liveness issue [27]. The security properties need to be re-defined accordingly. One can actually *transform* conventional protocols (in the static membership model) to protocols in the dynamic membership model [27,61].

Classification Based on the Timing Assumptions. Most industrial systems adopt consensus solutions in the synchronous or partially synchronous model, as summarized in Table 1. We believe the underlying reason is two-fold. First, the partial synchronous model is believed to well match the real network condition, i.e., the network is *stable* most of the time and becomes unstable occasionally. Additionally, if we set up a *timer* in a synchronous protocol to a large enough value, it is likely that all messages can be received before the timer expires. Accordingly, the synchronous protocol becomes a fit for the network condition. Second, most synchronous and partially synchronous protocols achieve a nice balance of latency and throughput and suit the needs of practical workloads.

Classification Based on the Adversary Models. As summarized in Table 1, most cryptocurrencies adopt the CTA or the TTA models. In contrast, general-purposed blockchain systems adopt the TA model, mostly because these blockchains are deployed in a private or consortium setting, and protocols in this category usually achieve great performance when the number of parties is small.

We would like to emphasize that from the design perspective, there is not a clear distinction between protocols in different adversary models. As mentioned above, as the TA models and TTA models can be interpreted in the same way, the design philosophy of protocols in these two categories is in fact quite similar.

Discussion. Designing a provably secure *and* practical consensus protocol is not easy, also as pointed out by many prior works [15]. The problem is a lot similar to the system engineering effort. There does not exist a one-size-fits-all solution, i.e., achieving both low latency, high throughput, and great scalability. One has to balance between the assumptions made (such that they are closest to reality) and the performance preference (depending on the expected workload of the system) before choosing the solution for the system.

Besides the assumptions mentioned above, additional assumptions are also interesting in the literature, e.g., static adversary vs adaptive adversary [58], building post-quantum secure protocols [26,99] vss non-quantum-secure protocols. We do not cover these topics in this paper due to space limitations.

> **Takeaway 1:** There does not exist a one-size-fits-all consensus mechanism.

2.3 Selective Results

In this section, we review the consensus mechanism proposed by both industry and academia. Due to space limitation, we show selective results and provide some additional results in Appendix A.

Proof-of-Work (PoW) Protocol . Proof-of-Work is one of the most well-known consensus protocols in permissionless blockchain systems. It was first introduced by Bitcoin [32] and has been adopted by many other cryptocurrencies like Ethereum 1.0 [12]. PoW protocols can be broadly categorized into the following types.

- *SHA-256 based PoW.* Bitcoin uses the SHA-256 hash function as its *mining* algorithm. Briefly speaking, parties compete to compute a hash value that is lower than a pre-specified *nonce* to become a block proposer. The competition to find such a value is called the *mining* process and is very computationally intensive. Specialized hardware (e.g. Application Specific Integrated Circuit, ASIC) was developed later to speed up the process.
- *ASIC-resistant PoW.* Protocols like Ethereum 1.0 [12] and Litecoin [57] use memory-hard algorithms such as Ethash and Scrypt [81]. These algorithms are designed to be resistant to ASIC mining. Some other protocols like Monero [66] use RandomX, which is more efficient for general-purpose CPUs.

- *Energy-saving PoW.* Some newer protocols are exploring ways to make PoW more economical. Chia [19] uses *Proof-of-Space*, which relies on storage capacity instead of computational power to reduce energy consumption. Other researchers study combining PoW with VDF (verifiable delay function), called Sprints [64], to force miners to perform PoW intermittently.

Although many PoW variants seek to improve efficiency, they all inherit the drawbacks of PoW, such as high energy consumption. Based on the knowledge known so far, these protocols can be provably secure (some of the protocols are not formally analyzed) only in a synchronous network, so the network assumption is the strongest among all consensus mechanisms.

> **Takeaway 2:** PoW protocol is the first protocol under the dynamic participation model but suffers from high energy consumption.

Proof-of-Stake (PoS) Protocols. PoS protocols have emerged as a popular and energy-efficient alternative to PoW. In PoS systems, parties are chosen to create new blocks based on the number of tokens they hold and are willing to *stake* (i.e., deposit). PoS protocols can be categorized into the following types.

- *Chain-based PoS.* Early PoS protocols like Peercoin [74] use a chain-based design where validators are pseudo-randomly selected to propose new blocks.
- *BFT-like PoS.* Algorand [39] proposes a variant of Byzantine agreement (BA) protocol and a committee sampling algorithm to build an efficient PoS protocol. Algorand assigns weights to the votes according to the stake each party owns to avoid Sybil attacks. It was found that one can directly use a BFT protocol as a PoS protocol as well and many industrial systems use variants of PBFT or HotStuff as their PoS protocols [3,10].
- *Hybrid-consensus PoS.* Ethereum's transition from PoW to PoS introduces a hybrid consensus protocol that combines chain-based PoS and BFT-style consensus. Besides proposing blocks, parties can also vote (called attest in the notion of Ethereum). Such a combination allows the protocol to *finalize* the blocks faster than prior works. Other variants of hybrid PoS include Cardano's Ouroboros [53] protocol and its follow-up works.
- *Delegated PoS (DPoS).* Some protocols like EOS [31] and Tron [89] allow token holders to vote for a limited number of parties and delegate their voting rights to the delegated parties. By running the consensus mechanism among delegated parties only, the system enjoys higher performance than other PoS approaches.

These PoS protocols overcome several PoW issues, such as high energy consumption. However, PoS protocols face other challenges including the difficulty of security analysis. Indeed, many PoS protocols have been found to suffer from various attacks.

> **Takeaway 3:** PoS protocols have become one of the most widely deployed consensus mechanisms, especially for cryptocurrencies.

Partially Synchronous BFT. As mentioned previously and also summarized in Table 1, partially synchronous BFT protocols are widely adopted in general-purpose systems. We categorize partially synchronous BFT into the following types.

- *All-to-all BFT.* These protocols involve all-to-all communication, where each party needs to send a message to all other parties, thus incurring $O(n^2)$ message complexity. Many classic BFT protocols fall into this category, e.g., PBFT [18] and its variants [10,27]. Such protocols are known to achieve a nice performance, i.e., low latency and high throughput, when the number of parties is small enough (say, <50 in wide area network). When the network further scales, the performance starts to degrade significantly.
- *BFT with linearity.* Protocols such as HotStuff [98] have attracted much attention in recent years, as they achieve $O(n)$ message complexity and $O(n)$ communication complexity. In these protocols, only one party communicates with all other parties. A pipelining feature (a new block can be proposed while disseminating the votes) can be used to improve the scalability. Compared to protocols in the all-to-all category, BFT with linearity achieves better scalability at the cost of higher expected latency. Several works reduce the number of phases from three in HotStuff to two to reduce the latency [38,49,86]. A very recent work Dashing [28] uses the concept of *weak QC* and *strong QC* to build more robust and efficient BFT with linearity.
- *Chain-based BFT.* Chain-based BFT organizes parties in a chain [24,43] and leverages the pipelining message pattern for high throughput. The communication paradigm is actually quite close to many PoS protocols. Among these protocols, BChain [24] is the first fully-fledged BFT protocol achieving both safety and liveness by itself and leverages the pipelining message pattern for high throughput. The cost is higher latency than other types of BFT.

> **Takeaway 4:** Partially synchronous BFT achieves a nice balance between low latency and high throughput when the network size is small.

Asynchronous BFT. The celebrated FLP result [34] says that *deterministic* BFT protocol will never be safe and live in an asynchronous network. Alternatively, BFT from randomization is the only solution to asynchronous BFT [16]. In these protocols, parties collaboratively compute a randomized *common coin* value, which can either be a binary value used for *binary agreement* [67,99] or several bits for a common *leader election* [14,26]. One notable research area is asynchronous common subset (ACS), a notion due to Ben-Or, Canetti, and

Goldreich (BCG) in the context of asynchronous multiparty computation [4]. Ben-Or, Kelmer, and Rabin (BKR) presented the ACS construction [5] from reliable broadcast (RBC) [8,9] and asynchronous binary agreement [67,99]. The BKR paradigm was found to be very powerful in recent years as RBC and ABA can be instantiated with very practical constructions [25,58,63]. Many works seek to further push the boundary of practical ACS constructions. There are two lines of research in this area: signature-free ACS (and is thus post-quantum secure) [26,99] and signature-based ACS [44,45]. The performance of ACS (used as a BFT) can be much higher than partial synchronous BFTs when there is a high concurrency of transactions.

> **Takeaway 5:** Practical asynchronous BFT achieves high throughput when there is a high concurrency of transactions.

3 Blockchain Standardization

3.1 Overview of the International Blockchain Standards

As mentioned above, blockchain integrates multiple technologies. The standardization of blockchain-related technologies requires a more comprehensive and systematic approach. Many organizations have initiated standardization efforts, as summarized in Fig. 2. The major players include ISO (International Organization for Standardization), ITU-T (International Telecommunication Union Telecommunication Standardization Sector), IEEE, W3C, IEC (International Electrotechnical Commission), IRTF (Internet Research Task Force), IETF (Internet Engineering Task Force), Standards Australia (SA), BSI (British Standards Institution), SAC (Standardization Administration of China), BRIBA (Belt and Road Initiative Blockchain Alliance), CESI (China Electronics Standardization Institute), and Hyperledger [50].

ISO/TC307, established by ISO under the leadership of SA in Sep 2016, is recognized as the first international working group dedicated to the development of blockchain standards [41]. In 2017, IEEE and ITU-T launched the blockchain standards program [47]. Notably, organizations like ISO, ITU-T, and IEEE are actively working on multiple blockchain standards. Additionally, many standard-setting activities are concentrated in countries such as China, the United States, and Australia. For instance, ISO/TC307 was established under the leadership of Standards Australia (SA), with its standardization framework developed based on the blockchain standards roadmap published by Standards Australia (SA). The NIST (National Institute of Standards and Technology) announced its collaboration with ISO to define the international blockchain standards in 2018 and has already published 7 blockchain standards. By the time of this paper, ITU-T and ISO have established 16 working groups and study groups for blockchain standardization efforts. China participates in 14 of these groups and has contributed to 19 out of the 45 blockchain standards released by ITU-T.

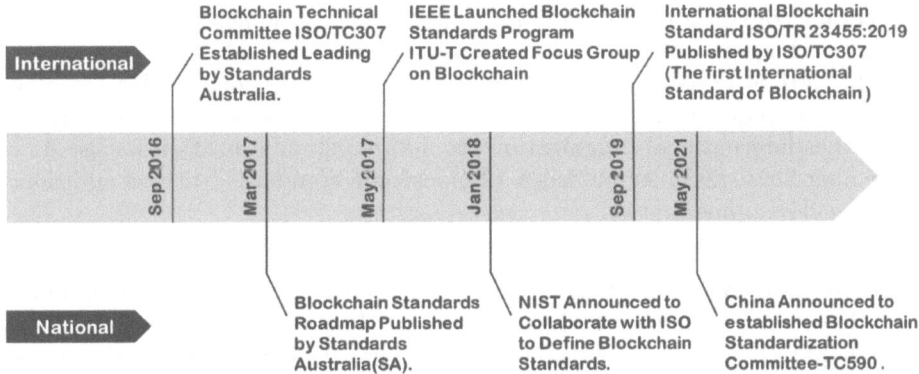

Fig. 2. Various organizations have started devoting efforts to standardize blockchains and DLT.

3.2 Mainstream International Standardization Organizations for Blockchain and DLT

An overview of mainstream international blockchain standardization organizations reveals that the primary blockchain standards are developed and published by ISO, ITU-T, and IEEE. As of September 2024, these three organizations have formally published 86 blockchain standards. A comparison of standards from ISO, ITU-T, and IEEE is presented in Fig. 3, where the horizontal axis represents different organizations and the vertical axis indicates the number of standards.

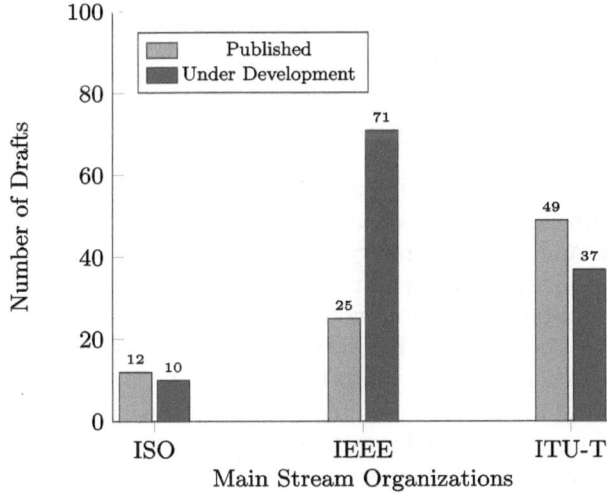

Fig. 3. Blockchain standards Status for mainstream international organizations.

Current Progress of ISO/TC307. Since the establishment of TC307 in 2016, several working groups and study groups have been formed. The secretariat of ISO/TC 307 is based in Australia and is primarily responsible for formulating international standards for blockchain and DLT, as well as collaborating with other international organizations to address standardization issues. As of September 2024, ISO has published 12 blockchain standards, with an additional 10 under development [48].

Current Progress of IEEE. IEEE is a non-profit professional organization that focuses on standard development. The research on standardizing blockchain technology can be traced back to May 2017.IEEE initiated the project titled"Standard for the Framework of Blockchain Use in IoT". Afterwards, it initiated an ongoing project related to blockchain technology. Additionally, IEEE has produced an industry connection document known as "Blockchain Asset Exchange" and has established an active Working Group dedicated to this subject. In January 2018, IEEE established the IEEE Blockchain Initiative, which serves as the main institution for blockchain-related projects and activities within the IEEE [46]. As of September 2024, IEEE has published 25 standards, while 71 are being developed [85].

Current Progress of ITU-T. The International Telecommunication Union (ITU) is a United Nations agency in charge of information and communication technology affairs. It is responsible for allocating and managing global radio frequency spectrum and satellite orbit resources, formulating global telecommunication standards, providing telecommunication assistance to developing countries, and promoting the development of global telecommunications [47]. As of September 2024, 49 blockchain-related standards have been approved by ITU-T, with 39 currently in development [78].

3.3   Analysis of Published International Standards

We analyze the 86 international blockchain standards currently published by leading standardization organizations. The standards will be categorized based on their content and scope of applications.

From an organizational perspective, both ISO and IEEE have organized dedicated blockchain standardization working groups. These working groups have clear divisions in their efforts. For instance, ISO/TC307, the earliest international standardization working group for blockchain, has well-structured internal divisions focusing on technical areas(e.g., smart contracts, interoperability, NFTs, etc.) and application and governance standards. In contrast, ITU-T does not have a specialized blockchain working group and largely relies on existing working groups (SG13, SG16, SG17, and SG20) to initiate and develop standards. This has resulted in inconsistencies in the classification of currently published standards among these organizations.

ISO/TC307. We classify the 12 standards published by ISO into four categories: *Use Cases and Design* (4 items), *Foundational Standards* (2 items), *Privacy and Security* (3 items), and *Governance and Management* (3 items). Overall, ISO/TC307 has a nice balance among standards related to applications, technology, and management. Foundational standards, such as vocabulary and reference architectures, have also been continuously updated since their release, while the technical specifications are comprehensive, especially in areas concerning security and privacy.

ITU-T. The 49 standards published by ITU-T can be classified into five categories: *Foundational Standards* (10 items), *Security and Privacy* (13 items), *Application Framework and System Design* (15 items), *Regulatory and Governance* (6 items), and *Performance and Evaluation* (5 items). Overall, ITU-T's blockchain-related standards have placed significant emphasis on applications and security, whereas technical specification standards remain relatively limited, especially in the standardization of specific technical components such as digital signatures, smart contracts, and consensus mechanisms.

IEEE. The 25 standards published by IEEE are classified into five categories: *Cryptocurrency and Transactions* (6 items), *Blockchain Applications and Management* (7 items), *Foundational Guidelines* (5 items), *Interoperability* (5 items), and *Governance and Risk Management* (2 items). Similar to ITU-T, IEEE places greater emphasis on standards related to blockchain applications, particularly in the context of cryptocurrency and transactions. The variety of standards in blockchain applications and management reflects the widespread adoption of this technology across different sectors. Furthermore, while the number of standards directly related to governance and risk management is limited, there are relevant aspects of security addressed within the interoperability and application management standards. Additionally, the number of drafts related to technical specifications in the IEEE standards is also relatively low.

Trends and Analysis

- *Overlapping in foundational standards.* Major organizations have established regulations for foundational blockchain standards (such as vocabulary, data formats, data flow, and reference architectures), with most of these regulations completed between 2019 and 2021. These foundational standards serve as the basis for subsequent security, application, and regulatory standards.
- *Sufficient application guidelines.* The development of application standards is substantial among standardization organizations. Such a trend shows that there exists a significant industry demand for the standardization of blockchain applications.
- *Insufficient core technical standards.* A gap across standardization organizations is the lack of technical specifications for core components such as consensus mechanisms and smart contracts. The development of technology is often limited by formalization and standardization.

– *Lack of standards for the security of the technical components.* Although there is a decent number of blockchain security standards, existing security standards primarily address issues closely related to systems such as IoT, power grids, and commercial applications. There remains a lack of security standards related to the technical components.

We also review the standardization of blockchain-related technology in China for the purpose of our case study in §4. Due to space limitations, we provide the details in Appendix B.

4 Standardization of Blockchain Consensus: Ongoing Progress and Challenges

4.1 Do We Need Standards for Blockchain Consensus?

The consensus mechanism is the core technique for Blockchain to achieve the security goals. As mentioned previously, many protocols have been proposed and used by different blockchain platforms. However, the standard(s) of blockchain consensus has yet to be made. One natural question is:

Do we really need standard(s) for blockchain consensus?

Our vision is *yes*. Namely, as pointed out by previous works [15], without being investigated and thoroughly analyzed by experts, consensus mechanisms are vulnerable to attacks. Many open-source industrial projects have experienced many examples [30,33,69,83]. In contrast, many consensus protocols used in consortium blockchains or private blockchains are not publicly available, making it even more challenging to discover the vulnerabilities.

The absence of unified security standards for consensus mechanisms has resulted in inconsistent design and implementation across blockchain platforms. One of the most notable examples is the Ronin Bridge attack in March 2022. Hackers managed to steal over $600 million worth of assets (173,600 ETH and 25.5 million USDC) by exploiting vulnerabilities in the Ronin sidechain's consensus mechanism [23,102]. The attackers gained control of validators, allowing them to bypass transaction verification. The Ronin Bridge was compromised because only nine validators existed and the attackers managed to control five of them, violating the assumption made by the mechanism.

Accordingly, the absence of standardized consensus mechanisms makes it challenging to trust the assets maintained by blockchain systems. To promote the safe and sustainable use of blockchain in safeguarding critical infrastructure and other use cases, it is desirable to establish unified standards for blockchain consensus mechanisms. In fact, consensus mechanisms are a lot like cryptographic protocols, which are commonly standardized nowadays.

4.2 Progress in Consensus Standards

Currently, there are no international or national standards that explicitly define specific implementation schemes for blockchain consensus mechanisms. Existing standards related to blockchain consensus mechanisms primarily focus on the following aspects:

- *Terminology and conceptual framework.* Current standards often define the basic terminology, concepts, and frameworks related to blockchain technology and its consensus mechanisms. For example, ISO 22739:2024 outlines the fundamental concepts of blockchain and consensus mechanisms but does not specify concrete technical implementations. A concluding viewpoint is that "the details regarding consensus differ among DLT systems and this can be a distinguishing characteristic between one DLT system and another" (definition 3.12, note 2).
- *Security and performance requirements.* Some standards address the security, performance testing, and application of consensus mechanisms across different industries. For example, China's national standard *Information Security Technology - Blockchain Security Framework* [84] outlines the security risks associated with consensus mechanisms and proposes security requirements for blockchain consensus protocols.

One of the main challenges in standardizing specific implementations of consensus mechanisms is that blockchain consensus technologies-especially those used in public blockchains-are still rapidly evolving. Solutions undergo frequent iterations, and new security vulnerabilities are continually discovered in existing mechanisms. In contrast, classical consensus mechanisms such as BFT protocols have been studied for over four decades and the proof and analysis are well provided by most research articles. Accordingly, the standardization of some consensus mechanisms such as BFT protocols is indeed feasible.

In fact, the National Information Security Standardization Technical Committee of China has released the first batch of national cybersecurity standards for 2023 [79], which includes the standards "Information Security Technology - Specification for Asynchronous Blockchain Consensus" and "Information Security Technology - Specification for Partial Synchronous Blockchain Consensus" led by the Institute of Software at the Chinese Academy of Sciences and Tsinghua University, respectively. The two standards aim to standardize two BFT protocols Dumbo [45] and Dyno [27], respectively.

On May 22, 2024, the IEEE Computer Society established the CFBS_p3215 WG - Consensus Framework for Blockchain Systems working group, which is expected to further advance the standardization of blockchain consensus mechanisms.

4.3   Future Directions and Recommendations

Based on the published international standards for blockchain, we find that the standardization efforts can be categorized into three phases: the initial phase, the development phase, and the maturity phase. In the initial stage, due to a lack of relevant understanding of blockchain, the primary focus is usually standardizing terminologies and reference architectures. This included defining key stakeholders, essential technological elements, and the interaction processes among various technological components. With the maturity of blockchain technology, standardization gradually transitioned into the development phase, primarily led by the industry. During this phase, use cases, application frameworks, and guidelines tailored to various scenarios were established. With the continuous convergence of technology and industry, standardizing some crucial building blocks is needed in the maturity phase, addressing security concerns, network attacks, and performance challenges.

Given the observation above, there are still some key challenges before or even after the standards are developed for blockchain consensus:

- *There is no one-size-fits-all consensus mechanism.* As mentioned previously, there is no one-size-fits-all consensus mechanism. One has to have a good understanding of the network conditions, deployment environment, and expected application workload, to *choose* the underlying consensus mechanism. Accordingly, also similar to the cryptographic standards, a family of standards for blockchain consensus might be needed.
- *Academia has been constantly developing new provably secure mechanisms.* The research in the consensus mechanism has lasted for four decades and is still an active research area. A good question is *which one should be chosen to standardize?* Additionally, the research results that are proven to achieve decent performance on paper might not be easy to implement and deploy in production systems. Accordingly, collaborations between the industry and academia are desirable in standardizing efforts.
- *Adopting a new consensus mechanism takes tremendous engineering efforts, especially for production systems.* Blockchain consensus mechanism is well known to be challenging to design, implement, and deploy, mostly because of a lack of well-trained experts. For a system to migrate to a new consensus mechanism, it usually takes a long time to implement, validate, and deploy. For instance, Ethereum spends 2 years to migrate from 1.0 to 2.0 [88]. If standards are developed for the consensus mechanism, many systems might be *reluctant* to adopt them.

We argue that standards do not aim to cherry-pick the *best* solutions, but rather to promote the use of *correct* mechanisms. Considering that the technical agreement in the industry regarding terminology and basic architecture has already been established, we have the following conclusion:

> **Takeaway 6:** Standardizing provably secure consensus mechanisms that have been validated by industrial systems and collaboration between industry and academia are desirable for standardizing blockchain consensus.

Additionally, the standardization roadmap for blockchain consensus mechanisms can be learned from the development of standards for cryptographic primitives. As discussed above, consensus mechanisms can be viewed as cryptographic protocols. Therefore, we have the following conclusion.

> **Takeaway 7:** Standardization for blockchain consensus mechanism can follow the roadmap of standards for cryptographic primitives.

Finally, attention should also be paid to the correct implementation, testing, and evaluation of consensus mechanisms to further improve the quality of the standard(s) and the adoption of the standards.

Acknowledgment. This work was supported in part by the National Key R&D Program of China under 2022YFB2701700, Beijing Natural Science Foundation under M23015, the National Natural Science Foundation of China under 92267203, China Postdoctoral Science Foundation under 2023M741949, and the Shuimu Tsinghua Scholar Program of Tsinghua University. Sisi is also with Zhongguancun Laboratory and Shandong Institute of Blockchain.

A   Additional Variants of Consensus Mechanism

Intel proposes the PoET (Proof-of-Elapsed-Time) mechanism that uses a trusted execution environment (TEE) to replace the mining process. Accordingly, PoET is both more performant and energy-efficient. Additionally, Proof-of-Authority (PoA), first introduced by Gavin Wood [95] as part of the Ethereum ecosystem, aims to be an efficient alternative of PoW. Intuitively, PoA is a variant of a GHOST-based consensus algorithm where parties take turns to propose blocks [101]. PoA is used in top cryptocurrencies such as VeChain [90] and Binance Smart Chain [7].

Directed Acyclic Graph (DAG) uses the data structure to model the proposed blocks. DAG-Rider uses DAG to build an asynchronous BFT protocol [52]. Each party stores the blocks proposed by other parties in a DAG data structure. Then, parties agree on the order by extracting some information from the DAG. This paradigm is also known as the type that de-couples block transmission (block proposal) from agreement on the order. Such a paradigm does not necessarily need DAG [28, 35, 40].

B   A Case Study: Chinese Standards

As of June 2024, according to incomplete data from the National Public Service Platform for Standards Information, the National Group Standards Information Platform and the Enterprise Standards Information Platform, China has researched or developed over 300 blockchain-related standards. These include 16 national standard plans, 8 officially published national standards, 22 industry standards, 42 local standards, and 215 group standards. The growth of various standards is shown in Fig. 4.

National Standards and Standardization Plans. As of June 2024, China has officially published and implemented eight national blockchain standards.

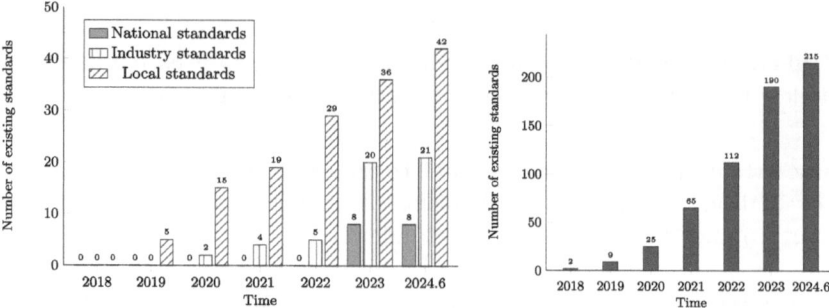

(a) Number of national standards, industry standards, and local standards.

(b) Number of group standards.

Fig. 4. Number of standard developments by blockchain-related organizations in China.

For example, the"Blockchain and Distributed Ledger Technology Terminology" (GB/T 43572-2023) aligns with the international standard ISO 22739:2020, and all of these standards were issued in 2023. Other notable standards include the "Blockchain and Distributed Ledger Technology Reference Architecture" (GB/T 42752-2023), "Information Security Technology - Blockchain Information Service Security Requirements" (GB/T 42571-2023), and "Information Security Technology - Blockchain Technology Security Framework" (GB/T 42570-2023). Two of these standards specifically address security issues and were among the first issued in May 2023. They provide foundational, general frameworks for guiding the application and development of blockchain technology in China by standardizing the functional architecture and core components of blockchain systems. These standards offer critical guidance for the industry in understanding blockchain concepts, building comprehensive blockchain systems, and selecting appropriate blockchain services.

The existing national standards cover a wide array of blockchain technologies, including application programming interfaces (APIs), notarization services, smart contract management, and system testing. This indicates a systematic and comprehensive approach to blockchain standardization, with a strong emphasis on security and governance.

In addition, 16 standards are currently under development, including four that are either identical to or modified versions of ISO standards. These developing standards reveal several key trends:

- *Integration of Blockchain with specific applications.* Draft standards address not only foundational technologies, such as blockchain appliances and distributed storage, but also specific industry applications like cold-chain food traceability and logistics tracking. This demonstrates the deepening integration of blockchain technology across various sectors.
- *Enhanced regulation and governance.* The inclusion of standards for blockchain regulatory platform access, service operation monitoring frame-

works, and governance guidelines highlights the growing importance of regulatory oversight as blockchain technology continues to advance.

- *Promoting maturity and interoperability of Blockchain services.* Draft standards include evaluation models for service capability maturity, reference architectures for distributed identity services, and technical specifications for cross-chain interoperability, reflecting efforts to enhance the maturity and interoperability of blockchain services.

Current national standards and plans demonstrate alignment with international standards in areas such as terminology and architecture while also reflecting differentiated approaches to specific applications.

> **Takeaway 8:** Chinese national standards partially align with the ISO standards, and have begun to establish standards for blockchain consensus technology.

Industry Standards, Local Standards, and Group Standards. We calculated the annual growth rates of industry standards, local Standards, and group Standards in Table 3.

Table 3. Annual addition of standard statistics

Standards	Time(year)						
	2018	2019	2020	2021	2022	2023	2024.1-2024.6
Industry standards	0	0	2	2	1	15	1
Local standards	0	5	10	4	10	7	6
Group standards	2	7	16	40	47	78	25

As of June 2024, 22 industry standards have been published. The first blockchain-related industry standard, "Blockchain Technology Financial Application Evaluation Rules" (JR/T 0193-2020), was released in 2020. The year 2023 saw a surge in growth, with 15 industry standards published. These industry standards highlight three major technological trends: 1) emphasis on security and performance testing in blockchain technology; 2) standardization of blockchain applications in specific industries, such as insurance and publishing, to foster technical norms and data management. 3) the convergence of blockchain with other technologies, such as the Internet of Things (IoT), smart cities, and industrial internet, is expanding blockchain's application scenarios and business potential.

In terms of local standards, 42 have been released, with the first blockchain-related local standard, "Blockchain Security Evaluation Index System" (DB61/T 1283-2019), published by Shanxi Province in 2019. The highest growth occurred in 2022, with 10 local standards issued. Local standards are characterized by their integration with regional features and industries. Multiple provinces emphasize security and regulatory requirements. For example, Shanghai's standard on blockchain security general requirements (DB31/T 1331-2021) and Jiangsu's standard on blockchain information system testing protocols (DB32/T 4197-2022) highlight the priority placed on security. Additionally, some regions are focusing on data notarization and smart contract security, reflecting a shared concern for security and technical standards across blockchain applications.

Regarding group standards, 215 have been published. The first blockchain-related group standard, "Blockchain Platform Basic Technical Requirements" (T/SIA 007-2018), was issued in 2018. The number of group standards has grown rapidly, with 78 published in 2023 alone. Various sectors are actively developing blockchain-related standards, ranging from financial e-invoicing, service credit, smart contracts, and supply chain management to educational credit token systems and genetic data applications. This broad applicability underscores blockchain's cross-industry relevance. Additionally, a significant portion of these standards focuses on data privacy protection, security technical guidelines, and smart contract security, underscoring the ongoing importance of security and privacy in blockchain development.

> **Takeaway 9:** China's blockchain standards prioritize security, industry applications, and integration with other technologies. The rapid growth in standards shows blockchain's increasing role in technology and regulation.

References

1. Abraham, I., Malkhi, D., et al.: The blockchain consensus layer and BFT. Bull. EATCS **3**(123) (2017)
2. Androulaki, E., et al.: Hyperledger fabric: a distributed operating system for permissioned blockchains. In: Proceedings of the Thirteenth EuroSys Conference, p. 30. ACM (2018)
3. Aptos. https://aptosfoundation.org/
4. Ben-Or, M., Canetti, R., Goldreich, O.: Asynchronous secure computation. In: STOC, pp. 52–61. ACM (1993)
5. Ben-Or, M., Kelmer, B., Rabin, T.: Asynchronous secure computations with optimal resilience. In: Proceedings of the 13th Annual Symposium on Principles of Distributed Computing, pp. 183–192. ACM (1994)
6. Bentov, I., Pass, R., Shi, E.: Snow white: provably secure proofs of stake. In: FC (2019)
7. Binance: BNB chain documentation (2024). https://docs.bnbchain.org/
8. Bracha, G.: An asynchronous [(n-1)/3]-resilient consensus protocol. In: Proceedings of the Third Annual ACM Symposium on Principles of Distributed Computing, pp. 154–162. ACM (1984)
9. Bracha, G.: Asynchronous byzantine agreement protocols. Inf. Comput. **75**(2), 130–143 (1987)
10. Buchman, E.: Tendermint: byzantine fault tolerance in the age of blockchains (2017)

11. Buterin, V., et al.: Combining ghost and Casper. arXiv preprint arXiv:2003.03052 (2020)
12. Buterin, V., et al.: Ethereum white paper. GitHub Repository **1**, 22–23 (2013)
13. Cachin, C., Guerraoui, R., Rodrigues, L.: Introduction to Reliable and Secure Distributed Programming. Springer Science & Business Media (2011)
14. Cachin, C., Kursawe, K., Petzold, F., Shoup, V.: Secure and efficient asynchronous broadcast protocols. In: Annual International Cryptology Conference, pp. 524–541. Springer (2001)
15. Cachin, C., Vukolic, M.: Blockchain consensus protocols in the wild. In: DISC (2017)
16. Canetti, R., Rabin, T.: Fast asynchronous byzantine agreement with optimal resilience. In: STOC, vol. 93, pp. 42–51. Citeseer (1993)
17. Cardano (2024). https://cardano.org/
18. Castro, M., Liskov, B.: Practical byzantine fault tolerance and proactive recovery. ACM TOCS **20**(4), 398–461 (2002)
19. Chia (2024). https://www.chia.net/
20. Clavin, J., et al.: Blockchains for government: use cases and challenges. Digital Gov. Res. Pract. **1**(3), 1–21 (2020)
21. Cosmos network. https://cosmos.network/
22. Distler, T.: Byzantine fault-tolerant state-machine replication from a systems perspective. ACM Comput. Surv. **54**(1), 24:1-24:38 (2021)
23. Duan, L., Sun, Y., Ni, W., Ding, W., Liu, J., Wang, W.: Attacks against cross-chain systems and defense approaches: a contemporary survey. IEEE/CAA J. Automatica Sinica **10**(8), 1647–1667 (2023)
24. Duan, S., Meling, H., Peisert, S., Zhang, H.: BChain: byzantine replication with high throughput and embedded reconfiguration. In: OPODIS, pp. 91–106 (2014)
25. Duan, S., Reiter, M.K., Zhang, H.: Beat: asynchronous BFT made practical. In: CCS, pp. 2028–2041. ACM (2018)
26. Duan, S., Wang, X., Zhang, H.: Practical signature-free asynchronous common subset in constant time. In: CCS (2023)
27. Duan, S., Zhang, H.: Foundations of dynamic BFT. In: 2022 IEEE Symposium on Security and Privacy (SP), pp. 1317–1334 (2022)
28. Duan, S., et al.: Dashing and star: byzantine fault tolerance from weak certificates. In: Eurosys (2024)
29. Dwork, C., Lynch, N., Stockmeyer, L.: Consensus in the presence of partial synchrony. J. ACM **32**(2), 288–323 (1988)
30. Ekparinya, P., Gramoli, V., Jourjon, G.: The attack of the clones against proof-of-authority. In: NDSS (2020)
31. Eos (2024). https://eosnetwork.com/
32. Eyal, I., Gencer, A.E., Sirer, E.G., Van Renesse, R.: Bitcoin-NG: a scalable blockchain protocol. In: NSDI, pp. 45–59 (2016)
33. Eyal, I., Sirer, E.G.: Majority is not enough: Bitcoin mining is vulnerable. Commun. ACM (2018)
34. Fischer, M.J., Lynch, N.A., Paterson, M.S.: Impossibility of distributed consensus with one faulty process, Technical report, Massachusetts Institute of Technology Cambridge Lab for Computer Science (1982)
35. Gao, Y., Lu, Y., Lu, Z., Tang, Q., Xu, J., Zhang, Z.: Dumbo-NG: fast asynchronous BFT consensus with throughput-oblivious latency. In: CCS (2022)
36. Garay, J., Kiayias, A., Leonardos, N.: The bitcoin backbone protocol: analysis and applications. J. ACM **71**(4), 1–49 (2024)

37. Garay, J.A., Kiayias, A., Leonardos, N.: The bitcoin backbone protocol: analysis and applications. In: Oswald, E., Fischlin, M. (eds.) EUROCRYPT, vol. 9057, pp. 281–310. Springer (2015)
38. Gelashvili, R., Kokoris-Kogias, L., Sonnino, A., Spiegelman, A., Xiang, Z.: Jolteon and Ditto: network-adaptive efficient consensus with asynchronous fallback. In: FC, pp. 296–315 (2022)
39. Gilad, Y., Hemo, R., Micali, S., Vlachos, G., Zeldovich, N.: Algorand: scaling byzantine agreements for cryptocurrencies. In: Proceedings of the 26th Symposium on Operating Systems Principles, pp. 51–68. ACM (2017)
40. Giridharan, N., Suri-Payer, F., Abraham, I., Alvisi, L., Crooks, N.: Autobah : seamless high speed BFT. In: SOSP (2024)
41. Gramoli, V., Staples, M.: Blockchain standard: can we reach consensus? IEEE Commun. Stan. Mag. **2**(3), 16–21 (2018)
42. Gudgeon, L., Moreno-Sanchez, P., Roos, S., McCorry, P., Gervais, A.: SoK: Layertwo blockchain protocols. In: Financial Cryptography and Data Security: 24th International Conference, FC 2020, Kota Kinabalu, Malaysia, February 10–14, 2020 Revised Selected Papers 24, pp. 201–226. Springer (2020)
43. Guerraoui, R., Knežević, N., Quéma, V., Vukolić, M.: The next 700 BFT protocols. ACM Trans. Comput. Syst. **32**(4), 12:1-12:45 (2015)
44. Guo, B., Lu, Y., Lu, Z., Tang, Q., Xu, J., Zhang, Z.: Speeding Dumbo: pushing asynchronous BFT closer to practice. NDSS (2022)
45. Guo, B., Lu, Z., Tang, Q., Xu, J., Zhang, Z.: Dumbo: faster asynchronous BFT protocols. In: CCS (2020)
46. IEEE blockchain technical community (2024). https://blockchain.ieee.org/
47. Introduction to ITU (2024). https://www.itu.int/en/Pages/default.aspx
48. Technical committee ISO/TC 307 blockchain and distributed ledger technologies (2024). https://www.iso.org/committee/6266604.html
49. Jalalzai, M.M., Niu, J., Feng, C., Gai, F.: Fast-hotstuff: a fast and robust BFT protocol for blockchains. IEEE Trans. Dependable Sec. Comput. (2023)
50. Jia, X., Xu, J., Han, M., Zhang, Q., Zhang, L., Chen, X.: International standardization of blockchain and distributed ledger technology: overlaps, gaps and challenges. CMES-Comput. Modeling Eng. Sci. **137**(2), 1491–1523 (2023)
51. Junqueira, F.P., Reed, B.C., Serafini, M.: Zab: high-performance broadcast for primary-backup systems. In: DSN, pp. 245–256. IEEE (2011)
52. Keidar, I., Kokoris-Kogias, E., Naor, O., Spiegelman, A.: All you need is DAG. In: PODC, pp. 165–175. ACM (2021)
53. Kiayias, A., Russell, A., David, B., Oliynykov, R.: Ouroboros: a provably secure proof-of-stake blockchain protocol. In: Annual International Cryptology Conference, pp. 357–388 (2017)
54. Lamport, L., Shostak, R., Pease, M.: The byzantine generals problem. ACM TOPLAS **4**(3), 382–401 (1982)
55. Li, H., et al.: FISCO-BCOS: an enterprise-grade permissioned blockchain system with high-performance. In: SC, pp. 1–17 (2023)
56. Li, R., Wang, Q., Wang, Q., Galindo, D., Ryan, M.: Sok: tee-assisted confidential smart contract. In: Proceedings on Privacy Enhancing Technologies (2022)
57. Litecoin (2024). https://litecoin.org/
58. Liu, C., Duan, S., Zhang, H.: Epic: efficient asynchronous BFT with adaptive security. In: DSN (2020)
59. Malkhi, D., Momose, A., Ren, L.: Towards practical sleepy BFT. In: Proceedings of the 2023 ACM SIGSAC Conference on Computer and Communications Security, pp. 490–503 (2023)

60. Malkhi, D., Nayak, K.: Hotstuff-2: optimal two-phase responsive BFT. Cryptology ePrint Archive (2023)
61. Meng, X., et al.: Rondo: Scalable and reconfiguration-friendly randomness beacon. In: NDSS (2025)
62. Miller, A.: Permissioned and permissionless blockchains. In: Blockchain for Distributed Systems Security, pp. 193–204 (2019)
63. Miller, A., Xia, Y., Croman, K., Shi, E., Song, D.: The honey badger of BFT protocols. In: ACM CCS, pp. 31–42 (2016)
64. Mirkin, M., Zhou, L., Eyal, I., Zhang, F.: Sprints: intermittent blockchain PoW mining. In: 33rd USENIX Security Symposium (USENIX Security 24) (2024)
65. Momose, A., Ren, L.: Constant latency in sleepy consensus. In: CCS, pp. 2295–2308 (2022)
66. Monero (2024). https://www.dash.org/
67. Mostefaoui, A., Moumen, H., Raynal, M.: Signature-free asynchronous Byzantine consensus with $t \leq n/3$ and $o(n^2)$ messages. In: PODC, pp. 2–9. ACM (2014)
68. Nakamoto, S.: Bitcoin: a peer-to-peer electronic cash system (2008)
69. Neu, J., Tas, E.N., Tse, D.: Ebb-and-flow protocols: a resolution of the availability-finality dilemma. In: SP (2021)
70. Neu, J., Tas, E.N., Tse, D.: Two more attacks on proof-of-stake ghost/ethereum. In: ConsensusDay, pp. 43–52 (2022)
71. Neuder, M., Moroz, D.J., Rao, R., Parkes, D.C.: Low-cost attacks on Ethereum 2.0 by sub-1/3 stakeholders. arXiv preprint arXiv:2102.02247 (2021)
72. Ongaro, D., Ousterhout, J.: In search of an understandable consensus algorithm. In: USENIX ATC, pp. 305–319 (2014)
73. Pass, R., Shi, E.: The sleepy model of consensus. In: Annual International Conference on the Theory and Application of Cryptology and Information Security (ASIACRYPT), pp. 380–409. Springer (2017)
74. peercoin (2024). https://www.peercoin.net/
75. Ponomarev, E.: DAPP developers survey results (2024). https://hackernoon.com/dapp-developers-survey-results-1c763901e756
76. Ponomarev, E.: Dapp survey results 2019 (2024). https://medium.com/fluence-network/dapp-survey-results-2019-a04373db6452
77. Project mbridge. https://www.bis.org/about/bisih/topics/cbdc/mcbdc_bridge.htm
78. Itu publications : Standardization (itu-t) (2024). https://www.itu.int/en/Pages/default.aspx
79. Notice on the release of the first batch of national standards for cybersecurity in 2023 (2024). https://www.tc260.org.cn/front/postDetail.html?id=20230413185511
80. Schwarz-Schilling, C., Neu, J., Monnot, B., Asgaonkar, A., Tas, E.N., Tse, D.: Three attacks on proof-of-stake Ethereum. In: FC, pp. 560–576 (2022)
81. Scrypt POW (2024). https://github.com/litecoin-project/litecoin/blob/master/src/crypto/scrypt.cpp
82. Sherman, A.T., Javani, F., Zhang, H., Golaszewski, E.: On the origins and variations of blockchain technologies. IEEE Sec. Privacy **17**(1), 72–77 (2019)
83. SlowMist: The analysis of etc 51 (2024). https://slowmist.medium.com/the-analysis-of-etc-51-attack-from-slowmist-team-728596d76ead
84. Standardization Administration of the People's Republic of China: Information security technology - specifications for Blockchain security framework, Technical report, GB/T 42570-2023 (2023)

85. Standards by IEEE blockchain (2024). https://blockchain.ieee.org/standards
86. Sui, X., Duan, S., Zhang, H.: Marlin: two-phase BFT with linearity. DSN (2022)
87. TESTNET Sepolia (ETH) blockchain explorer. https://sepolia.etherscan.io/
88. The merge (2024). https://ethereum.org/en/roadmap/merge/
89. Tron (2024). https://tron.network/
90. Vechain: Vechain: Web3 for better (2024). https://vechain.org/
91. Wang, Q., Li, R., Wang, Q., Chen, S.: Non-fungible token (NFT): overview, evaluation, opportunities and challenges. arXiv preprint arXiv:2105.07447 (2021)
92. Wang, X., Duan, S., Clavin, J., Zhang, H.: BFT in blockchains: from protocols to use cases. ACM Comput. Surv. (2022)
93. Werner, S., Perez, D., Gudgeon, L., Klages-Mundt, A., Harz, D., Knottenbelt, W.: Sok: decentralized finance (DeFi). In: Proceedings of the 4th ACM Conference on Advances in Financial Technologies, pp. 30–46 (2022)
94. Wood, G.: Ethereum: a secure decentralised generalised transaction ledger. Ethereum Proj. Yellow Pap. **151** (2014)
95. Wood, G.: PoA private chains (2015). https://github.com/ethereum/guide/blob/master/poa.md
96. Wu, K., Ma, Y., Huang, G., Liu, X.: A first look at blockchain-based decentralized applications. Softw. Pract. Exp. (2021)
97. Xu, J., Paruch, K., Cousaert, S., Feng, Y.: Sok: decentralized exchanges (DEX) with automated market maker (AMM) protocols. ACM Comput. Surv. **55**(11), 1–50 (2023)
98. Yin, M., Malkhi, D., Reiter, M.K., Gueta, G.G., Abraham, I.: Hotstuff: BFT consensus with linearity and responsiveness. In: PODC (2019)
99. Zhang, H., Duan, S.: Pace: fully parallelizable BFT from reproposable byzantine agreement. In: CCS (2022)
100. Zhang, M., Li, R., Duan, S.: Max attestation matters: making honest parties lose their incentives in Ethereum POS. In: USENIX Security (2024)
101. Zhang, X., Li, R., Wang, Q., Wang, Q., Duan, S.: Time-manipulation attack: breaking fairness against proof of authority aura. In: Proceedings of the ACM Web Conference 2023, pp. 2076–2086 (2023)
102. Zhao, Q., et al.: A comprehensive overview of security vulnerability penetration methods in blockchain cross-chain bridges. Authorea Preprints (2023)
103. Zheng, P., Jiang, Z., Wu, J., Zheng, Z.: Blockchain-based decentralized application: a survey. IEEE Open J. Comput. Soc. (2023)

Security and Privacy Evaluation of IP Cameras on Shodan

Cheok Ieng Ng[✉] and Maryam Mehrnezhad

Royal Holloway, University of London, Egham, UK
ngcheokieng@gmail.com, maryam.mehrnezhad@rhul.ac.uk

Abstract. IP cameras have become a popular option in residential spaces, especially for family members, pet owners, and others who wish to monitor their home from afar, providing both security and peace of mind. The ease of use, the ability to stream real-time data and the affordable price make them an attractive choice not just in homes, but also in commercial environment. However, just like any other IoT devices, any misconfiguration during the manufacturing or deployment process can result in an insecure device and privacy leakage.

In this study, we compared and analysed different legislation related to IoT devices across the globe. We have identified multiple privacy and security implications by accessing and evaluating 281 footage from publicly accessible Internet Protocol cameras (IP cameras) available on Shodan in the UK. We evaluate such risks by using ChatGPT, in addition to a manual assessment. Our results show that general large language models such as ChatGPT are highly accurate in detecting the content of such footage e.g., detecting the presence of people in those images. Our findings highlight the need of security awareness among the users and manufacturers, as well as addressing the inconsistencies across different legislation worldwide.

Keywords: IP camera · Shodan · User Privacy · User Security

1 Introduction

Online Security has become a widely discussed topic nowadays, with the main reason being the contribution of cyber-attacks and ransomware. The public's concerns about security are rising, and this can be evidenced by the increased number of surveillance camera throughout the years. Research from Clarion UK indicates that from 2012 to 2022, there was a 238.16% increase in the number of CCTV cameras in London Boroughs, with an estimated total of over 7 million CCTV cameras in the UK [7]. This research takes into account the rise of home CCTV cameras, doorbell cameras, council investment in CCTV systems, and more commercial CCTV systems being installed.

The use of surveillance cameras has evolved from eyes to IPs, from analog camera to IP camera. IP cameras have become a popular option in residential

© The Author(s), under exclusive license to Springer Nature Switzerland AG 2025
X. Lu and C. J. Mitchell (Eds.): SSR 2024, LNCS 15559, pp. 57–80, 2025.
https://doi.org/10.1007/978-3-031-87541-0_4

spaces, especially for family members, pet owners, and others who wish to monitor their home from afar, providing both security and peace of mind. The ease of use, the ability to stream real-time data and the affordable price make them an attractive choice not just in homes, but also in commercial environment.

However, just like any other IoT devices, any misconfiguration during the manufacturing or deployment process can result in an insecure device. There is no "one-size-fits-all" security and privacy answer, it is important for the manufacturer to accurately identify their usersdaily usage of the IP camera and apply appropriate security measures [26]. It is also crucial for end-users to be aware of the security settings of IP cameras, which they can adjust to enhance the security of the device, and to further protect themselves. The purpose of this research is to analyse the implications of publicly available IP camera data and provide guidance on how to protect privacy and improve security in the rapidly growing IoT environment.

As the technology and popularity of IoT devices rise, their security concerns become an inevitable topic. Within the categories of IoT, the security of IP cameras is the most crucial, not only because IP cameras are IoT devices and massive distributed denial-of-service (DDoS) attacks like Mirai [6] are powerful, but also because of the substantial amount of sensitive information they provide and the severe consequences if compromised. It is noteworthy to see that the general public becomes more used to the presence of IoT devices, there appears to be a trend of general opinion that the conveniences of IoT devices come with the price of insecurity and the leakage of information, which is erroneous. The security awareness of both users and manufacturers should be improved to correct this view. Standards and regulations should also be adjusted to improve the security of IoT devices, specifically IP cameras.

Contributions. In this paper, we investigate how publicly accessible data of IP cameras on Shodan, an online search engine that scans for devices connected to the Internet and collects information about them, affects the device owners and the general public, as well as how current practice can be improved. By performing a security and privacy evaluation, our results highlight that serious risky practices exist in these IP cameras. This work contributes to the understanding of IP camera security within the broader context of IoT devices.

More specifically, we highlight the gap between existing IoT-specific legislation and real world security challenges, concentrating into the inadequacy of current regulations across the globe related to these technologies.

We then provide an in-depth analysis of the risks associated with publicly accessible IP camera data on platforms like Shodan, highlighting the potential privacy breaches even when data is not personally identifiable. By evaluating a dataset of 281 publicly accessible IP camera footage both via ChatGPT and a manual assessment, this study identifies the risks these devices may present to both users and the wider public.

The findings of this study contribute to the ongoing discussion about the need for legislative improvements to keep up with the rapidly evolving IoT landscape, in addition to the advances made in large language models such as ChatGPT, providing a basis for future work in developing more robust security frameworks for IP cameras and other IoT devices.

2 Background and Related Work

The rise of IoT devices has transformed household appliances into a network of interconnected smart devices, bringing various benefits in all areas of life. Among these devices, IP cameras have become increasingly popular and ubiquitous, providing not only homeowners but also business owners with surveillance and security. However, the availability of search engines like Shodan, which index network-connected devices, has raised concerns about potential vulnerabilities and privacy issues with these IoT devices.

2.1 IP Cameras

An IP camera is a digital camera that uses the internet to send and receive video. Unlike traditional CCTV cameras, IP cameras don't need a local recorder. They can be accessed directly over a network, making them ideal for surveillance. Additionally, IP cameras support advanced features such as motion detection, two-way audio, and cloud-based storage, further enhancing their capability for both residential and commercial security systems.

There are many studies focused on the security of IP cameras that echo the same idea: stronger security features should be implemented by the device manufacturer. For example, Abdalla et al. [2] investigated the security weaknesses of a specific brand of wireless IP cameras and showed that the device has various flaws and weaknesses, including default credentials and lack of encryption.

Seralathan et al. [35] analysed the existing security features and weaknesses of IP cameras using Nmap and Wireshark to collect and analyse data. They found that the IP camera used non-encrypted communication, resulting in sensitive data being transferred in plaintext, including credentials, which could be retrieved when traffic was captured using tools like Wireshark. The RTSP URL used to stream data was predictable and there was no authentication required. Exploiting these vulnerabilities could result in unauthorised access to data, and potentially allowing attackers to use the device as a botnet.

Alharbi and Aspinall [4] also analysed and compared the security measures of five different smart cameras from various perspectives, including communication methods, smart camera devices, web interface settings, and Android applications. Their analysis revealed a wide range of vulnerabilities across all components, such as non-encrypted video stream, default password, lack of password policy and account lockout mechanisms, and over-privileged Android application with unnecessary permissions. They pointed out that these vulnerabilities indicated that security was not a priority for vendors. Furthermore, the security measures of the devices did not match the advertisements, which gave an impression of high security and privacy oriented.

While the research mentioned above focused on the software and the communication between Android applications and IP cameras, Almazrouei et al. [5] focused on the hardware layer of an IP camera. They examined the circuit board and were able to identify the communication protocol as UART because the manufacturer kept the labelling on the circuit board. They were then able to interact with the system using a USB-to-UART serial cable, start the device in safe mode, and gained root access. With root access, they were able to modify the authorised SSH keys file and establish a SSH connection to the device from the internal network.

Many reports [8,25] have expressed the public concerns about the insecurity of IP cameras. Xu et al. [40] showed that despite the public concerns regarding IP cameras having weak security and the possibility of infringing user privacy, there was an incredible number of IP cameras found to have empty or null passwords.

2.2 RTSP Security

The Real-Time Streaming Protocol (RTSP) is an application level protocol for controlling the delivery of real-time data, such as audio and video [34]. There are many other protocols for IP cameras, for example, HTTP, ONVIF, WebRTC, RTMP. We discuss why RTSP is widely used and what strengths make it irreplaceable and ubiquitous in IP cameras.

The Open Network Video Interface Forum (ONVIF) Streaming Specification stated that any devices providing real-time streaming of video, audio and metadata, shall support media transfer using RTSP [30]. Moreover, most systems, even if they do not use RTSP as the primary streaming protocol, support RTSP as a fallback or secondary streaming protocol [29].

Nuñez and Toasa [28] compared the performance of RTMP, RTSP and HLS protocols on mobile network. In their research, RTSP had the lowest RAM and battery consumption, however, the performance was unstable.

Aloman et al. [1] compared the performance of MPEG-DASH, RTSP and RTMP. They concluded that RTSP had the lowest latency but suffers in Quality of User Experience (QoE) due to packet loss.

The studies above explain why RTSP is still widely used despite the existence of better options. This is because the most important security property for an IP camera is availability. An IP camera should always be able to show the video and audio data in "real-time" or with the lowest possible latency. Additionally, long battery life ensures the availability of the IP camera's data [18,28]. With the focus on availability as the top priority, packet loss and user experience quality become secondary concerns. This is also why most of the IP cameras keep RTSP as a fallback solution - to guarantee availability.

A commonality among all existing literature that focused on security analysis of IP cameras, is the discoverability and predictability of the RTSP URLs, which can be used to retrieve live videos from the devices. TCP port 554 is frequently found open without proper security measures [2,4,35]. A large scale empirical investigation of IP cameras with no password protection was carried out by Xu et al. [40] also suggested that TCP port 554 (used by the RTSP service) is commonly opened and could be easily exploited by attackers as a pivot point to the internal network.

This vulnerability allows attackers to use a simple Nmap brute-force attack to find the RTSP URL of an IP camera. If thedefault password remains unchanged and no security measures are applied, the attacker will be able to gain unauthorised access to the live video stream using a password brute-force attack.

Whilst RTSP is a commonly used protocol in IP cameras, its security concerns are often overlooked by manufacturers and users.

2.3 Shodan

Shodan, an online search engine that scans for devices connected to the Internet and collects information about them, has slowly become the researchers' favourite toolkit when conducting large-scale analysis because of its convenience, especially for researches related to the industrial control systems (ICS) and IoT because of their discoverability and criticality. Shodan has the ability to discover vulnerable IP cameras, using the technique of detecting non-password-protected devices [3].

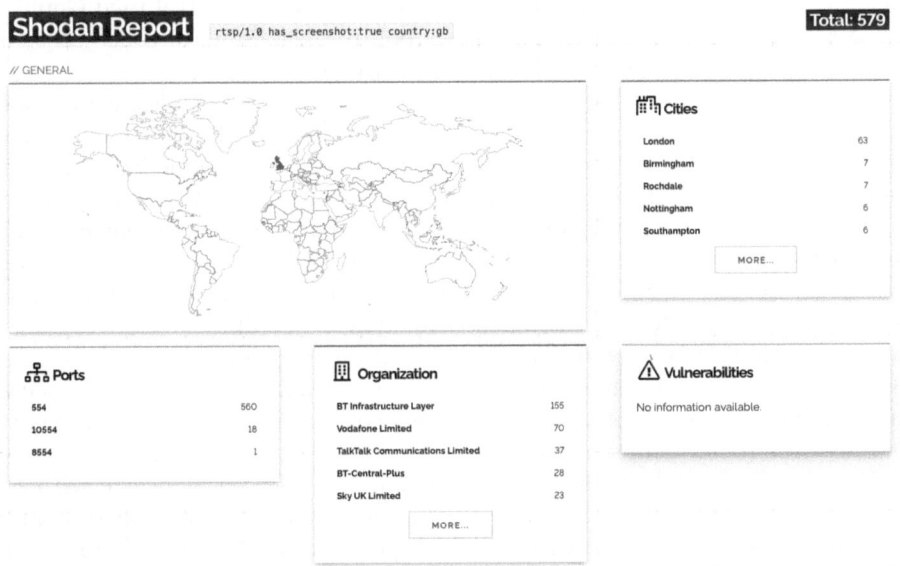

Fig. 1. Shodan report on the Query 'rtsp/1.0 has_screenshot:true country:gb'

Figure 1 shows the Shodan report based on the query 'rtsp/1.0 has_screenshot:true country:gb'. The total number of discovered results at the time of capture of this screenshot (Sep 2024) is 579. The query limits the results to devices located in Great Britain, so the map highlights the UK in red, indicating that all the discovered devices are within the UK. The report also breaks down the results by city, showing that London has the highest number of IP cameras matching the query. Devices were discovered across several ports, including: port 554, the default RTSP port, with 560 devices, port 10554 with 18 devices, and port 8554 with 1 device. The report also identifies the internet service providers or organisations responsible for hosting these devices, including BT Infrastructure Layer, Vodafone Limited, TalkTalk Communications Limited, BT-Central-Plus, and Sky UK Limited. The report states that no vulnerability information is available for these devices, meaning that no vulnerabilities can be implied based on the metadata Shodan has collected. This suggests that neither the software version, hardware version, nor configurations of these IP cameras indicate a vulnerability.

Genge and Enăchescu [20] developed a Shodan-based passive vulnerability assessment tool for Internet-facing services, ShoVAT. Rae et al. [32] assessed the effectiveness of ShoVAT. They concluded that ShoVAT is a powerful tool for vulnerability scanning and assessment within the IoT landscape. Shodan API can be integrated with existing security systems which makes it easier to manage and address vulnerabilities. In contrast, this integration also makes life easier for less experienced hackers to compromised devices.

Phan et al. [31] developed an immersive visualisation tool, ShodanVR to visualise text records from Shodan's database. Ercolani et al. [15] used Gephi, a network graphs visualising and analysing tool, to visualise data collected using Shodan and proposed a methodology to identify SCADA devices.

Shodan claims that they crawl the entire Internet at least once a week and an on-demand scan can be performed immediately using the API [36]. Bodenheim et al. [10] evaluated the ability of the Shodan search engine in 2014. They deployed four internet-facing programmable logic controllers (PLCs) and showed that all four PLCs were initially scanned by Shodan in less than four days and Shodan was able to index all four PLCs within 19 days. They expressed concerns regarding the easy discoverability of ICS systems on Shodan and proposed mitigating strategies like service banner manipulation [10].

Chen et al. [11] evaluated Shodan scans through a honeypot analysis. They concluded that Shodan scans the entire Internet at lease every 66 h and focuses on scanning common ports below 10000, only some specific service related ports that are over 10000 were scanned.

Das and Tuna [14] suggested that Shodan can be used alongside with IP-based location identifier tools and web mapping services to obtain location information. They suggested that there is a high potential that personal information which should be kept private may be captured and used for illegal purposes.

3   Review of Standards and Legislation

In this section, we analyse a selection of standards and legislation focusing on IoT devices, especially IP cameras and discuss our findings. The standards that we look at include ISO/IEC 27402:2023 [38] and NIST IR 8259 [39]. The legislation that we look at include those from the UK [27], EU [16,17,22], and California [19,21].

3.1   Standards

There are currently no mandatory standards that manufacturers must comply to when producing IoT devices. ISO/IEC 27402:2023 focuses on securing the hardware and software aspects of IoT devices, whereas NIST IR 8259 focuses on activities such as planning, defining use cases in the pre-market phase, and communicating with customer in the post-market phase. Both standards have not specified security requirements for hardware and software, rather, they focus on the process. For example, ISO/IEC 27402:2023 specifies that data at rest and in transit should be protected from unauthorised access, modification and disclosure, without specifying the minimum protection mechanism.

3.2   Legislation

Legislation such as GDPR [22] and CCPA [19] enhances data protection and privacy by enforcing data controllers and collectors, such as manufacturers, to be compliant and adopt robust security measure during data collection. Newer legislation, such as the Product Security and Telecommunications Infrastructure Act (PSTI) [27], the California IoT Security Law [21], and the Cyber Resilience Act (CRA) [17] regulates the hardware and software security requirements of IoT devices. While the PSTI and the California IoT Security Law focus specifically on IoT devices, the CRA mandates compliance for any products with digital elements, such as laptops, smartphones, sensors and cameras, routers, ICS, OS, firmware, apps, games, software libraries and CPUs. This means that IP cameras and their mobile applications fall into this category, and it is the obligations of manufacturers, importers and distributors to ensure compliance with the CRA.

However, the requirements in these laws are not always specific and often lack clear definition. This ambiguity can lead to different interpretations and implementations, resulting in inconsistencies in the level of security provided in IoT devices.

Also, there is a inconsistency across different legislation worldwide. While some regions, such as the EU, have stricter regulations, others may have more lenient regulations, allowing malicious actors to target specific regions with more relaxed regulations. This inconsistency required manufacturers to be compliant with different set of requirements, increasing their costs to improve the security measures of the devices.

4   Methodology

In this section, we explain how we prepared our data set, provide an overview of the data collection and analysis methods used in this research. The methodology is described in Fig. 2.

First, data is collected from Shodan using command line. Next, ChatGPT-4o is trained with appropriate instructions and the collected data is sent for analysis. The IP addresses of the IP cameras are converted into location in the

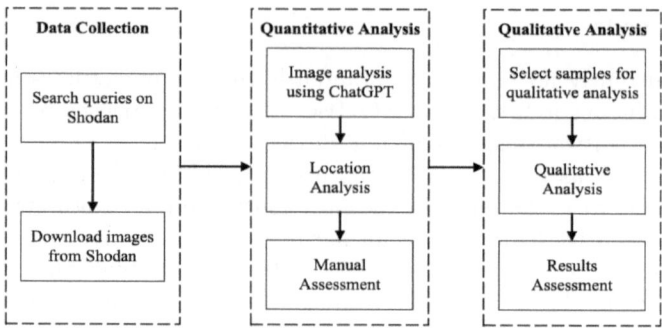

Fig. 2. Research Methodology

format [city, region, country] using Python. The results are then summarised into a table. For qualitative analysis, a few images are selected based on their categories for further analysis. The results are then summarised and reviewed.

4.1   Data Collection

Shodan provides a command-line interface (CLI) [37] and Python library that allow users to execute commands with the their API key. Since it is only possible to download search results using either the CLI or the official Python library for Shodan, and a free user account do not support the use of CLI and Python library, an academic membership account is used in this research.

This research focuses on the IP cameras within the UK. In order to find vulnerable IP cameras, below search query is used:

rtsp/1.0 has_screenshot:**true** country:gb

The query 'rtsp/1.0' searches for devices with RTSP version 1.0 enabled. Since RTSP is commonly used in IP cameras, it is expected that the query will return a list of IP cameras. The query 'has_screenshoot:true' searches for devices that have a screenshot available in the Shodan database, this could include footage from IP cameras, desktop screenshots, or lock screens from computers or servers. The query 'country:gb' searches for devices with IP addresses located in the UK. Combining these queries, the full query returns a list UK-based IP cameras with RTSP 1.0 enabled, for which Shodan has a screenshot of the device available in its database.

At the time of conducting the research, there were a total of 622 results. The following CLI command was used to download and output the results into a file 'results.json.gz':

```
$ shodan download results rtsp/1.0 has_screenshot:true
  country:gb
```

The file 'results.json.gz' was then parsed and converted to images using the following commands:

```
$ shodan parse results.json.gz
$ shodan convert results.json.gz images
```

4.2   Data Cleansing

When reviewing the data, there was a significantly large number of duplicate results, such as footage from the same camera taken in different times of the day, as well as outdated footage that was over a year old. Shodan claims that it crawls the internet once a week [36]. We decided to only include footage taken within a week of the research date (in July 2024) would be included and analysed. This method ensures that all IP cameras are operational and active at the time of conducting research. Additionally, it allows for an assessment of what information a third party might obtain if given access to IP camera footage that is no more than a week old.

Data was cleaned based on the timestamp on the image and the last online date of the device on Shodan. During the data cleansing process, it was observed that some footage appeared to be taken from the same camera but had different IP addresses, with the last online date of one being more recent than the other. Therefore, because most of the residential IP addresses are allocated dynamically, it is deduced that Shodan may cache the images captured from the same device under old IP address, and only update or clean the cache within a certain time interval, which could potentially allow a third party to gain more information about a specific area.

After the data cleansing process, the total number of results was reduced from 622 to 281. This significant reduction suggests that Shodan stores a substantial amount of screenshots from devices that are either no longer alive, or have changed IP addresses. This information could potentially allow a malicious actor to profile a specific IP camera.

4.3   Data Analysis

Footage Content Analysis: ChatGPT-4o was used the analysed the cleaned data. Due to the limitation of a ChatGPT free account, which restrict the number of attachments a user can upload and the number of requests a user can make using ChatGPT-4o within a specific time frame, a ChatGPT Plus account was necessary for handling the analysis accurately and efficiently.

The model is trained with instructions before starting the analysis. Below instructions were used to ensure the accuracy and relevance of the results.

> Analyse attached images and export the results into a CSV file. The CSV should contain below columns:
> 1. Residential or commercial. You should specify whether the image is from a residential property (e.g., a house) or a commercial property (e.g., a supermarket).
> 2. Reason. You should provide the reason why the image is residential or commercial.

3. Indoor or outdoor. You should tell whether the image was taken indoor or outdoor.
4. People present in the photo. You should also tell whether or not there are people in the photo.
5. Detailed description. This should include the full content of your analysis.
6. Put 'unknown' if you are uncertain about the setting of the scene.

We tested several instructions and based on some initial results concluded that the above set of instructions are the most effective ones for building the dataset we aimed for.

Location Analysis: We used a Python script was used instead to convert IP addresses to locations. This was feasible because the format of the downloaded image filename is 'ip-port.jpg'. The Python script was used to create a list of IP addresses from the collected data, send HTTP request to 'http://ip-api.com/', parse the responses, return a string that includes the city, region, and country, and append the results into a text file. To ensure that the rate limit of the API is not exceeded, the script sends 2 requests per second using the Python 'time.sleep' function. This Python code is provided in Appendix A.

Manual Assessment: After collecting the data, cleansing, and analysing the content of the footage via the above approach, we then manually assess our results by reviewing the ChatGPT results. All 281 results were reviewed to verify the scene settings and categorization provided by ChatGPT. ChatGPT was accurate in identifying the settings of the images and correctly categorise all of the images except for two: One nighttime image that was completely black was miscategorised as indoor, and another nighttime image that was also completely black was miscategorised as residential instead of unknown. These images were included in the qualitative analysis. The results of converting IP addresses into locations were also integrated with the image analysis results for further analysis.

4.4   Ethical Considerations

This research was conducted with adherence to the professional standards outlined in the code of conduct established by the British Computer Society, The Chartered Institute for IT [9]. Data were stored in an encrypted hard disk securely that is accessible only to the research team. This research does not include any analysis of personal identifiers to protect individual privacy. The software and services used for conducting the research on IP cameras do not attempt to connect to the IP camera, login to the IP camera, exploit vulnerabilities of the camera, and access hidden URLs of the IP camera. Since this research uses publicly available information from the internet and does not reveal of exploit vulnerabilities of any IP cameras, there is no risk of exposing information that could disclose vulnerabilities.

Table 1. ChatGPT Scene categories and subcategories (N=281)

Scene Category	%	Subcategory	%
Residential	76.5	Indoor	28.3
		Outdoor	57.0
Commercial	13.2	Indoor	5.2
		Outdoor	9.5
Unknown	10.3		
Indoor	34.2	With people	3.2
		Without people	34.9
Outdoor	55.5	With people	59.9
		Without people	2.0
Unknown	10.3		
People present	4.6		
No people present	95.4		

4.5   Limitations

The dynamic assignment of residential IP addresses poses a challenge, as it can result in outdated or inaccurate data being captured, leading to potential errors in location information. This research relies on an IP geolocation API, which has an accuracy of 89% at the city level and 99% at the country level in Europe [23]. However, the API may not always provide precise location data and is subject to request rate limits, leading to potential inaccuracies and unreliabilities. Additionally, the quality of the images analysed varies, with some footage being low resolution or captured during nighttime. Furthermore, the study is focused exclusively on IP cameras in the UK, limiting the applicability of the findings to other regions with different security practices, user behaviours, and regulatory frameworks. All of the above provide research opportunities for future work.

5   Results

281 images downloaded from Shodan are analysed using ChatGPT-4o. We summarize the scene categories, subcategories, and the percentage distribution of IP cameras in different scene settings in Table 1.

Out of the 281 analysed images, the top 10 cities with the most occurrence are London with 21 occurrences; Nottingham and Birmingham with 5 occurrences each; Leicester, Crewe, Wolverhampton, Greenwich, and Manchester with 4 occurrences each; and Fulham and Norwich with 3 occurrences each. Considering that London is the largest city in the UK with over 8.9 million people living there [24], London may have a higher density of IP cameras and, therefore, a higher density of insecure IP cameras.

5.1   Distribution of IP Cameras and Footage

This section discusses the distribution of IP cameras by residential/commercial, indoor/outdoor, and the presence of people in the collected footage.

Residential vs. Commercial: As shown in Table 1, the number of IP cameras found in residential properties in our study is nearly six times greater than those in commercial properties. This suggests that these IP cameras are more commonly used for remote home monitoring. Whereas in commercial properties, property owners may be more likely to hire professional CCTV installation teams instead of installing IP camera themselves due to the specific needs and security requirements of commercial environments. Some commercial properties may even require their cameras to be integrated with security infrastructure, such as gates. Also, it is important to secure value assets and the safety of customers and employees in a commercial environment. CCTV or IP cameras installed by professionals are generally more secure due to the higher standards and legal obligations they must adhere to, such as due diligence and regulatory compliance.

It is notable that there are 29 IP cameras in the Unknown category. This is potentially due to dark images taken at nighttime, lack of details, low resolution, or unclear images, which make it difficult for ChatGPT-4o to perform accurate analysis. ChatGPT-4o was trained to return 'Unknown' if it is uncertain about the scene. This ensures that the analysis maintain a high level of accuracy and that ChatGPT-4o does not attempt to analyse images with poor quality, which helps to reduce the number of inaccurate results.

Indoor vs. Outdoor: As shown in Table 1, the number of IP cameras placed outdoors is over 1.5 times greater than those placed indoors. This suggests that in the UK, IP camera users prioritise monitoring and securing the surrounding of their properties. By placing IP cameras outdoor, property owners able to detect potential intruders, monitor entry points of the property such as gates and doors, and record and provide evidence of any suspicious activities around the property. The higher distribution of outdoor IP cameras also suggests that the growing awareness of the importance of the external security measures, as well as internal measures.

Residential/Commercial and Indoor/Outdoor: Table 1 also presents the total counts of the distribution of IP camera by residential or commercial properties and indoor or outdoor settings. It shows that the total counts of both residential outdoor IP cameras and commercial outdoor IP cameras are greater than residential indoor and commercial indoor IP cameras. The fact that residential outdoor IP cameras constitute the majority of the sample supports the point that the awareness of the importance of the external security measures is growing in the UK, especially among the general public.

This pattern indicates that compared to commercial properties, which are likely to have more robust security measures in-house, such as hardened doors and gates, alarm systems for intruders, and 24/7 guards, residential property owners are more likely to invest in external security measures, such as placing IP cameras outdoors. This could be due to the lack of indoor security measures and possibly the difficulty of implementing indoor security measures.

Furthermore, the accessibility, affordability, and easy installation of IP cameras have provided a cost-effective and simple way to enhance security for homeowners. Also, the advancement in IP camera technology, such as weather resistance and night vision capability have made them more reliable for outdoor monitoring.

The count differences between residential indoor and residential outdoor, and commercial indoor and commercial outdoor are roughly the same, with outdoor cameras being twice as many as indoor cameras. This consistent pattern across both residential and commercial properties highlights a boarder trend of prioritising the safety of the surrounding environment. This further suggests that both residential and commercial property owners acknowledge the importance of monitoring and securing the surrounding of their properties.

The Presence of People: Among 281 samples, there are 268 images with no people present and 13 images with one or more people present. This significant difference could be due to various reasons such as empty scene because of the time of the day when the images were taken. It also indicates that the majority of IP cameras are likely placed to monitor unoccupied areas where people are not expected to present.

Our results also suggest that among 281 samples, 8.33% of indoor images have people present, whereas 3.21% of outdoor images have people present. This suggests that indoor IP cameras are more likely to capture images with people than outdoor IP cameras. This meets the expectation since indoor IP cameras are commonly used to monitor places where human activity is frequent, while outdoor IP cameras are typically used to monitor entry points and the surroundings of the properties, where human activity is less frequent.

5.2   Qualitative Analysis on Selected Samples

To test the accuracy of the analysis and identify anomalies, seven results have been selected for further analysis based on their categories. The selected images are shown in Fig. 3. These include Sample-4, an outdoor residential scene with people present; Sample-85, an indoor commercial scene with people present; Sample-187, an indoor residential scene with no people present; Sample-188, an unknown scene; Sample-269, an outdoor commercial scene with people present; Sample-36 and Sample-273, two anomalies that require further analysis.

Sample-4. Sample 4 is an image with the filename 2.30.82.201-554.jpg, downloaded from Shodan. The result of the Python script used to convert IP addresses

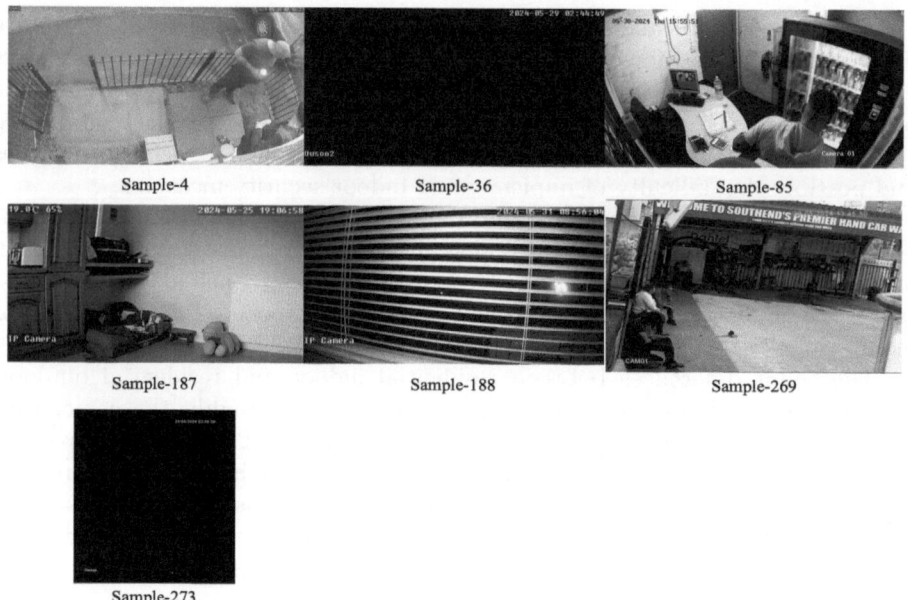

Fig. 3. Seven Selected Images For Further Analysis

into locations suggests that this IP address is located in Leeds. The images includes an entrance area of a residential property. The ground is paved with stone slabs and there is grass along the road. It is considered to be a residential property due to the layout of the fence and the present of a car parked on the road. There are two individuals present in the image, the person positioned closer to the fence is holding a cup. It appears that they are both looking at the same object in the same direction, probably discussing the fence or some objects located close it.

ChatGPT-4o identified it as residential, outdoor, and with people present, described as "The typical residential entryway with a gate and people present. The photo shows an outdoor entryway with paving stones and a fence, with two people standing near the gate." The identification and description are accurate but missing details such as the parked car and the behaviour of the two individuals. The individual holding a cup has a tattoo on the right forearm, which may be used to identify identity.

Sample-85. Sample-85 has a filename of 81.134.6.207-8554.jpg. The Python script suggests that this IP address is located in Great Barton. The image suggests an indoor setting with a desk, a chair, and a vending machine filled with various beverages. There is an individual standing near the vending machine and facing away from the camera. There are various objects placing on the desk, including a notebook, a calculator, and an unlocked desktop. The screen of the desktop displaying what seems to be surveillance footage from other cameras.

With the presence of the desktop, the calculator and two fire extinguishers hanging on the white brick wall, it is suggested that this is an image with commercial indoor scene.

ChatGPT-4o identified it as commercial, indoor with people present, described as "The photo shows an indoor area with a vending machine, a desk with office supplies, and an industrial setup. A person is visible in the foreground, indicating this is a working environment, likely in a commercial or industrial setting." The identification is accurate. However, the description lacks details. For example, ChatGPT-4o fails to describe the appearance of the individual, who has short hair and wearing a light gray hoodie, and the presence of two fire extinguishers.

The fact that Great Barton has a population of 2000 people only, makes it relatively easy to find the exact location of this image.

Sample-187. Sample-187 has a filename of 86.172.173.243-554.jpg. The Python script suggests that this IP address is located in Bedford. The image appears to be a corner of a kitchen, indicating a residential indoor scene. On the left side of the image, there is a toaster on top of a kitchen worktop. On the right side of the image, there is a radiator against the wall. A pet bed with blankets and pillows is placed on the floor, along with a stuffed teddy bear.

ChatGPT-4o identified it as residential, indoor with no people present, described as "The photo shows an indoor area with a kitchen, household items, and a teddy bear, indicating a residential area." The identification and description are accurate. There are not many details in this image that can be used to identify an individual. However, the purpose of this IP camera appears to be to monitor the pet, as the pet bed is located in the centre of the camera's view. If the pet were captured in the image, this could be used to identify a specific pet in the area and potentially identify its owner.

Sample-188. Sample-188 has a filename of 86.174.91.105-554.jpg. The Python script suggests that this IP address is located in Fulham. The images seems to be captured through a window with blinds. The camera is placed indoor, facing outward, as fences can be identified through the blinds.

ChatGPT-4o fails to identify the scene, with the reason described as "The photo shows window blinds in low light, making it difficult to determine the setting." It is appropriate to classify this image as Unknown due to the lack of details and low light.

Sample-269. Sample-188 has a filename of 193.237.245.201-554.jpg. The Python script suggests that this IP address is located in London. The image appears to be taken at a hand car wash business. The sign at the top says "WELCOME TO SOUTHEND'S PREMIER HAND CAR WASH", indicating it is located in Southend. The background of the image includes equipment and tools used for car wash. There are three individuals present in the image, possibly employees. It is unlikely that the individuals are customers due to no cars are captured in the image.

ChatGPT-4o identified it as commercial, outdoor with people present, described as "The photo shows an outdoor area of a car wash with workers sitting and resting. The area is well-lit and organized." The identification and description are accurate, even though the sign at the top is not mentioned. The sign indicates that the car wash is located in Southend. In fact, images from the first Google review result of Google search for "car wash Southend" match the sign in this image, making it possible to identify the working location of these individuals.

Sample-36 and Sample-273. Sample-36 and Sample-273 are identified as anomalies during the analysis of the distribution of IP camera. They are completely dark, yet ChatGPT-4o identified Sample-36 as residential and Sample-273 as indoor.

For Sample-36, ChatGPT-4o identified it as residential, unknown about indoor or outdoor settings, and no people present, described as "The photo is dark, and it is difficult to discern any details. The dark image indicates nighttime, likely in a residential area." ChatGPT-4o suggests that it is likely in a residential area without providing any valid reason.

For Sample-273, ChatGPT-4o identified it as unknown whether it is a residential or commercial scene, indoor and no people present, described as "The image is completely dark, suggesting it might be a garage or storage room with the lights off." While the possibility of it being a garage or storage room with the lights off exists due to the word 'Garage' presence in the image, this is not what the image shows and is only a prediction from ChatGPT-4o.

To confirm the accuracy of dark image analysis by ChatGPT-4o, all dark images and the corresponding results were reviewed. It appears that for other dark images, ChatGPT-4o identified them as Unknown successfully with description similar to "The photo is very dark, making it difficult to determine the setting or any details." It is unclear why ChatGPT-4o fails to identify Sample-36 and Sample-273 correctly. This issue should be avoidable by refining the pretraining of the model.

5.3   ChatGPT Accuracy

During the analysis of IP camera footage, ChatGPT-4o's accuracy in identifying images was evaluated. Out of the 281 results, only two images, Sample-36 and Sample-273, were flagged as anomalies due to ChatGPT's failure to correctly identify them. Despite both images being completely dark, ChatGPT-4o identified Sample-36 as residential and Sample-273 as indoor. Upon reviewing all other dark images, which ChatGPT-4o correctly labeled as "Unknown", with descriptions specifying the difficulty in determining the setting due to the darkness. These inconsistencies in accurately identifying Sample-36 and Sample-273 suggest that while ChatGPT-4o is generally reliable with image classification, further model refinements could improve its accuracy in specific scenarios.

In addition to content analysis, we also initially experimented to use ChatGPT-4o for converting IP addresses into locations. However, the accuracy and the responding time were slow. Our location analysis approach is still automated via a Python script.

ChatGPT is a general-purpose AI model, there are other specialised AI models specifically designed for more accurate analysis in particular contexts, such as people detection in video or image [13]. These specialised models may outperform general models like ChatGPT by leveraging more advanced or tailored algorithms for detecting objects, identifying scenes, or classifying environments more accurately under challenging conditions. Combining the strengths of these specialized models with the versatility of general AI could lead to more robust and precise outcomes in complex analysis.

6   Discussion

In this section, we interpret the findings and propose mitigation strategies for both technical and social aspects. We aim to provide a detailed analysis of how these factors contributed to the observed outcomes.

6.1   Individual's Identifiability

The level of personal identifiability of the footage found on Shodan varies significantly depending on the content of the footage. It is essential for the image to include people in order to be personal identifiable. Please note that there are more advanced ways to identify people and their location even if the image does not include a person, as we discuss in other sections. However, we do not consider footage without people present to be personally identifiable. Our results show that only 5% of the samples (13 images) have people present. Given that the scale of our experiments was small, these numbers might not look significant. If these experiments are scaled up, the identifiability issue can pose a greater risk to the citizens.

In addition, extra configuration can increase the chance of having people in more footage. Note that the exact data collection and indexing time of Shodan scan engine are unknown. However, it is likely that the percentage would increase if outdoor footage were captured during daytime compared to nighttime, and residential indoor footage were captured during nighttime when people are more likely to be present.

Complex and targeted attacks such as cyber-stalking and other forms of tech abusability can be enabled by such risks [33]. For instance, in Sample-4, it is possible to identify a person due to the tattoo on the right forearm. If the pattern is unique, with the correct use of photo editing apps, it is possible to enhance and clarify blurry photos, extract the tattoo pattern. A malicious actor can then use such data, in addition to the location analysis and other contextual information, to identify the individual and pose risk to the privacy and safety of that person.

Another example is Sample-85, where it would not be possible to identify an individual just by analysing the image. However, it is possible to deduce the height and the body size of the individual appearing in the image. Also, the image was captured from a device located in Great Barton based on its IP address. Great Barton is a small town with a population less than 2,000 people [12]. Given that this is a commercial property, it is relatively easy to locate the exact location of this property and find the individual with a certain body size and height.

In Sample-269, it is clear that the individuals appearing in the image are employees of the car wash. The fact that images from the first Google review result of Google search for "car wash Southend" match the sign in this image makes it easy for anyone to visit this car wash in person and find the individuals.

From the samples described above, it is obvious that IP cameras footage on Shodan can significantly expose individuals' identity and privacy. Although the footage may not contain personal identifiers or may be too blurry to identify, the context of the footage can often lead to indirect identification of individuals through observation of surrounding environment, living patterns, and habits. Also, geolocation data from the footage helps to locate the physical location of cameras. Combined with other information, such as the living patterns of individuals, further targeted attack such as stalking can be performed by malicious actors. To mitigate these risks, it is important to implement technical solution onto the IP cameras, such as encryption and authentication, as well as policy changes that encourage stricter data protection practices.

6.2   Open Access IP Cameras

There are 144,712 IP cameras located in the UK that were found and indexed by Shodan scan engine at the time of this research. Only 1.9% of these cameras, which amounts to 281 IP cameras, have footage captured and the last online date within one week. The low percentage suggests that the majority of the IP cameras have reasonable authentication and encryption mechanisms implemented. While we cannot comment on the security of the IP cameras that are not included in our analysis, there is a chance that some other forms of vulnerabilities may exist in those systems.

However, The presence of 281 unprotected cameras indicates that such vulnerabilities still exist. These cameras have no authentication enabled and are at risk of being exploited by malicious actors. It is possible that malicious actors gain unauthorised access into the cameras and further infiltrate the home networks where the IP cameras are connected to, and conduct further attack. Once the malicious actors are inside the network, they can potentially compromise other connected devices, for example, mobile phones, laptops, routers, and install malware or even use the compromised devices as a bot to conduct extensive cyber attacks such as DDoS attacks.

Furthermore, Shodan also exposes other vulnerabilities such as outdated firmware or unpatched system, which can be used by the malicious actors to compromise protected IP cameras with security measures implemented. These vulnerabilities can be exploited to bypass existing security measures. It is important to keep firmware updated and systems patched to prevent vulnerabilities from being exploited. Manufacturers play a crucial role in enhancing the security of IP cameras in both pre-market and post-market phases as NIST IR 8259 [39] suggests.

This findings also highlights the need for user education regarding the security of IP cameras. 1.9% may not seem like a lot, but 281 unprotected cameras means there are 281 households or shops at risk. Many users may not be aware of the risks associated with unsecured IP and the consequences of a security breach.

6.3   Legislation and Standards

Industry standards, policies and regulatory frameworks play an important role in mitigating the risks associated with publicly accessible IP camera data on online platform like Shodan. They ensure responsible practices across the entire IoT lifecycle. Industry standards such as ISO/IEC 27402 [38] and NIST IR 8259 [39] provides general guidelines for securing both the hardware and software aspects of IoT devices and communication with customers. Adherence to these standards ensure IoT devices have a strong default security settings and receive regular firmware updates, significantly reducing the risk of unauthorised access and compromised devices. These standards combined provide a comprehensive framework for robust IoT security.

However, it is important to note that compliance to these standards is not mandatory. Manufacturers are not legally required to adhere to these standards, which can result in inconsistent security measures across different IoT devices and IoT manufacturers, leading to certain devices being more vulnerable to specific types of attacks. Without mandatory compliance, it solely depends on the commitment of manufacturers to security practices, which may not always be correct and consistent.

Legislation such as GDPR [22] and CCPA [19] enhances data protection and privacy by enforcing data controllers and collectors, such as manufacturers, to be compliant and adopt robust security measure during data collection. Newer legislation, such as the Product Security and Telecommunications Infrastructure Act (PSTI) [27], the California IoT Security Law [21], and the Cyber Resilience Act [17] regulates the hardware and software security requirements of IoT devices. However, the requirements in these laws are not always specific and often lack clear definition. This ambiguity can lead to different interpretations and implementations, resulting in inconsistencies in the level of security provided in IoT devices.

Also, there is a inconsistency across different legislation worldwide. While some regions, such as the EU, have stricter regulations, others may have more lenient regulations, allowing malicious actors to target specific regions with more relaxed regulations. This inconsistency required manufacturers to be compliant with different set of requirements, increasing their costs to improve the security measures of the devices. All of above can be future research directions to be explored by researchers and practitioners across disciplines and sectors.

6.4 Mitigation Strategies

To address these challenges, a holistic approach that combines user education, manufacturer responsibility, and regulatory oversight is required. User education can be enhanced by providing easily accessible resources that emphasise the importance of securing IoT devices and detailing steps for users to enhance their own devices' security measures. This includes changing default passwords, installing firmware updates, and understand the risks associated.

Manufacturers must also take greater responsibility and integrate security features into the design and production phases of their devices, achieving the goal of security-by-design. This includes setting strong default and one-time password, ensuring regular firmware updates even in the post-market phase, and performing thorough security testing before launching the products. Also, manufacturers should provide clear, easy-to-understand instructions to help users maintain a high standard of security.

Regulatory oversight also plays a crucial role in establishing, enforcing, and maintaining consistent security standards across different regions. Governments and regulatory bodies should work together to create harmonised regulations that offer clear guidelines for IoT security, mandating essential security measures such as encryption and authentication to set up a baseline level of security for all IoT devices. Consistent security standards and regulations across different regions also helps in international cooperation when dealing with international IoT security threats. Countries can establish an unified approach to secure IoT devices, making it difficult for malicious actors to exploit regulatory gaps.

7   Conclusion

We investigated the privacy and security implication of publicly accessible IP cameras available on Shodan using ChatGPT, in addition to a manual assessment. The study shows that the widespread deployment of IP cameras in the UK, combined with the ease of discovering and accessing these devices through the internet and the accuracy of ML systems, presents significant privacy and security risks to individuals.

Our analysis suggested that a large number of IP cameras were exposed online with inadequate security controls. This included IP camera live stream that can be accessed without authentication, potentially revealing sensitive information about individuals' daily routines and the layout of their house or surrounding area. The use of RTSP and similar protocols without encryption implemented makes it easier for malicious actors to exploit the devices for unauthorised purposes. In addition, ChatGPT showed a very high accuracy in analysing the content of such footage, posing a serious risk to users that can easily be automatically exploited.

We also examined current standards and regulations governing IoT devices. While frameworks such as ISO/IEC 27402:2023 [38] and NIST IR 8259 [39] are in place, the analysis revealed that gaps exist in effectively enforcing these standards across different regions and manufacturers. The recent adoption of the Product Security and Telecommunications Infrastructure Act [27] in the UK, the Cyber Resilience Act [17] in the EU, and the California IoT Security Law [21] represent a positive step toward enhancing IoT security, though its practical impact is yet to be determined.

Future research should focus on exploring legislative enhancements to keep pace with the rapid evolution of IoT technologies, as well as developing automated tools to aid in identifying and mitigating vulnerabilities in IoT devices using Shodan and other platforms. Additionally, further research could focus on improving image quality before analysis, particularly for low resolution footage, by using more advanced image processing techniques or AI models. Expanding the scope of the study beyond the UK to include IP cameras from other regions would also provide a more comprehensive understanding of global security practices, user behaviours, and regulatory frameworks.

Acknowledgments. The second author is a part of research supported by the UK Research and Innovation (UKRI), through the Strategic Priority Fund as part of the Protecting Citizens Online programme (Grant: AGENCY: Assuring Citizen Agency in a World with Complex Online Harms, EP/W032481/2).

Disclosure of Interests. The authors have no competing interests to declare that are relevant to the content of this article.

A   Appendix - Python code

```python
import requests
import time

def get_location_by_ip(ip):
    try:
        response = requests.get(f'http://ip-api.com/json/{ip}')
        data = response.json()
        if data['status'] == 'success':
            return f"{data['city']}, {data['regionName']}, {data['country']}"
        else:
            return "Location_not_found"
    except Exception as e:
        return str(e)

def get_locations(ip_list):
    locations = []
    for ip in ip_list:
        location = get_location_by_ip(ip)
        locations.append(location)
        time.sleep(0.5)
    return locations
```

```
def read_ip_list(file_path):
    with open(file_path, 'r') as file:
        ip_list = [line.strip() for line in file.readlines()]
    return ip_list

def write_locations(file_path, locations):
    with open(file_path, 'w') as file:
        for location in locations:
            file.write(location + '\n')
```

References

1. Aloman, A., Ispas, A.I., Ciotirnae, P., Sanchez-Iborra, R., Cano, M.D.: Performance Evaluation of Video Streaming Using MPEG DASH, RTSP, and RTMP in Mobile Networks. IEEE, Munich, Germany (2015). https://ieeexplore.ieee.org/abstract/document/7396692
2. Abdalla, P.A., Varol, C.: Testing IoT Security: The Case Study of an IP Camera. IEEE, Beirut, Lebanon (2020). https://doi.org/10.1109/ISDFS49300.2020.9116392
3. achillean: How shodan takes screenshots? (2019). https://security.stackexchange.com/a/203334
4. Alharbi, R., Aspinall, D.: An IoT analysis framework: An investigation of IoT smart cameras' vulnerabilities. IET, London (2018). https://doi.org/10.1049/cp.2018.0047
5. Almazrouei, O., Magalingam, P., Hasan, M.K., Almehrzi, M., Alshamsi, A.: Penetration Testing for IoT Security: The Case Study of a Wireless IP Security CAM. IEEE, Houston, TX, USA (2023). https://doi.org/10.1109/ICAIC57335.2023.10044176
6. Antonakakis, M., et al.: Understanding the mirai botnet. In: 26th USENIX Security Symposium (USENIX Security 17), pp. 1093–1110. USENIX Association, Vancouver, BC (2017). https://www.usenix.org/conference/usenixsecurity17/technical-sessions/presentation/antonakakis
7. Barker, R.: How many CCTV cameras are in London? (2022). https://clarionuk.com/resources/how-many-cctv-cameras-are-in-london/
8. BBC: MWC 2017: '22,000 hackable webcams in Barcelona' (2017). https://www.bbc.co.uk/news/technology-39101533
9. BCS, T.C.I.f.I.: Code of conduct for BCS members. https://www.bcs.org/media/2211/bcs-code-of-conduct.pdf
10. Bodenheim, R., Butts, J., Dunlap, S., Mullins, B.: Evaluation of the ability of the Shodan search engine to identify Internet-facing industrial control devices. Int. J. Crit. Infrastruct. Prot. **7**(2), 114–123 (2014). https://doi.org/10.1016/j.ijcip.2014.03.001
11. Chen, Y., Lian, X., Yu, D., Lv, S., Hao, S., Ma, Y.: Exploring Shodan from the perspective of industrial control systems. IEEE Access **8**, 75359–75369 (2020). https://doi.org/10.1109/ACCESS.2020.2988691
12. Council, G.B.P.: Great barton. https://greatbarton-pc.gov.uk/our-village/
13. CVEDIA: CVEDIA-RT. https://docs.cvedia.com
14. Das, R., Tuna, G.: Packet tracing and analysis of network cameras with Wireshark. IEEE, Tirgu Mures, Romania (2017). https://doi.org/10.1109/ISDFS.2017.7916510

15. Ercolani, V.J., Patton, M.W., Chen, H.: Shodan visualized. IEEE, Tucson, AZ, USA (2016). https://doi.org/10.1109/ISI.2016.7745467
16. European Commission: The Eu cybersecurity act. https://digital-strategy.ec.europa.eu/en/policies/cybersecurity-act
17. European Commission: The European cyber resilience act. https://www.european-cyber-resilience-act.com
18. Firmansyah, M.I.M., Suharto, N., Prasetyo, Y.H.: RTSP and HTTP protocol analysis for streaming services on manet networks in state polytechnic of Malang. J. Telecommun. Netw. **12**(3), 172–177 (2022). https://doi.org/10.33795/jartel.v12i3.473
19. GENERAL, S.O.C.D.O.J.O.O.T.A.: California consumer privacy Act. https://oag.ca.gov/privacy/ccpa
20. Genge, B., Enăchescu, C.: ShoVAT: Shodan-based vulnerability assessment tool for Internet-facing services. Secur. Commun. Netw. **9**(15), 2577–3044 (2015). https://doi.org/10.1002/sec.1262
21. Information, C.L.: SB-327 information privacy: connected devices. https://leginfo.legislature.ca.gov/faces/billTextClient.xhtml?bill_id=201720180SB327
22. Information Commissioner's Office: Overview – Data Protection and the EU. https://ico.org.uk/for-organisations/data-protection-and-the-eu/overview-data-protection-and-the-eu/
23. IP-API: Frequently asked questions. https://members.ip-api.com/faq
24. for London, T.: London's geography and population. https://trustforlondon.org.uk/data/geography-population/
25. Munford, M.: Could your 'smart' home be a weapon of web destruction? (2016). https://www.bbc.co.uk/news/business-37776964
26. National Cybersecurity Alliance: You Can't Have Privacy Without Security (2016). https://staysafeonline.org/cybersecurity-for-business/you-cant-have-privacy-without-security
27. NCSC: Smart devices: new law helps citizens to choose secure products. https://www.ncsc.gov.uk/blog-post/smart-devices-law
28. Nuñez, L., Toasa, R.M.: Performance evaluation of RTMP, RTSP and HLS protocols for IPTV in mobile networks. IEEE, Seville, Spain (2020). https://doi.org/10.23919/CISTI49556.2020.9140848
29. OccupyTheWeb: IP Camera Hacking: Hacking IP Cameras with Cameradar (2023). https://www.hackers-arise.com/post/ip-camera-hacking-hacking-ip-cameras-with-cameradar
30. ONVIF: ONVIF Streaming Specification (2023). https://www.onvif.org/specs/stream/ONVIF-Streaming-Spec.pdf
31. Phan, T., Krum, D.M., Bolas, M.: ShodanVR: immersive visualization of text records from the Shodan database. IEEE, Greenville, SC, USA (2016). https://doi.org/10.1109/IMMERSIVE.2016.7932379
32. Rae, J.S., Chowdhury, M.M., Jochen, M.: Internet of Things Device Hardening Using Shodan.io and ShoVAT: A Survey. IEEE, Brookings, SD, USA (2019). https://doi.org/10.1109/EIT.2019.8834072
33. Rogers, M.M., Fisher, C., Ali, P., Allmark, P., Fontes, L.: Technology-facilitated abuse in intimate relationships: a scoping review. Trauma, Violence, Abuse **24**(4), 2210–2226 (2023)
34. Schulzrinne, H., Rao, A., Lanphier, R.: Real Time Streaming Protocol (RTSP) (1998). https://www.ietf.org/rfc/rfc2326.txt

35. Seralathan, Y., et al.: IoT security vulnerability: a case study of a Web camera. IEEE, Chuncheon, Korea (South) (2018). https://doi.org/10.23919/ICACT.2018.8323686

36. Shodan: On-Demand Scanning. https://help.shodan.io/the-basics/on-demand-scanning

37. Shodan: Shodan command-line interface. https://cli.shodan.io

38. for Standardization, I.O.: Cybersecurity — IoT security and privacy — Device baseline requirements (2023). https://www.iso.org/standard/80136.html

39. of Standards, N.I., Technology: NISTIR 8259 foundational cybersecurity activities for IoT device manufacturers (2020). https://doi.org/10.6028/NIST.IR.8259

40. Xu, H., Xu, F., Chen, B.: Internet protocol cameras with no password protection: an empirical investigation. In: Passive and Active Measurement. PAM 2018. LNCS. vol. 10771, pp. 47–59. Springer, Cham. https://doi.org/10.1007/978-3-319-76481-8_4

Limitations of Wrapping Protocols and TLS Channel Bindings: Formal-Methods Analysis of the Session Binding Proxy Protocol

Enis Golaszewski[1]([✉]), Edward Zieglar[2], Alan T. Sherman[1],
Kirellos Abou Elsaad[1], and Jonathan D. Fuchs[1]

[1] Cyber Defense Lab, University of Maryland, Baltimore County (UMBC),
1000 Hilltop Circle, Baltimore, MD 21228, USA
`{golaszewski,sherman,abou3,jfuchs2}@umbc.edu`
[2] National Security Agency, 9800 Savage Road, 20755 Fort George G. Meade, USA
`evziegl@uwe.nsa.gov`

Abstract. We present the first formal-methods analysis of the *Session Binding Proxy (SBP)* protocol, which mitigates theft of a server-issued authentication cookie from a client communicating with a vulnerable, legacy server. To protect the cookie, SBP cryptographically binds the cookie to an underlying *Transport Layer Security (TLS)* channel using the channel's master secret and a secret key known only to a reverse proxy, which SBP introduces between the server and the client. An adversary who steals the bound cookie cannot reuse this cookie to create malicious requests on a separate connection because the cookie's channel binding will not match the adversary's channel. Because SBP does not modify the client or server software, it renders the client and server "oblivious protocol participants" that are not aware of the SBP session. Our analysis verifies that SBP mitigates cookie theft under the client's cryptographic assumptions but fails to authenticate the client under the proxy's assumptions: the proxy lacks assurance that the client generates a fresh TLS pre-master secret, and the legacy server relies on usernames and passwords to authenticate the client. Our analysis of this obscure protocol sheds insight into the role and limitations of TLS channel bindings when augmenting legacy protocols.

Keywords: Channel binding · cryptographic binding · cryptographic protocols · Cryptographic Protocol Shapes Analyzer (CPSA) · cryptography · cybersecurity · formal methods · oblivious protocol participants · Session Binding Proxy (SBP) · Transport Layer Security (TLS) · wrapping protocols

1 Introduction

Flawed legacy systems are a security professional's nightmare: they are challenging to patch against known vulnerabilities, store large accumulations of sensitive

© The Author(s), under exclusive license to Springer Nature Switzerland AG 2025
X. Lu and C. J. Mitchell (Eds.): SSR 2024, LNCS 15559, pp. 81–119, 2025.
https://doi.org/10.1007/978-3-031-87541-0_5

data, and often contribute to spectacular data breaches [47]. In the 2015 attack on the United States *Office of Personnel Management*, which leaked over 22 million sensitive records to geopolitical adversaries, attackers exfiltrated data from decades-old computer systems incapable of encrypting [37]. To protect legacy systems, organizations often attempt to isolate such systems by using *Virtual Local Area Networks (VLANs)*, firewalls, air gaps, and reverse proxies. In spite of these attempts, poorly designed solutions continue to enable existing or new attacks, while instilling a false sense of security.

Legacy systems often communicate using outdated cryptographic protocols or legacy protocols, with known weaknesses. A prevalent approach for hardening legacy protocols is to bind them to modern protocols, such as *Transport Layer Security (TLS)*, and to rely on this binding to mitigate known vulnerabilities. Cryptographic *channel binding* (see Sect. 2.2), a common binding technique, binds the cryptographic values of the legacy protocol to a cryptographic channel established by a modern protocol (e.g., TLS). Because it is difficult to develop sound cryptographic protocols, due diligence requires that we analyze cryptographic bindings using formal methods.

We present a formal-methods analysis of the 2013 *Session Binding Proxy (SBP)* protocol by Burgers, Verdult, and van Eekelen [10], originally designed to mitigate a known session-hijacking vulnerability with their university's Blackboard Learn software [14].

Before SBP, an adversary could hijack a Blackboard session as we explain by example. After an instructor logs into Blackboard, Blackboard issues an authentication cookie to the instructor. The adversary steals the cookie, perhaps by a *cross-site scripting (XSS)* attack that exploits inadequate input validation in discussion posts. Using the stolen cookie, the adversary modifies the gradebook. To defend against this attack, Blackboard binds the cookie to the client's IP address and self-reported browser information. This defense fails, however, because the adversary can spoof their IP address and browser information.

SBP is a cryptographic protocol that wraps a vulnerable web application server and introduces a *reverse proxy*. SBP binds the HTTP *session authentication cookie*—a token with which a client identifies themselves to the server—to an underlying TLS channel between the client and the proxy. The reverse proxy receives requests on behalf of the server and manages the cookie binding. A design goal of SBP is to avoid modifying the client or the server: neither the client nor the server are aware that they participate in a session of SBP with the proxy.

1.1   Our Work

Despite the protocol's obscurity and lack of adoption, there are several lessons to learn from SBP. SBP improves legacy authentication protocols (e.g., password-based authentication via TLS 1.2) without modifying the legacy systems. SBP applies a channel binding to the session cookie without awareness of the client or the server, which are both unable to verify the binding, resulting in structural flaws. Rather than incorporating an existing TLS channel-binding standard, SBP specifies a flawed, non-standard channel binding that violates existing TLS libraries by exposing the session master secret. Because the original SBP protocol specifies TLS 1.2 with *Rivest-Shamir-Adelman (RSA)* key exchange, the protocol depends on the freshness of a pre-master secret, for which there is no guarantee because the client is solely responsible for generating this secret. Protocol designers can incorporate these lessons to build more robust wrapping protocols, and to understand better the limits and appropriate environments for the protocols.

To analyze SBP, we model a baseline scenario without SBP (pre-SBP), the original SBP, and five custom variations in the strand-space model [50] using the *Cryptographic Protocol Shapes Analyzer (CPSA)* [20]. Throughout, we focus on SBP's goal of preventing cookie-stealing attacks. Our model of the original SBP incorporates and binds to TLS-1.2-RSA (TLS 1.2 using RSA key exchange), consistent with the SBP authors' description and their prototype implementation. Each of our custom variations binds to alternate versions of TLS, of which several use *Diffie-Hellman (DH)* key exchange: *mutual TLS (mTLS)*-1.2-RSA, TLS-1.2-DH, mTLS-1.2-DH, TLS-1.3, and mTLS-1.3. Using our models, we explore how variations between underlying TLS channels affect SBP's cookie-stealing resistance and compare these variations to pre-SBP and the original protocol.

Using CPSA, we formalize security goals of the SBP design by extracting authentication goals to define an SBP session context. From each of the protocol's distinct cryptographic perspectives (client, proxy), we prove or disprove *context agreement*, in which legitimate parties agree on the session context after executing the protocol, via an exhaustive proof or counterexample. From the cryptographic perspectives of the client and proxy, our analysis identifies the properties of the underlying communication channel that SBP requires to function within the *Dolev-Yao (DY)* network intruder model [13]. To our knowledge, we are the first to perform a formal-methods analysis of the SBP protocol.

From our analysis, we identify several vulnerabilities resulting from the design of the original SBP protocol: (1) The client cannot verify the cryptographic binding that the proxy applies to the cookie (see Sect. 8). (2) The proxy cannot authenticate the client because the client does not produce a certificate; the client may transmit stolen credentials; and the protocol leaks freshness of the TLS pre-master secret when using RSA. (3) As a consequence of (2), the proxy may communicate with the adversary, who forwards the client's credentials and requests from a different SBP session. As we show in Sect. 8.2, an adversary can also exploit these vulnerabilities to launch a *"credential-stealing attack."*

From these vulnerabilities of the original SBP protocol, the most serious attack is a credential-stealing attack, in which the adversary operates a corrupt proxy to harvest the user's credentials. With the user's credentials, the adversary can simply sign into the protected server without stealing any cookies. Furthermore, because the original SBP protocol uses TLS-1.2-RSA in which the proxy cannot verify the freshness of the pre-master secret, the proxy may bind a cookie to a compromised channel, enabling session hijacking as if SBP were not present.

For anyone who wishes to use SBP, we recommend using SBP with the strongest choices for TLS. In particular, we recommend using SBP with mTLS-1.2-DH or mTLS-1.3, which are the only two versions we found to satisfy the security objectives from both the client and proxy perspectives. By applying DH rather than RSA, these versions ensure freshness of the TLS master secret. Even better would be to use a variant of SBP with mTLS-1.3, replacing SBP's non-standard channel binding with a TLS exporter binding [54] (see Sect. 11.5).

1.2 Wrapping Protocols

Wrapping protocols such as SBP, which encapsulates an older, flawed protocol, exist to solve a practical problem facing many organizations: hardening legacy systems against adversaries who target these systems with known vulnerabilities. Such adversaries exploit known vulnerabilities in these systems that can be impossible for organizations to patch. Systems may become impossible to patch because vendors discontinue support, developers of custom software become unavailable, and patches break the system's functionality. Although it may be tempting to eliminate the legacy system from an organization's network, doing so can be prohibitively expensive and disruptive. Solutions such as SBP attempt to wrap and isolate legacy systems to keep them available while mitigating known attacks.

TLS channel binding is the key idea of SBP, which seeks to improve cookie-based authentication in HTTP by applying a custom channel binding to the cookie. Many protocols assume authenticated communication channels negotiated by protocols such as TLS, which is widely available, supported, and ubiquitous with web browsing. To bind values in a new protocol to an underlying TLS channel, protocol designers apply channel bindings: they encrypt or hash their sensitive values together with secret values originating from the TLS channel. The purpose of such bindings is to enable protocol participants to detect protocol interactions in which an adversary attempts to transfer information bound to one TLS channel to a session taking place on a different TLS channel. We explore the ability of SBP's channel binding to mitigate cookie-based hijacking, and discuss SBP's decision to use a custom binding in Sect. 11.5.

Wrapping protocols introduce the problematic notion of *oblivious protocol participants* (see Fig. 1), which we define informally as participants that participate in cryptographic protocols without knowledge that they are participating. Often, these participants are flawed legacy systems that are not possible to patch. To enable such systems to function in a network without presenting soft targets for adversaries, wrapping protocols fool the participants into participating in stronger protocols that mitigate known flaws. The existence of protocols such as SBP illustrates a need for such protocols and their oblivious participants.

Oblivious protocol participants introduce new dangers, particularly in the DY model, because they are not aware of the protocols or sessions in which they communicate. Cryptographic bindings (see Sect. 2.2) are vital primitives for preventing *man-in-the-middle (MitM)* attacks but are impossible for oblivious participants to apply or verify.

1.3   Our Contributions

This work evolves a preliminary formal-methods analysis of SBP by Elsaad [2], who verified that the original SBP protocol resists protocol interactions from the client's perspective. Additionally, as we present in Sect. 8.2, Elsaad identified and implemented a "tailgating attack" against SBP, which (beyond the DY model) assumes that the adversary can execute code in the client's browser. Our expanded study analyzes additional models. We also identify issues with TLS channel binding and passwords and make recommendations for designing and deploying protocols like SBP.

Our primary contributions are: (1) We present a formal-methods analysis of the SBP protocol, in which we state and prove security goals from the client and proxy perspectives for a model of the original SBP, five variations, and a baseline model without SBP. (2) We interpret our formal analysis in terms of vulnerabilities, attacks, and risks. (3) For people who wish to use SBP, we recommend using using a variant of SBP with mTLS-1.3 and exporter bindings. (4) We recommend principles and improvements for SBP and similar wrapping protocols. (5) We discuss lessons learned for protocol designers developing wrapping protocols like SBP. Source code for our CPSA models is available on GitHub [51].

In the remainder of this paper, we introduce SBP and wrapping protocols that perform channel binding, review relevant background, explain the SBP protocol, state our adversarial model, present our CPSA model for each variation of SBP, state security goals in strand space for each model, prove or disprove the security goals using CPSA, point out potential vulnerabilities, attacks, and risks, make recommendations, summarize previous work, and discuss issues and open problems raised by our work.

1.4   Summary of Technical Findings

From the cryptographic perspectives of the client and proxy, our analysis (as summarized in Table 1) identifies the properties of the underlying communication channel that SBP requires to function within the *Dolev-Yao (DY)* network intruder model [13]. The client and proxy must mutually authenticate each other, and the channel binding must incorporate fresh values from each communicant. From the proxy's perspective, only models that use mTLS with DH (e.g., mTLS-1.2-DH, mTLS-1.3) authenticate mutually. Without these features, the proxy cannot determine if they are communicating with a legitimate client or the network adversary. Within a DY network, traditional passwords are an inadequate authentication mechanism because clients may inadvertently transmit these values to the adversary (see Sect. 11.4). Additionally, when using TLS or mTLS with RSA (e.g., as in the original SBP), the proxy has no assurance that the client contributes a fresh pre-master secret to the protocol—consequently, the proxy may bind the cookie to a compromised TLS channel.

In our models that use mTLS with DH, the proxy authenticates the client using a client certificate; the proxy is guaranteed freshness of the TLS master secret; and the protocol does not leak this freshness—preventing session hijacking. In this variation, the client receives a cookie bound to the fresh TLS master secret. Of the models we analyze, only models incorporating mTLS with DH (e.g., mTLS-1.2-DH, mTLS-1.3) guarantee that the client and the proxy perspectives agree on an SBP session context, including the identities of the user, server, and cookie. It is important, as we do in our mTLS models, that client certificate binds to the client's username and not just to the user's machine. If the certificate binds only to the client's machine, it may be possible for any entity accessing the client's machine to transmit stolen credentials to an honest proxy. That is, unless the certificate binds to the user name, a major benefit of using mTLS (certificate authentication of the client) is lost.

2   Background

We present relevant background regarding session hijacking, cryptographic binding, formal-methods protocol analysis, strand spaces, CPSA, proxies, and TLS.

2.1   Session Hijacking

In session hijacking, an adversary presents a legitimate user's session credentials as their own, potentially enabling malicious transactions. Examples include *cross-site scripting (XSS)*, in which the adversary injects code into the client's browser to steal a session authentication token [45], and malicious browser plug-ins [23–25], which can modify web pages in the client's browser or steal sensitive information, such as an HTTP cookie. Existing mitigations include HTTP-only cookies [55]. SBP seeks to eliminate cookie-based session hijacking by binding the user's cookie to an underlying TLS session.

2.2   Cryptographic Binding

Cryptographic binding is vital for preventing a DY adversary from creating adverse protocol interactions [26]. It applies cryptographic primitives, such as encryption, digital signature, or hashing, to associate session context (e.g., identities and nonces) with a message from a specific protocol session. Cryptographic binding may or may not involve secrets. It is important that an adversary cannot undo bindings and that recipients be able to verify them. As early as 1996, Abadi and Needham's [1] informal guidelines on designing sound cryptographic protocols stated a need to bind to session contexts cryptographically. An example of cryptographic binding is a digital certificate, which associates a public key with a network identity via a signature. SBP uses a particular type of binding—channel binding—in which SBP binds an authentication token to an underlying TLS channel between the client and the proxy.

Protocols that do not bind appropriately are vulnerable to protocol interactions. The well-known 1995 attack by Gavin Lowe [31] on the *Needham-Schroeder (NS)* [35] protocol exploits a lack of binding between the responder's nonce and the responder's identity. Binding failures continue to appear in modern protocols such as FIDO UAF [18], illustrating the need for formal-methods tools in protocol design. We discuss requirements for effective cryptographic bindings in Sect. 11.6.

2.3 Formal-Methods Protocol Analysis

Formal-methods protocol analysis involves expressing a protocol in a formal mathematical model, stating theorems that reflect the protocol's desired security properties, and proving those theorems. Often, this process requires the assistance of specialized theorem-proving tools. Notable existing tools for protocol analysis include ProVerif [9], Tamarin Prover [34], Maude-NPA [16], and CPSA [30]. It is also possible to carry out security analysis using more general high-order logic theorem provers such as Isabelle [38]. Unlike most theorem provers, CPSA is capable of discovering protocol security goals given a set of assumptions and a partial execution. In this sense, CPSA is a "model-finding tool." Like other theorem provers, CPSA is also capable of verifying stated theorems within the model. For our analysis, we use CPSA because we are familiar with the tool, have access to experts, and find the tool's model-finding properties useful for identifying protocol security goals and protocol interactions.

Such formal-methods analysis of protocols will not detect implementation errors, cryptographic weaknesses, nor application of protocols to inappropriate settings.

2.4 Strand Spaces

Strand spaces [50] are a formalization of interactions between protocol participants on a DY network. A protocol's *strand space* comprises a set of *strands*, which express actions by legitimate parties or a network penetrator. Each strand expresses a sequence of incoming and outgoing messages via positively or negatively signed *terms*: positive terms denote messages going out into the network, and negative terms denote messages coming in from the network. A pair of strands with corresponding terms, such that one strand transmits the terms that the other strand receives, are *complementary* strands. We model the strand space of a protocol by extracting the protocol's roles from its specification, extracting complementary strands from these roles, and including penetrator strands that express the capabilities of our adversary.

Together with a set of keys known to the adversary, penetrator strands express the adversary's available actions on the network. The adversary composes these strands to construct attacks within a protocol's strand space. A standard set of penetrator strands models the following actions: (1) Emit or extract arbitrary messages. (2) Replay messages. (3) Concatenate message or separate messages into components. (4) Using knowledge of a secret key, encrypt or decrypt messages. When necessary, one can include additional penetrator strands that express additional behaviors.

Interactions between strands occur in subsets of strand spaces called *bundles*: a bundle consists of a portion of legitimate party strands and penetrator strands from a strand space and captures causal relationships between the terms that these strands transmit and receive. Strands within bundles follow three rules: First, a strand cannot send and receive a message concurrently. Second, a strand must receive a message from a unique node on another strand that emits that message. Third, if a strand emits a message, any strand expecting such a message may receive it. The same strand can appear multiple times in a bundle. Bundles express unique execution sequences within a protocol's strand space, including sequences that describe attacks by an adversary.

Because proving properties of strand spaces is subtle, time consuming, and laborious, we rely on CPSA to prove theorems for us automatically.

2.5 CPSA

CPSA [30] is an open-source tool for analyzing cryptographic protocols within the strand-space model. While capable of proving theorems, CPSA distinguishes itself as a model-finder: given an input model—which comprises strands consisting of roles, messages, variables, and a set of initial assumptions—when executing to completion, CPSA identifies all essentially different executions of the protocol within a DY network and outputs these executions as *shapes* [29]. CPSA's model finding enables users to identify the strongest achieved security goal for an input model [46]. Additionally, for each shape, CPSA outputs shape analysis sentences from which users can extract the security goals [21,22,40] and corresponding proofs.

Users define CPSA models using LISP-like s-expressions that implement a custom language. In these models, which superficially resemble (but are not) executable source code, users specify one or more roles, associated variables and messages, and skeletons. *Skeletons* specify one or more initial strands and impose assumptions on the strand variables, such as "uniquely originating" a value or identifying a value, most often a secret or key, is unavailable to the adversary. When CPSA executes, the tool attempts to satisfy skeleton nodes by repeatedly applying actions available to a DY intruder in strand space theory. A *shape* is a skeleton consisting of only the strands of legitimate protocol participants, in which CPSA satisfies all nodes under the skeleton's assumptions.

Within a CPSA skeleton, we constrain variables by applying one or several origination assumptions: uniquely originating, uniquely generating, non-originating, and penetrator non-originating. *Uniquely originating* terms are unknown to protocol participants and the network until a legitimate strand emits them as part of a message, enabling us to model random nonces, fresh secret keys, and other values that must be unique for each execution of a protocol. Unlike uniquely originating terms, *uniquely generating* terms do not need to originate in messages and might appear as part of a strand's computations (e.g., terms derived from DH exponents). *Non-Originating* values are values such as private keys, which the adversary does not know, cannot guess, and will never appear on the network in a decryptable form. *Penetrator non-originating* values include passwords, which only legitimate strands can originate, that the adversary does not know without obtaining them from some run of the protocol.

2.6 Proxies

Proxies, also known as proxy servers, are systems that pass messages on behalf of other systems, often between web clients and servers [33,53]. There are two major types of proxies: *forward proxies*, which accept communication from entities and pass them to remote destinations on a network, and *reverse proxies*, which appear outwardly as servers and pass traffic to other systems.

Proxies intercept and manipulate network traffic by design and can appear indistinguishable from an adversary, making them problematic for protocol security. A rogue proxy enables an adversary to create, delete, and modify network messages to exploit flaws in network protocols. Because communicants often are unable to determine that they are communicating via a proxy, the scenario of a rogue proxy can be challenging to detect and mitigate. Within the DY model, a potentially corrupt proxy may make achieving many security goals impossible. We discuss the potential vulnerabilities and attacks affecting SBP's reverse proxy in Sect. 8.

2.7 Transport Layer Security (TLS)

Transport Layer Security (TLS) [41–43] is a widely deployed cryptographic protocol for negotiating encrypted communication channels on insecure networks. Frequently, protocols that require a confidential channel with authentication and integrity bind with TLS. The most common deployments of TLS assume a client-server architecture in which the server produces for the client a certificate, signed by a certificate authority, that attests the server's public key. This common deployment results in one-way authentication: the client authenticates the server, but the server does not authenticate the client. In a variation of TLS known as *mutual TLS*, or *mTLS*, both the client and the server produce certificates to authenticate each other.

To establish a TLS channel, a client and a server engage in the TLS handshake protocol to compute a session key with which they encrypt subsequent traffic. During the handshake, the communicants generate and share random nonces. The communicants then compute the session key (*"master secret"*) using the nonces and a *pre-master secret*, which results from a *Rivest-Shamir-Adleman (RSA)* [44] or *Diffie-Hellman (DH)* key exchange. When using RSA, the client generates the pre-master secret and transmits it to the server encrypted under the server's public key. When using DH, the client and the server compute the pre-master secret together. Crucially, when using TLS with RSA, only the client contributes freshness to the pre-master secret. By contrast, when using TLS with DH, both the client and the server contribute freshness to the pre-master secret.

Currently, two versions of TLS are in active use: TLS-1.2 and TLS-1.3. TLS-1.2 supports several types of key exchanges, which include the popular options DH and RSA. TLS-1.3 improves on TLS-1.2, including eliminating RSA as an option for key exchange in favor of DH. Consequently, TLS-1.3 with DH guarantees that both the client and the server contribute to the freshness of the pre-master secret.

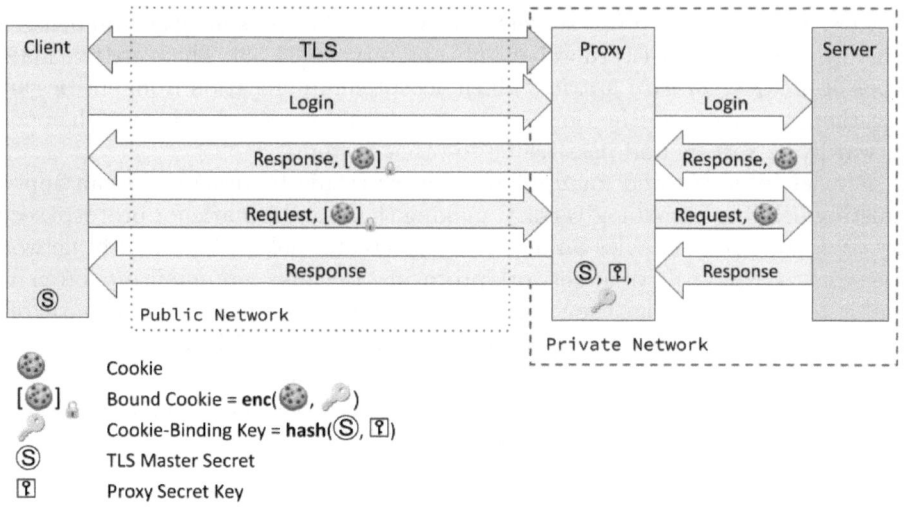

Fig. 1. Architectural diagram for the SBP protocol in which the client and application server are oblivious protocol participants. A client establishes a session with the SBP (reverse) proxy over the Internet and issues further requests to this proxy. The proxy strips SBP-specific information from the client's messages before forwarding them to the application server across a private network. The server, believing the proxy to be the client, replies with responses which the proxy relays to the client.

3   Session Binding Proxy (SBP) Protocol

Developed in 2013 by Burgers, Verdult, and van Eekelen [10], the *Session Binding Proxy (SBP)* protocol is a custom protocol that wraps a vulnerable web server to improve resistance against cookie-based session hijacking. The protocol assumes an adversary who executes a malicious script (e.g., via XSS) in the client's browser to steal the cookie, but cannot accomplish more difficult attacks such as stealing the client's TLS session secrets, compromising the client's stored certificates, or accessing the client's file system. To defend against this adversary, SBP specifies a reverse proxy that manages communication on behalf of the server and cryptographically binds a client's authentication cookie to the master secret of the underlying TLS channel (version 1.2 with RSA, in the original SBP). This binding hinders an adversary from stealing a client's cookie and presenting it as their own by enabling the proxy to invalidate cookies that fail to bind to the correct TLS channel. SBP specifies messages between three distinct roles (client, proxy, server) and comprises three separate protocol phases: key establishment, session establishment, and request handling. Figure 1 illustrates the binding of the cookie, the main idea behind SBP.

Key Establishment. The client initiates this phase by completing a standard TLS handshake with the proxy. In this handshake, the proxy sends a certificate to the client, enabling the client to authenticate the proxy. Following the TLS handshake, the client and proxy each possess a master secret K_{TLS}, which the proxy uses to bind the session cookie in the following phase. The remaining phases communicate over this encrypted TLS channel.

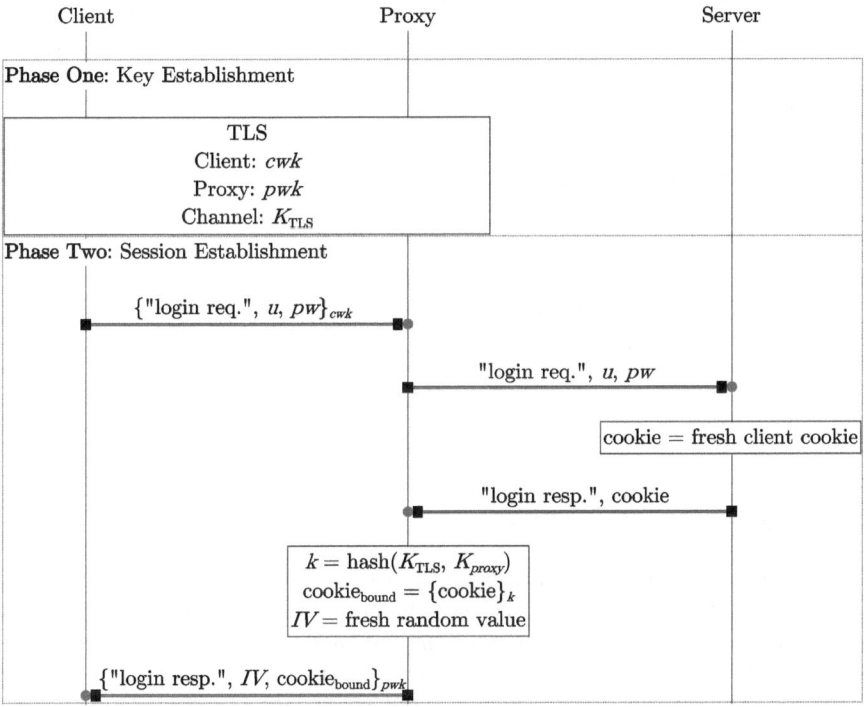

Fig. 2. Idealized message sequence diagram of SBP's first two phases: key establishment and session establishment. Vertical lines correspond to protocol roles; arrows indicate sending or receiving a message; and arrow labels specify message content. The proxy passes all messages between the client and the server, binding the cookie in the second phase using the master secret of the client-proxy TLS channel and a system private key known only to the proxy.

Session Establishment. To establish a session with the server, the client, server, and proxy exchange the following messages: (1) The client transmits to the proxy an authentication request containing credentials intended for the server, including a username u and a password pw. (2) The proxy forwards the client's request to the server. (3) The server generates a session cookie (an authentication token representing the client's authenticated identity) and a response for the client, and transmits these values to the proxy. (4) The proxy encrypts the session cookie using a cookie-binding key k, which key comprises a hash of the master secret K_{TLS} from the previous phase, a proxy secret key K_{proxy} known only by the proxy, and a random initialization vector IV. The proxy transmits to the client the server's response, the IV, and an encryption of the session cookie under k. By so encrypting the cookie, the proxy binds the cookie to the TLS session. The client, upon receiving the final message of this phase, stores the IV and the encrypted cookie for future requests. Figure 2 illustrates the message flow of SBP's first two phases. Appendix B.1 defines the messages and their variable names.

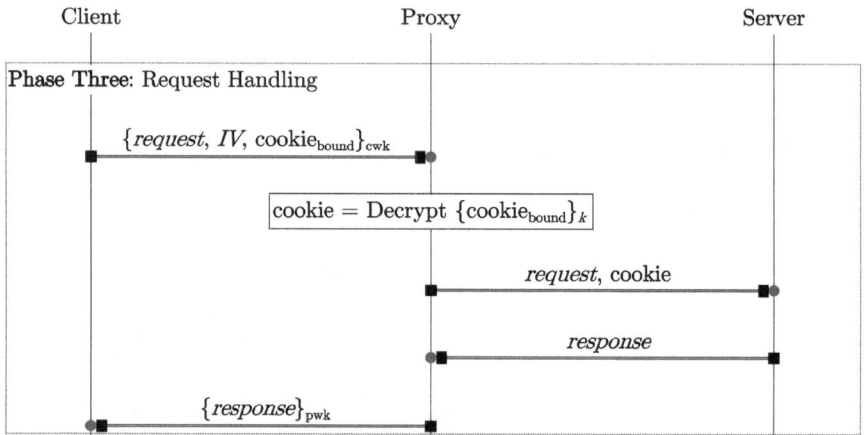

Fig. 3. Idealized message sequence diagram of SBP's third phase: request handling. Using knowledge of the TLS channel with the client, the proxy decrypts the client's bound cookie cookie$_{bound}$ and substitutes the unbound cookie in the request prior to forwarding it to the server. The server is never aware of the exchange of messages between the client and the proxy; rather, it assumes the proxy is the client and responds to the proxy appropriately. Similarly, the client is unaware of the exchanges between the proxy and the server, and the client is unaware that its cookie is a bound cookie.

The SBP authors intended the IV to prevent replay attacks in which the adversary replays an old bound cookie. In this sense, the IV functions more like a nonce than a traditional IV. However, because the cookie does not bind to the IV, the IV does not achieve its intended purpose.

Request Handling. The client, now in possession of the bound session cookie, initiates further requests in this last phase: (1) The client transmits a request, the IV from the previous phase, and the bound session cookie to the proxy. (2) Using knowledge of the IV, k, and K_{proxy}, the proxy decrypts the client's bound cookie, replaces the encrypted cookie with the decryption of the bound cookie, and forwards the request to the server. (3) The server receives the request and the session cookie, validates the cookie, and if the cookie is correct, transmits a response to the proxy. (4) The proxy forwards the response to the client. The ladder diagram of Fig. 3 specifies request handling within an existing SBP session.

The authors of SBP provide a proof-of-concept implementation that implements the proxy as an embedded component of the server, as we recommend (see Sect. 9). The authors, however, potentially dangerously do not require this configuration: the protocol's abstract design specifies the proxy and the server as two separate network entities that communicate over a dedicated, private channel, whose characteristics could greatly impact the security of the protocol.

4 Adversarial Model

We evaluate SBP against a DY-style adversary that hijacks an honest user's session via two primary methods: stealing a user's cookies using techniques such as XSS (see Sect. 2.1), and exploiting protocol interactions between two separate SBP sessions. To hijack a user's session, the adversary attempts to provide a legitimate SBP proxy with an honest user's authentication cookie. The DY network intruder model is a commonly used and widely accepted adversarial model that captures strong realistic threats for many network applications. It is important to understand how SBP performs in the DY model, even if the authors of SBP did not consider this realistic threat.

As a classic DY adversary, the adversary has full control over all messages on the network and manipulates an unbounded number of protocol sessions. Additionally, to evaluate SBP's goal of mitigating stolen cookies, the adversary may steal cookies from legitimate users at will. The adversary cannot break cryptographic primitives. They must acquire session keys to compromise TLS channels or any corresponding channel bindings for any cookies they obtain. Additionally, the adversary may operate a SBP proxy with which legitimate users intentionally communicate. Within the strand-space model, we formalize these capabilities as penetrator strands (see Appendix 2.4). To reflect the adversary's ability to steal cookies, we grant these strands the ability to originate any cookie in the protocol.

To enable TLS channel negotiation between legitimate network participants, we assume there exists an honest certificate authority on the network for which all legitimate participants possess an authentic certificate. This certificate authority produces a legitimate certificate for any network entity, including SBP proxies and users operated by the adversary. Additionally, we assume that all network participants rely on the same version of TLS, which varies for our different protocol models. Finally, we assume that the server behaves honestly and that the adversary cannot compromise messages between an SBP proxy and its corresponding server. We make this assumption because the reference implementation of SBP embeds the proxy and the server on a single network entity, and SBP will fail to achieve any security properties if this assumption is false.

Our adversary is willing to risk detection and criminal charges to access a legitimate user's accounts unlawfully and to engage in a range of malicious activities, such as transferring assets to steal them, collecting private information to blackmail users, or selling user credentials to criminals. Potential targets include universities (SBP's original use case), financial institutions, E-commerce services, social media, and other lucrative stores of sensitive data.

5   CPSA Models of SBP

Using CPSA's modeling language, we specify roles, variables, messages, and assumptions to model a baseline protocol (with no SBP) and six variations of the SBP protocol: *Pre-SBP*, *SBP-TLS-1.2-RSA*, *SBP-mTLS-1.2-RSA*, *SBP-TLS-1.2-DH*, *SBP-mTLS-1.2-DH*, *SBP-TLS-1.3*, *SBP-mTLS-1.3*. The baseline pre-SBP model contrasts with SBP to illustrate how SBP helps resist our adversary. For each SBP model, a *client* communicates with a *proxy* using a version of TLS that corresponds to the protocol's name. For these models, we state security goals in Sect. 6 and analyze the goals in Sect. 7. Augmenting the ladder diagrams in Sect. 3, Appendix B defines the messages and their variables and gives selected source code for our CPSA models. For our complete source code, see GitHub [51].

For TLS authentication, we incorporate separate models reflecting different TLS versions into our pre-SBP and SBP models. We assume RSA key exchange for models with the "RSA" suffix and DH key exchange for other models. As part of this work, we analyzed the authentication properties of our TLS models and found these properties to be consistent with existing proofs (e.g., Tamarin proofs [12]). Every legitimate strand completes TLS authentication prior to sending or receiving further messages. For non-mutual TLS sessions, only proxy strands transmit certificates. For mutual TLS sessions, client and proxy strands transmit certificates. Following the negotiation of a TLS session, all legitimate strands in our models encrypt messages under the appropriate TLS key.

Each strand in each model corresponds to a complementary strand such that messages in one strand mirror messages in a complementary strand. Client strand terms correspond to proxy strand terms. Proxy strand terms correspond with client strand terms. TLS authentication messages reflect these relationships between strands.

The SBP protocol enables two branches of operation for a client: the client can authenticate to the proxy, receive a bound session cookie, and make requests, or the client can recall a cookie from a previous session to make requests. We reflect this branching behavior by specifying two variations of each strand (client, proxy). Strands with the suffix -a (*a-strands*) authenticate using credentials then process requests. Strands with the suffix -r (*r-strands*) recall cookies from previous sessions and process requests. We include both types of strands in our strand spaces to enable CPSA to explore behaviors resulting from strands, executing these two distinct cases, interacting with each other.

In our models, we distinguish between a client and a user. A *user* is an entity that communicates with the proxy via a process called the *client* that is connected to a network. This distinction can be important when introducing certificates, as we do in SBP-mTLS-1.2-RSA, SBP-mTLS-1.2-DH, and SBP-mTLS-1.3. In our models, the user certificate binds to a username. There may be other applications (e.g., involving TLS tunneling) in which a certificate binds to a client machine identifier (see Sect. 11.5).

The pre-SBP and SBP models share several common terms that include the client's username u and password pw, an authentication cookie cookie, and an HTTP request and response.

5.1 Pre-SBP Model

For comparison, we begin with a pre-SBP model in which a *client* communicates with a *server* over a TLS-1.2-RSA channel without SBP. We model four strands: client-a, client-r, server-a, and server-r. Each strand establishes a TLS session with a complementary strand and carries out its respective steps: (1) Client-a transmits u and pw, receives and stores cookie, transmits cookie together with request, and receives response. (2) Client-r retrieves cookie from storage, transmits it with request, and receives response. (3) Server-a receives u and pw, creates, transmits and stores cookie, receives request together with cookie, and transmits response. (4) Server-r receives request together with cookie, retrieves cookie from storage, and transmits response. Each client strand assumes the client perspective, and each server strand assumes the server perspective.

We also model the pre-SBP protocol over TLS-1.2 with DH, TLS-1.3, and with mutual TLS. The security properties of each model are equivalent, so we refer to all of these models as a single model: Pre-SBP.

5.2 SBP Models

For each of our SBP models, we model four strands: client-a, client-r, proxy-a, and proxy-r. SBP strands include three additional terms over the Pre-SBP model: a system private key K_{proxy} for binding the cookie, the TLS channel's master secret K_{TLS}, and a bound cookie $\mathsf{cookie_{bound}} = \mathsf{Enc}(\mathsf{cookie}, k)$, where $k = \mathsf{Hash}(K_{\mathsf{TLS}}, K_{\mathsf{proxy}})$. We specify the following strands: (1) Client-a transmits u and pw, receives and stores $\mathsf{cookie_{bound}}$, transmits $\mathsf{cookie_{bound}}$ with request, and receives response. (2) Client-r retrieves $\mathsf{cookie_{bound}}$ from storage, transmits it together with request, and receive response. (3) Proxy-a receives u and pw, creates and stores cookie, transmits $\mathsf{cookie_{bound}}$, receives request and $\mathsf{cookie_{bound}}$, and transmits response. (4) Proxy-r retrieves cookie, receives request together with $\mathsf{cookie_{bound}}$, and transmits response. Client strands assume the client perspective, and proxy strands assume the proxy perspective.

6 Security Goals in Strand Spaces

We formalize SBP's security properties within the strand-space model by specifying *context agreement* security goals: following a run of SBP, instances of a client and a proxy strand must agree on a session context. Failure to agree on context indicates the possibility of protocol interaction, which may lead to vulnerabilities and subsequent attacks on our SBP models. For a protocol to be correct, all legitimate parties that execute a protocol must agree on the resulting session context. We precisely formulate Goal 1 as an injective agreement [32]. Goal 1 implies the main security goal of SBP: to prevent cookie stealing in the DY adversarial model. In Sect. 7, we prove or disprove Goal 1 for different versions of our SBP models.

6.1   Session Context

A *session context* consists of authentication goals on which complementary pairs of role strands must agree. These facts express equivalences of values such as communicant identities, key material, nonces, or cookies. In SBP, a client and a proxy must agree on the username, the server's identifier, and a relationship between an unbound cookie and a bound cookie: for any cookie, the client must have assurance that the cookie binds to the underlying TLS channel between itself and the proxy. For the pre-SBP model, we rely on a simpler context in which a client and a server agree on a cookie, the username, and the server's identifier. Using CPSA, we iteratively arrived at minimal session contexts for the pre-SBP and SBP models, which we describe in Context 1 and Context 2, respectively.

Session Context 1 (Pre-SBP). *Let $\mathcal{C}$ and $\mathcal{S}$ be instances of complementary client strands and server strands in a pre-SBP strand space. For any pair $(\mathcal{C}, \mathcal{S})$, the following facts hold: $\mathcal{C}$ and $\mathcal{S}$ agree on the username u, the server identifier s, and the cookie* cookie.

Session Context 2 (SBP). *Let $\mathcal{C}$ and $\mathcal{P}$ be instances of complementary client strands and proxy strands in an SBP strand space. For any pair $(\mathcal{C}, \mathcal{P})$, the following facts hold: $\mathcal{C}$ and $\mathcal{P}$ agree on the username u, the proxy identifier p, and for any cookie* cookie *that $\mathcal{P}$ originates, $\mathcal{C}$ must hold a corresponding bound cookie* cookie$_{bound}$ *that incorporates* cookie.

We specify three sets of origination assumptions (Sect. 2.5) for our distinct roles: client, proxy, and the pre-SBP model's server. Origination assumptions express a role's cryptographic perspective by establishing assumptions about values in the protocol, such as the secrecy of private keys and freshness of session values. Due to differences in origination assumptions, security goals that hold for one set of assumptions may fail to hold for another set of assumptions. Often, such a discrepancy suggests a flaw in a protocol. Below, we provide definitions for each of our assumption sets.

Assumption 1 (Client Assumptions). *For any initial client strand $\mathcal{C}$ in a bundle, we make the following assumptions: (1) Private keys of legitimate parties are unknown (non-originating) to the adversary. (2) $\mathcal{C}$ generates (uniquely originates) a fresh client-random nonce for TLS, and [for TLS-1.2] a fresh pre-master secret or [for TLS-1.3] a fresh DH value. (3) [SBP models only] The proxy system key is not available to the adversary.*

Assumption 2 (Proxy Assumptions). *For any initial proxy strand $\mathcal{P}$ in a bundle, we make the following assumptions: (1) Private keys of legitimate parties are unknown to the adversary. (2) $\mathcal{P}$ generates a fresh proxy-random nonce for TLS, and [for TLS-1.3] a fresh DH value.*

6.2   Session Context Agreement

To define *session context agreement*, we first specify two predicates: successful completion and unique completion. *Successful completion* states that for any initial strand that executes fully, there exists a complementary strand in the bundle that executes the protocol and agrees on a context. *Unique completion* states that within a bundle, no complementary strand exists that completes the protocol and does not agree on the context with the initial strand. We provide mathematical definitions for each of these predicates below.

Within the following definitions, for any bundle $\mathcal{B}$, $\mathcal{B}$-height refers to the number of nodes of a strand that are in bundle $\mathcal{B}$: a strand of integer height i has executed at least i steps of a protocol run. When executing the protocol between an initial and complementary strand, the complementary strand need not execute fully to satisfy the terms of the initial strand—the complementary strand's height can be less than a full run.

Definition 1 (Successful Completion). *Let π be any two-party protocol; let $\mathcal{B}$ be any bundle in any strand space Σ_π; let $\mathcal{R}_a$ and $\mathcal{R}_b$ be roles in Σ_π; let s and s' be any pair of complementary strands in Σ_π; let $Ctx[\pi]$ be any session context for π; and let $Orig[\mathcal{R}_a]$ be any set of origination assumptions for s. Let i and j be any natural numbers.*

$Succ(\mathcal{R}_a, \mathcal{R}_b, Ctx[\pi], Orig[\mathcal{R}_a], i, j)$ if and only if (iff) for all bundles $\mathcal{B}$ that yield from Σ_π and strands $s \in \mathcal{R}_a \cap \mathcal{B}$, there exists a strand $s' \in \mathcal{R}_b \cap \mathcal{B}$ such that under $Orig[\mathcal{R}_a]$, s with $\mathcal{B}$-height i and s' with $\mathcal{B}$-height j satisfy $Ctx[\pi]$.

Definition 2 (Unique Completion). *Let $\mathcal{R}_a$ be any role in Σ_π; let $Ctx[\pi]$ be any session context for π; and let $Orig[\mathcal{R}_a]$ be any set of origination assumptions for s. Let i and j be any natural numbers.*

$Uniq(\mathcal{R}_a, Ctx[\pi], Orig[\mathcal{R}_a], i, j)$ iff for all roles $\mathcal{R}_b, \mathcal{R}_c$ in Σ_π, $Succ(\mathcal{R}_a, \mathcal{R}_b, Ctx[\pi], Orig[\mathcal{R}_a], i, j) \wedge Succ(\mathcal{R}_a, \mathcal{R}_c, Ctx[\pi], Orig[\mathcal{R}_a], i, j) \implies \mathcal{R}_b = \mathcal{R}_c.

Using these predicates and assumptions, we define Goal 1 as a context agreement that captures the main security goal of SBP to prevent cookie stealing in the DY adversarial model. In Goal 1, a role holding a set of assumptions must demonstrate successful completion and unique completion with some complementary role. Goal 1 is an authentication goal that requires *injective agreement* between an initial and a complementary strand—there exists a one-to-one mapping of the session context between these strands. Any protocol execution that yields a counterexample to the injective agreement of Goal 1 proves the failure of Goal 1 for that protocol. Counterexamples to Goal 1 describe attacks on the protocol under the initial role's perspective.

Goal 1 (Context Agreement). *Let Σ_π be any strand space; let $\mathcal{R}_a$ and $\mathcal{R}_b$ be any complementary roles in Σ_π; let $Orig[\mathcal{R}_a]$ be any set of origination assumptions for role $\mathcal{R}_a$; and let $Ctx[\pi]$ be any session context for π. For any role ρ, let $height(\rho)$ be the height of any fully executing strand in role ρ. Let i and j be natural numbers such that $i = height(\mathcal{R}_a)$ and $j \leq height(\mathcal{R}_b)$.*

Session context agreement means $\exists j$ such that
$$Succ(\mathcal{R}_a, \mathcal{R}_b, Ctx[\pi], Orig[\mathcal{R}_a], i, j) \land Uniq(\mathcal{R}_a, Ctx[\pi], Orig[\mathcal{R}_a], i, j).$$

In Sect. 7, using CPSA, we evaluate context agreement goals for each of our models from each role's perspective.

7   CPSA Analysis of Security Goals

We state and prove theorems that evaluate context agreement goals for each of our models (Pre-SBP, SBP-TLS-1.2-RSA, SBP-mTLS-1.2-RSA, SBP-TLS-1.2-DH, SBP-mTLS-1.2-DH, SBP-TLS-1.3, SBP-mTLS-1.3). For each model, we prove a context-agreement theorem for a distinct strand with a corresponding perspective. All strands (client, proxy, or server) use the corresponding perspectives and contexts that we detail in Sect. 6. While we do not mention intruder strands in our theorems, CPSA considers them when proving or disproving context agreement.

For our SBP models, context-agreement prevents cookie stealing and subsequent session hijacking by an adversary. Unique completion, one of the two requirements for context agreement, states that, for any legitimate client or proxy strand, no strand exists in a bundle that does not agree on the SBP context: the client's username, the proxy's identifier, and the correspondence between the unbound and bound cookie. To make requests using the stolen cookie, the adversary must construct a bundle in which a client and a proxy strand exist, but hold non-matching contexts resulting from communicating with penetrator strands. When such a bundle exists, the adversary successfully manipulates a bound cookie from one SBP session to another to make requests, illustrating a successful cookie-stealing attack.

7.1   Summary of CPSA Analysis

Table 1 summarizes the results of our analysis. For each strand represented by a column, we indicate for which of our models the strand satisfies a context agreement goal with its complementary strand (e.g., client and server, or client and proxy). In the baseline Pre-SBP model, cookie-stealing is clearly possible—SBP seeks to prevent this specific attack. In TLS-1.2 and TLS-1.3, the responder cannot authenticate the initiator within the DY model. In mTLS-1.2-RSA, the responder cannot guarantee freshness of the pre-master secret. Consequently, only SBP-mTLS-1.2-DH and SBP-mTLS-1.3 guarantee context agreement for all of their strands.

Table 1. Summary of security goal analysis for the pre-SBP and SBP models. For each model, a check (✓) indicates that all strands holding the corresponding perspective satisfy context agreement (cookie-stealing prevention) theorems. A crossmark (×) indicates that CPSA finds a counterexample that disproves context agreement for that perspective. When using mTLS-1.2-DH or mTLS-1.3, in which both the client and the server contribute to the pre-master secret, SBP satisfies the client and proxy security goals.

Model	client	proxy	server
Pre-SBP	×	N/A	×
SBP-TLS-1.2-RSA	✓	×	N/A
SBP-mTLS-1.2-RSA	✓	×	N/A
SBP-TLS-1.2-DH	✓	×	N/A
SBP-mTLS-1.2-DH	✓	✓	N/A
SBP-TLS-1.3	✓	×	N/A
SBP-mTLS-1.3	✓	✓	N/A

In our strand spaces, we include r-strands (see Sect. 5) that model the scenario in which a client or proxy recall a previously stored cookie to process a fresh request on a new TLS connection. Because their appearance implies that a cookie migrates from one TLS session to another, these strands only appear in an SBP bundle if something has gone wrong. Our analysis primarily concerns a-strands, which express terms for both authentication and a subsequent request. Our theorems assume a-strands for each role.

Each theorem asserts a context agreement goal as either true or false for a distinct strand and perspective. Proofs take one of two forms: an exhaustive proof that evaluates all possible, essentially different executions of the SBP model, or a counterexample consisting of a CPSA shape that disproves the security goal. Termination of CPSA is necessary only for exhaustive proofs; a single counterexample is sufficient to disprove context agreement. For each model, we prove theorems for the model's two role perspectives. When a theorem disproves context agreement for a strand, we provide and discuss a counterexample that illustrates a protocol interaction by the adversary. In Sect. 8, we discuss vulnerabilities, attacks, and risks that result from counterexamples.

7.2 Method

To analyze SBP using CPSA, we: (1) model protocol roles by extracting messages and variables from a protocol specification, (2) specify origination assumptions for crucial variables that each role originates—often, these assumptions are specific to certain protocol perspectives and ultimately reside in skeletons, (3) specify skeletons for different role perspectives or special scenarios, (4) execute CPSA to produce output shapes, and (5) extract and prove security goals from the resulting shapes.

7.3 Pre-SBP Analysis

We analyze a baseline scenario of password-based authentication over TLS 1.2 (without SBP) and confirm the known flaw that SBP seeks to mitigate. From the client and proxy perspectives, the legacy protocol fails to achieve the session context agreement goal, particularly agreement on the authentication cookie. Under the client's cryptographic assumptions, the client may accept cookies from incorrect sessions, enabling mismatches between the client and the server's cookies. Under the server's cryptographic assumptions, the server lacks the means to authenticate the client and may complete the entire protocol with the intruder. To confirm these issues, we state and prove Theorems 1 and 2.

Theorem 1. *For any initial client role holding the client assumptions and any complementary server role in the Pre-SBP strand space, Goal 1 is false.*

Proof (Counterexample). For our Pre-SBP model, CPSA finds one shape illustrating a counterexample to Goal 1 in which an initial client strand fails to agree with a complementary server strand on the username associated with a cookie. This failure results from the adversary acquiring the cookie from a session with the server and reissuing it to the legitimate client in a separate session. Because the client can complete the protocol using a cookie issued for another user, this counterexample shows that stealing a cookie and using it to hijack a session is possible under the client's perspective in the Pre-SBP model.   □

Theorem 2. *For any initial server role holding the server assumptions and any complementary client role in the Pre-SBP strand space, Goal 1 is false.*

Proof (Counterexample). CPSA finds a single counterexample shape to Goal 1 in which the initial server strand completes the protocol entirely with penetrator strands owned by the adversary. In this shape, no legitimate client strand exists. Because the server has no assurance that the client's password is secret and has no other means by which to authenticate the client, the adversary completes arbitrary runs of the protocol with the server. As a result, there will never exist a legitimate complementary strand on which the server will agree to a Pre-SBP session context.   □

7.4 SBP Analysis

As we did in the Pre-SBP model, we specify and prove theorems for the client and the proxy perspectives in the models of the original SBP and variations. Theorems 3 and 4 refer to multiple models that produced equivalent analyses. In Theorem 4, the models fail to achieve the session context agreement goal due to a proxy's inability to distinguish a legitimate client from the adversary. Section 7.5 provides two shapes output from CPSA that highlight our analysis.

In Theorem 4, proxy strands cannot distinguish between a client and an adversary because (1) the client's password may be known by the adversary, and (2) when using TLS 1.2 with RSA, the client's pre-master secret may lack freshness. Resulting from (1), our TLS 1.2 and TLS 1.3 models produce bundles which do not contain any client strands. The proxy strand completes an entire SBP session solely with penetrator strands, providing the proxy with no guarantee of session context agreement with any legitimate entity. In contrast, mTLS 1.2 with RSA fails primarily due to (2): while any bundle must include a proxy strand and a client strand, the proxy has no assurance that the adversary has no compromised the TLS channel by anticipating the client's pre-master secret, which may not be fresh.

Theorem 5 proves session context agreement when using mTLS-1.2-DH and mTLS-1.3, in which the client authenticates to the proxy by producing a client certificate. In contrast with mTLS-1.2, mTLS-1.3 establishes a confidential pre-master secret using a DH key exchange, assuring the proxy that the pre-master secret is unknown to the adversary. Because providing a client certificate to every client may be unreasonable, we suggest alternate authentication methods in Sect. 9.

Theorem 3. *For any initial client role holding the client assumptions and any complementary proxy role in the SBP-TLS-1.2-RSA, SBP-mTLS-1.2-RSA, SBP-TLS-1.2-DH, SBP-mTLS-1.2-DH, SBP TLS-1.3, and SBP-mTLS-1.3 strand spaces, Goal 1 is true.*

Proof (Enumeration). For each SBP model, CPSA terminated and found a single shape that satisfies context agreement between a client-a and a proxy-a strand. Because CPSA terminated and provably found all possible shapes, no counterexample exists. □

Theorem 4. *For any initial proxy role holding the proxy assumptions and any complementary client role in the SBP-TLS-1.2-RSA, SBP-mTLS-1.2-RSA, SBP-TLS-1.2-DH, and SBP-TLS-1.3 strand spaces, Goal 1 is false.*

Proof (Counterexample). For each of the five models, CPSA finds a single counterexample shape to Goal 1 that illustrates the initial proxy strand completing the protocol with the adversary. SBP-TLS-1.2-RSA, SBP-TLS-1.2-DH, and SBP-TLS-1.3 produce identical shapes in which the proxy fails to authenticate the client because the client's password is known to the adversary, which is a common scenario in password-based authentication. Resulting from a leaked pre-master secret, SBP-mTLS-1.2 produces a shape in which a proxy strand begins a TLS handshake with a client strand, but completes the rest of the protocol with penetrator strands.

Because the nonces are transmitted in the clear, the adversary learns the client and server nonces. Consequently, to hijack the TLS channel and any subsequent SBP session, the adversary requires only knowledge of the pre-master secret. □

Theorem 5. *For any initial proxy role holding the proxy assumptions and any complementary client strand in the SBP-mTLS-1.2-DH and SBP-mTLS-1.3 strand spaces, Goal 1 is true.*

Proof (Enumeration). CPSA terminated and found a single shape consistent with Goal 1 in which a proxy-a strand completes the protocol and agrees on the SBP session context with a client-a strand. Because the client transmits an authenticated certificate, the proxy has no doubts about the client's identity even in the event that the user's password and username are known to the adversary. The proxy contributes to the freshness of the pre-master secret via the DH key exchange in each model, preventing instances where the client does not generate a fresh pre-master secret. Because, upon termination CPSA explores all essentially different protocol executions, Goal 1 is true.   □

7.5   CPSA Shapes

We provide two selected CPSA shapes (Figs. 4 and 5) that affirm or provide counterexamples for the proofs in Sect. 7.

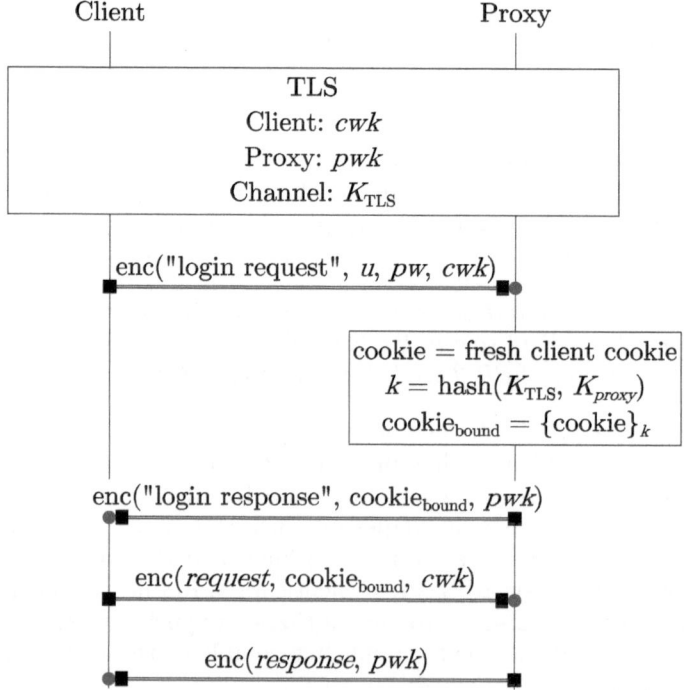

Fig. 4. CPSA shape for the client's perspective in the SBP-TLS-1.2-RSA, SBP-mTLS-1.2-RSA, SBP-TLS-1.2-DH, SBP-mTLS-1.2-DH, SBP-TLS-1.3, and SBP-mTLS-1.3 models. From the perspective of a client-r strand, under the client's cryptographic assumptions, the protocol completes as expected with a proxy-r strand. This outcome results from the client authenticating the server via its certificate, and guaranteeing freshness of the pre-master secret.

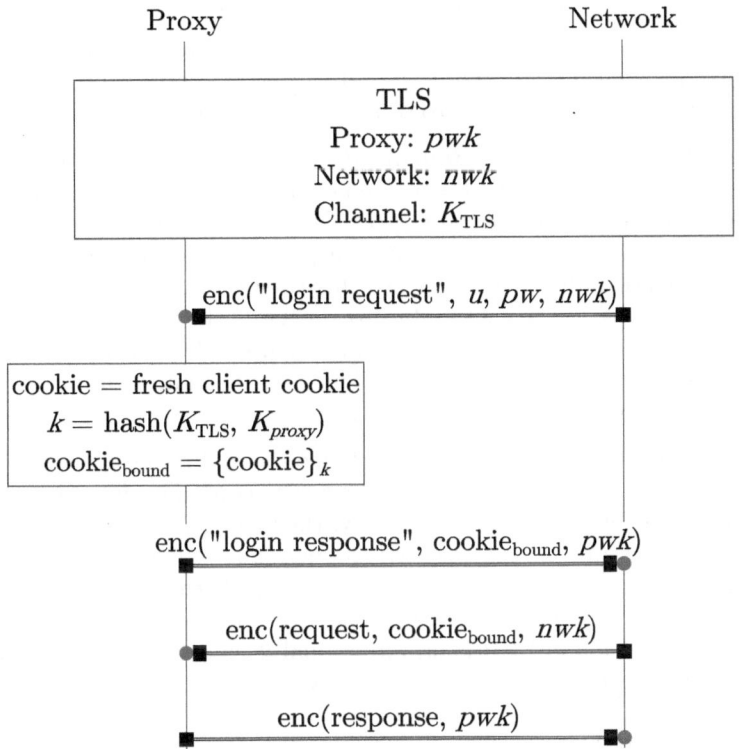

Fig. 5. CPSA shape for the proxy's perspective in the SBP-TLS-1.2-RSA, SBP-mTLS-1.2-RSA, SBP-TLS-1.2-DH, and SBP-TLS-1.3 models. From the perspective of a proxy-r strand, the protocol completes with the network (adversary). The proxy is unable to authenticate an honest client because the client credentials are known to the network and the client does not transmit any other proof of identity, such as an authenticated certificate. In the SBP-mTLS-1.2-DH and SBP-mTLS-1.3 models, the proxy-r strand instead completes the protocol with a client-r strand, rather than with the network.

8   Vulnerabilities, Attacks, and Risks

We discuss vulnerabilities, attacks, and risks resulting from our analysis of SBP.

8.1   Vulnerabilities

In decreasing order of severity, we list vulnerabilities exposed from our analysis.

The Proxy Cannot Authenticate the Client. In the SBP-TLS-1.2-RSA, SBP-TLS-1.2-DH, and SBP-TLS-1.3 models, the proxy cannot authenticate the client. As a result, the proxy readily executes the SBP protocol with an adversary that presents stolen client credentials, requests using SBP cookies from compromised sessions, or requests originating from other SBP sessions.

The Proxy Learns the Client's Password. In SBP, the proxy learns the client's password and transmits this password to the legacy server. Within the DY model, it is possible for a client to initiate the protocol with a corrupt proxy, which may use the password to authenticate to other services, including other SBP proxies.

The Client Cannot verify the Binding of the Cookie. Because the SBP proxy binds the cookie using a secret key unknown to the client, the client cannot verify the channel binding of the cookie. Consequently, the client may accept an inappropriately bound cookie, which may bind to a TLS channel in which the client does not participate, and use this cookie to make requests. It would be desirable for the client to be able to detect if they receive such a cookie and abort the protocol. However, this goal is impossible to achieve under SBP's requirements, because the unmodified client does not know the binding exists, and lacks the means to verify the binding.

The Server is an Oblivious Protocol Participant. Confirming an obvious aspect of SBP's design, we identify that if an adversary communicates directly with a legacy server and bypasses the SBP proxy, they can pass stolen authentication cookies as we illustrate in the Pre-SBP model. This vulnerability is the result of the server being an *oblivious protocol participant*: the server participates in the SBP session without awareness of the SBP protocol. The legacy server's oblivious participation in SBP is an intentional design—a major goal of SBP is to avoid modifying the server.

8.2   Attacks

We describe a credential-stealing attack and tailgating attack that exploit the stated vulnerabilities.

Credential-Stealing Attack. Because SBP does not modify the client, the client is unaware of the proxy and believes itself to communicate with the legacy server using the legacy protocol across a TLS connection. This limitation enables a straightforward attack that harvests the client's credentials using a corrupt proxy. SBP's design restricts the client's authentication method to traditional passwords and compels the client to transmit their password to the proxy, thereby leaking the password. In this attack, there is no need to compromise any TLS channel because the client connects to what it believes is the legacy server, but is in fact the proxy. If the proxy is corrupt, it may misuse the client's password in attempts to authenticate to other services, including those behind additional SBP proxies. Figure 6 illustrates the execution of this attack.

Tailgating Attack on SBP. Elsaad [2] confirmed that, consistent with the author's assumptions, SBP is vulnerable to a *cross origin request forgery (CSRF)* attack, which we call a "tailgating" attack. In this attack an adversary executes a script inside of a client browser (e.g., via XSS) as a "man-in-the-browser" to issue requests within the client's SBP session. As an alternative to stealing authentication cookies, this attack is problematic because, to the proxy, the malicious requests originate from the correct client and are bound to the correct TLS

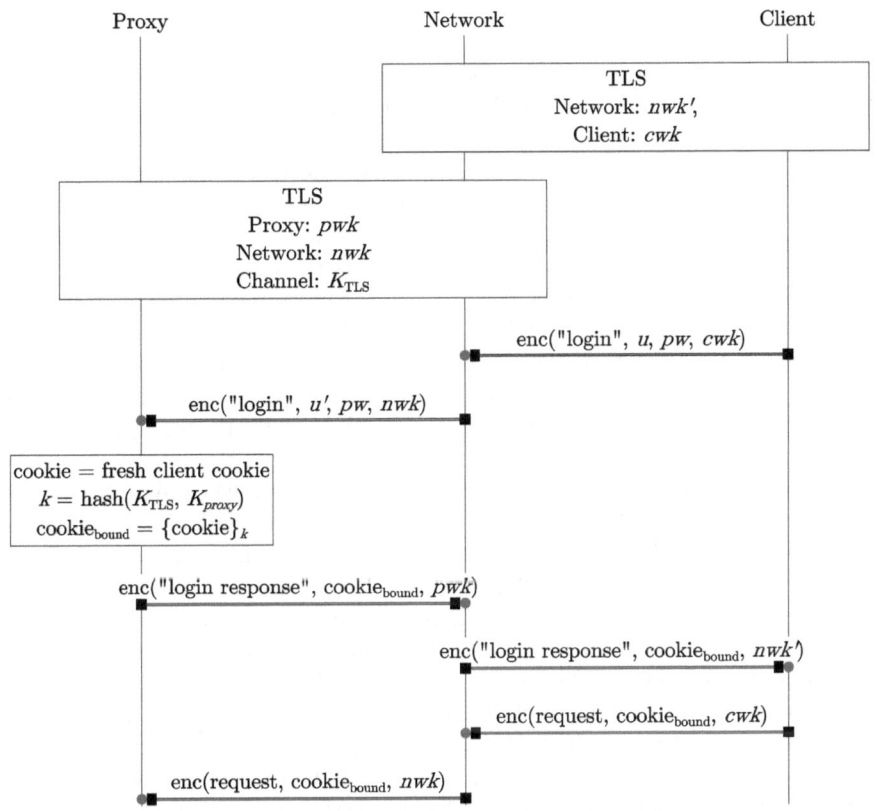

Fig. 6. Protocol diagram illustrating a credential-stealing attack. The client connects to a proxy under the control of the network and issues their login request, leaking their password to the adversary. The adversary then uses the client's password in a separate SBP session, enabling them to authenticate as the client and make requests on the client's behalf. This attack, which does not require compromising any TLS channel, results from SBP leaking the password to the proxy. Additionally, the client's failure to verify the binding of a cookie enables the adversary to forward requests between the client and the proxy without the client's knowledge.

channel. Because these requests originate from the client on the appropriate TLS channel, and because they contain the corresponding bound authentication cookie, the proxy will accept the requests. While not possible within the DY model—a DY adversary cannot compromise a client in this manner—this attack is available within an adversarial model that the SBP authors specify: they allow one of their adversaries to execute arbitrary code in a client browser. Elsaad implemented a proof-of-concept of this attack against a custom SBP implementation [15].

8.3 Risks

We compare risks associated with legacy servers in typical environments, such as universities, with and without the protection of SBP.

Without SBP, the adversary poses a serious risk to a legacy server. By stealing authentication cookies from legitimate users and hijacking their sessions, the adversary gains access to accounts, which might range from basic user accounts to administrator accounts. Stealing cookies is simple against outdated servers and browsers and is possible for even unsophisticated adversaries to achieve. Upon gaining access to accounts, the adversary can impersonate the corresponding users, steal sensitive data to which the users have access, and perform actions using the user's privileges. If the account has elevated privileges, the adversary's access may result in a complete loss of the system—the adversary might freely take the system offline or exploit it to attack other systems on an organization's network.

When SBP wraps the legacy server, the adversary faces a significant obstacle: even when using known exploits to steal cookies, the adversary must find a way to breach a TLS connection or break the cookie's channel binding. Each of these tasks is challenging for all but the most sophisticated adversaries. Likely, it would be easier for the adversary instead to corrupt a SBP proxy, harvest a user's credentials (username and password), and search for opportunities resulting from credential reuse. The risk of this credential-stealing attack depends on the properties of the TLS channel: in the original SBP which uses TLS-1.2-RSA, the adversary could reuse the stolen credentials, but if the SBP proxy authenticates users using mTLS-1.2-DH or mTLS-1.3, the adversary would have to break the TLS channel. The damage of a successful attack is equivalent to that of breaching a legacy server that is unprotected by SBP.

9 Recommendations

Building on our analysis of SBP, we make recommendations for wrapping protocols that mitigate known attacks under the common constraint of not modifying the legacy server, and potentially not modifying the legacy client. While SBP is partially successful at achieving its intended goal, mitigating XSS-based cookie stealing without modifying the client or the server, it inexplicably devises its own channel binding method and builds on weak legacy authentication methods.

Use Standard TLS Channel Bindings. At the time of SBP's development, several TLS channel binding standards were already available [3]. When incorporating channel binding, which is an effective strategy for hardening legacy protocols, wrapping protocols should rely on one or more standard channel bindings, rather than devising their own. SBP-like protocols should require the clients to communicate with proxies over TLS 1.3 channels, and proxies should bind the authentication cookie using a TLS "exporter" binding [54] (see Sect. 11.5). We formally verified that SBP using mTLS-1.3 with a TLS exporter binding also satisfies

Goal 1 from both the client and server perspectives, as does SBP-mTLS-1.3 (see GitHub [51]).

Use Stronger Authentication Methods. A major challenge facing SBP and SBP-like wrapping protocols is that they may be forced to rely on a legacy server's outdated, password-based authentication methods. When communicating across a one-way authenticated TLS channel, password-based authentication struggles to achieve security, especially in intruder models such as DY. As a side effect of using passwords, the SBP proxy learns the user's password. Whenever possible, we recommend using one of several stronger authentication methods, including (1) requiring clients to produce certificates for mTLS 1.3, (2) authenticating clients using more robust authentication protocols such as FIDO UAF, in which authenticator devices assert a client's identity using attestation certificates, (3) relying on multiple factors of authentication where legacy services permit. In an ideal world, all clients produce authenticated certificates and communicate over mutually authenticated TLS channels.

Verify Bindings. In wrapping protocols such as SBP, all protocol principals must verify channel bindings on values they receive. Verifying channel bindings is challenging in SBP because the proxy, not wishing for the client to learn the unencrypted authentication cookie, transmits only the channel-bound cookie without any additional information for the client to verify. Without modification, this bound cookie is indistinguishable from an unbound cookie to a legacy client. When introducing channel binding, we recommend that wrapping protocols modify clients to verify bindings, for example by providing additional information to verify the presence and source of a channel binding, and to carry out zero-knowledge proofs.

10   Previous Work

To our knowledge, our work is the first formal-methods analysis of SBP.

In their original paper, Burgers et al. [10] informally evaluated SBP's security against a variety of known attacks against TLS and cookies. They consider attacks against six levels of a system executing SBP: (1) JavaScript, (2) HTML, (3) plug-ins, (4) browser, (5) TLS library, (6) operating system kernel. They conclude that SBP resists known cookie hijacking attacks against Levels 1 and 2, but fails to mitigate session hijacking when attacks target Level 3 (see the Tailgating Attack in Sect. 8.2) and higher. Concluding that an adversary requires the TLS master secret and the proxy secret key to break the system, their analysis fails to consider the properties of their custom channel binding within a TLS 1.2 channel, such as a client's inability to detect a forwarded SBP cookie.

Previous formal-methods analyses using CPSA include the CAVES multi-party attestation protocol [11], Zooko's forced-latency protocol [27], the *Secure Remote Password (SRP)* protocol [49], TLS-1.3 [6], the FIDO *Universal Authentication Framework (UAF)* [17,18].

Like SBP, other designs for hardening flawed protocols running on legacy software frequently incorporate proxies. SessionShield [36] incorporates client-side proxies that prevent the client's browser from learning session identifiers, making these values unavailable to XSS attacks by an adversary. Pournaghshband et al. [39] improve the security of mobile medical devices, which communicate wirelessly via flawed legacy protocols, by introducing a physical proxy that manages authenticated, encrypted sessions between these devices and their base stations. In the automotive space, works such as Wang and Sawhney's VeCure [52] and Schmandt et al.'s Mini-MAC [48] augment the existing protocols of legacy controller area networks (CAN buses) to mitigate serious flaws. As with SBP, formal-methods analyses of these systems were not part of their design process and often do not exist.

11 Discussion

We discuss several issues raised by our work, including lessons learned, the benefits of isolation in wrapping solutions, inadequate adversarial models, authenticating via passwords, SBP's custom channel binding, requirements for effective cryptographic binding, why we chose symbolic analysis, how SBP's design prevents meaningful improvement, and open problems and future work.

11.1 Lessons Learned

Our study provides helpful lessons for security engineers enhancing the security of legacy protocols with channel binding: (1) When unable to modify a crucial legacy protocol, wrapping the protocol to enhance its security is a reasonable technique for improving the legacy protocol's resistance to known attacks. (2) Because wrapping protocols like SBP result in "oblivious" communicants, strong authentication and secrecy properties are impossible to achieve in the DY model. (3) Relaxing SBP's constraints to enable modifying the client to improve authentication between the client and the proxy (e.g., via mTLS or multifactor authentication) results in a wrapping protocol with stronger security properties. (4) Recipients of cryptographic channel bindings must verify the bindings. In SBP, the client is unable to verify the binding, resulting in a logical flaw in which the client may accept and use a cookie that binds to an incorrect TLS channel.

11.2 Benefits of Isolation

Within the DY model, legacy systems that participate in protocols obliviously are vulnerable to adversaries that bypass network controls to communicate with the systems directly. To mitigate this vulnerability, one can isolate the systems physically and logically. To isolate the system physically, configure the network so that it physically communicates only with a proxy executing the wrapping protocol. To isolate the system logically, establish a VLAN [28] to separate network traffic logically. The objective is to prevent any network entity other than an authorized proxy from communicating with the wrapped legacy system.

11.3   Inadequate Adversarial Models

When designing and analyzing protocols, researchers should use well-defined adversarial models and formal-methods tools. Without a well-defined adversarial model, it is impossible to articulate and analyze the security properties. The SBP authors [10] did not analyze their protocol using any formal model such as the DY model. Although their analysis identifies several attacks and mitigations, they did not consider issues such as the client communicating with a corrupt proxy, the server being unable to authenticate the client, and the client's inability to verify the binding of a cookie (see Sect. 8). Furthermore, experience has shown that, without the aid of formal-methods tools, protocol design and analysis is highly error-prone.

11.4   Authenticating via Passwords

SBP wraps systems that authenticates users using traditional passwords, which are often a poor method of authentication. Users often rely on weak passwords, store passwords insecurely, and reuse passwords across multiple services. Passwords also suffer from poor storage practices (e.g., storing plaintext passwords in a database) and precomputation by adversaries. Relaxing SBP's requirements to modify the client enables switching to stronger authentication mechanisms, such as those that we suggest in Sect. 9. Under SBP's requirement not to modify the client, the protocol is limited to the authentication mechanisms of the underlying legacy server, of which implementers of wrapping protocols like SBP should insist on the strongest mechanisms.

11.5   SBP's Channel Binding vs Channel-Binding Standards

Rather than relying on existing TLS 1.2 channel binding standards, which bind to *communication endpoints* to facilitate cross-session bindings, SBP introduces a custom TLS channel binding in which messages bind directly to a *TLS session's master secret*. A consequence of this binding is that bound cookies in SBP become invalid when communicants negotiate a new TLS channel, though are also impossible to transfer between different TLS sessions. Additionally, SBP's custom binding incorporates the session master secret in a manner that may expose it, particularly to known-plaintext attacks against a bound cookie.

TLS-based wrapping protocols should implement standard channel bindings. We recommend using TLS 1.3's exporter binding [54], which uses *exported keying material (EKM)* that TLS implementations provide to users without exposing the master secret. TLS 1.3 computes the EKM by a pseudorandom function (e.g., hash function) applied to the following security parameters: master_secret, client_random, server_random, a label string, and an (optional) context value.

We recommend that SBP bind the cookie to more than just the endpoints— for example, also bind to the username or user certificate. The following limitation would result if SBP bound cookies only to endpoints: if multiple users shared one endpoint (e.g., they log into a shared machine that communicates with a legacy server across a dedicated TLS connection), it might be possible for an adversary to transfer cookies for different users between sessions that share common endpoints.

11.6 Requirements for Cryptographic Binding

Effective cryptographic bindings must achieve several goals: (1) Each role in a protocol is able to verify, append, and sign a session context. (2) The bindings are unique to a protocol instance, version, and session; and (3) upon completing execution, each legitimate protocol role must agree on the context. In practice, many protocols, including SBP, fail to bind in a manner that achieves these goals. Oblivious protocol participants are unable to participate in effective binding because they are, by design, unaware of the protocol context. Other protocols fail to bind values consistently, neglecting to bind crucial values such as challenges or nonces, or binding in a manner that prevents other legitimate protocol roles from verifying the bindings.

Using zero-knowledge proofs [19], protocol roles can potentially verify bindings without disclosing sensitive values, such as the unbound cookie in SBP.

11.7 Why We Chose Symbolic Analysis

We chose to analyze SBP *symbolically* because we wish to search for possible structural weaknesses and we wish to carry out our analysis automatically, to avoid possible errors in human-constructed proofs. An advantage of using CPSA is that it can discover security goals automatically (see Sect. 2.5). An alternate approach is to use a *computational model*, such as that of Bellare and Rogaway [5], which researchers have adapted to analyze FIDO2 and related protocols [4,7]. An advantage of computational models is that they discover cryptographic weaknesses and they can model specific components such as TLS. Although computational approaches can yield useful results, they are more complicated and tend to be less automated [8].

11.8 Two Inherent Limitations of SBP's Design

SBP's requirement to mitigate cookie-based session hijacking without modifying the client or server software results in two serious limitations: the client cannot verify SBP's cookie channel bindings, and the SBP proxy learns the client password. SBP's core requirement (not to modify the client or server) represents a tradeoff: it makes SBP broadly applicable but limits its effectiveness at reducing security vulnerabilities.

Because clients believe they communicate with a legacy service and not with an SBP proxy, they are unaware of the channel binding on their authentication cookie and thus cannot authenticate the binding. Because the client cannot authenticate the cookie binding, an adversary can give the client a cookie which the client accepts, even though the cookie is bound to an incorrect channel (see

Fig. 6). This limitation, which can prevent injective agreement on the bound cookie, is impossible to correct without relaxing SBP's requirement not to modify client software.

The SBP proxy learns the client's password when forwarding it to the wrapped application, resulting in the user's password leaking to the adversary who compromises a legitimate proxy or operates a malicious proxy. There is no way to mitigate this issue without modifying the client and the proxy, such as by using *Password Authenticated Key Exchange (PAKE)* protocols [49].

11.9   Open Problems and Future Work

The benefits and drawbacks of enhancing systems with wrapping solutions demands further study. Our analysis of SBP and oblivious protocol participants underscores the needs to specify best practices for designing and implementing wrapping protocols, and to devise better bindings for such protocols. Our work raises awareness of cryptographic binding and formal-methods verification for practitioners working to wrap flawed systems. It would be useful to develop standards for wrapping protocols. As future work, we are developing tools for applying cryptographic bindings to protocol specifications automatically.

12   Conclusion

We performed a formal-methods analysis of six models of SBP—the original SBP protocol and five variations—and compared them with a baseline model without SBP. In our original SBP model and variations, the client has assurance that our DY adversary cannot hijack the session with a stolen cookie. The proxy, however, has no assurance that the user's password is confidential, nor that the session cookie is unique to the proxy's session, which enable MitM attacks.

In models that do not use mTLS with DH, the proxy's cryptographic perspective does not guarantee resistance to cookie stealing by an adversary because of several issues. SBP's non-standard channel binding does not enable clients to verify the binding of the cookie because they do not possess sufficient information. Except for mTLS connections with DH, the proxy cannot authenticate the client because passwords are insufficient to authenticate users in the DY model. These issues result in part from a lack of adoption of client certificates and stronger authentication protocols, a design flaw in the RSA key exchange of TLS-1.2-RSA and mTLS-1.2-RSA, and SBP's requirement to conform to legacy password authentication mechanisms. To our knowledge, we are the first to analyze SBP using formal methods and the first to highlight the phenomenon of oblivious protocol participants in wrapping protocols.

Protocol designers should be aware that SBP's limitations are challenging to correct without modifying the legacy client, which SBP does not permit. If able to modify the client, our recommendations include implementing standard channel bindings, incorporating stronger authentication methods such as client certificates or multifactor authentication between the client and the proxy, and providing the client with information to verify the binding of the cookie. When unable to modify the client, we recommend running protocols like SBP over mTLS-1.2-DH or mTLS-1.3 channels, which help ensure freshness and confidentiality of the pre-master secret and mutually authenticate the communicants.

With many organizations struggling to protect flawed legacy systems on their networks, wrapping protocols are inevitable and necessary. In the DY model, such protocols must take great care to establish and bind to encrypted channels with the necessary properties. Where possible, these protocols should eliminate flawed authentication mechanisms, such as traditional passwords, in favor of more robust solutions. Because it is often not possible or practical to modify the legacy systems or the client software that interacts with them, wrapping protocols such as SBP may represent the most attractive practical mitigation to known flaws, and SBP significantly complicates an adversary's attempt to hijack sessions via stealing the user's cookie. Our formal-methods analysis sheds insights on the strengths and limitations of wrapping protocols that depend on channel binding.

Acknowledgments. We thank Joshua Guttman for helpful comments, especially concerning performing analyses with CPSA. This work evolves research initiated by Kirellos Elsaad [2] in his 2022 MS thesis. Alan Sherman, Enis Golaszewski, and Jonathan Fuchs were supported in 2023 in part by the National Security Agency under an INSuRE+C grant via Northeastern University. Alan Sherman was also supported in part by the National Science Foundation under DGE grants 1753681 (SFS), 1819521 (SFS Capacity), and 2138921 (SaTC).

A   Acronyms and Abbreviations

CPSA	Cryptographic Protocol Shapes Analyzer
DY	Dolev-Yao
DH	Diffie-Hellman
EKM	exported keying material
FIDO	Fast Identity Online
HMAC	hashed-based message authentication code
HTTP	Hypertext Transfer Protocol
MitM	man-in-the-middle
NS	Needham-Schroeder
PAKE	password authenticated key exchange
RSA	Rivest-Shamir-Adelman
SBP	Session Binding Proxy Protocol
TLS	Transport Layer Security
UAF	Universal Authentication Framework
VLAN	virtual local area network
XSS	cross-site scripting

B   Detailed CPSA Models of SBP

We precisely define our CPSA models of SBP in terms of messages and CPSA source code. See Sect. 3 for ladder diagrams.

B.1   Messages

Below, we specify messages that we use to model honest SBP strands.

- Let u be a username for some arbitrary user.
- Let pw be a password for the user u.
- Let IV be a fresh initialization vector for the session.
- Let K_{TLS} be the TLS master secret for the channel between the client and the proxy.
- Let K_{proxy} be a system private key for binding cookies at the proxy.
- Let cookie be the unbound session cookie that the legacy server generates for the client.
- Let cwk and pwk be TLS client and proxy write keys.
- Let $k = \mathsf{Hash}(K_{\mathsf{TLS}}, K_{\mathsf{proxy}})$ be the cookie-binding key.
- Let $\mathsf{cookie_{bound}} = \mathsf{Enc}(\mathsf{cookie}, k)$.
- Let *request* (*req.*) and *response* (*resp.*) be arbitrary requests and responses for an application-layer protocol (e.g., HTTP).

We specify the SBP protocol between a *client*, *proxy*, and legacy *server*. In our models, we combine *proxy* and *server* into a single entity *proxy*. Thus, our models omit messages between *proxy* and *server*, which we assume take place over a private network. We assume that *client* and *proxy* establish a TLS channel and use this channel for establishing the session and handling subsequent requests.

Session Establishment

1. *client* $\longrightarrow$ *proxy*: $\{$ "login request", $u, pw\}_{cwk}$
2. *proxy* $\longrightarrow$ *server*: $\{$ "login request", $u, pw\}$
3. *proxy* $\longleftarrow$ *server*: $\{$ "login response", cookie$\}$
4. *client* $\longleftarrow$ *proxy*: $\{$ "login response", IV, cookie$_{\mathsf{bound}}\}_{pwk}$

Request Handling.

1. *client* $\longrightarrow$ *proxy*: $\{request, IV, \mathsf{cookie_{bound}}\}_{cwk}$
2. *proxy* $\longrightarrow$ *server*: $\{request, \mathsf{cookie}\}$
3. *proxy* $\longleftarrow$ *server*: $\{response\}$
4. *client* $\longleftarrow$ *proxy*: $\{response\}_{pwk}$

B.2   Selected CPSA Source Code

We give selected source code for our CPSA models of SBP. Specifically, Fig. 7 gives our CPSA specification for an authenticating *client* role in session establishment, and Fig. 8 gives our CPSA specification for an authenticating server (*proxy*) role in session establishment. See GitHub [51] for our complete source code.

```
(defrole clienta ;; Role in which the client authenticates with password
  (vars
    (u s ca name) ;; u - username, s - server, ca - certificate authority
    (cr sr random32) ;; cr - client random, sr - server random for TLS
    (spk akey) ;; server's public key
    (pms random48) ;; pms - premaster secret generated by client for TLS
    (p password) ;; user's password
    (cookie mesg) ;; authentication cookie provided by the server
    (any mesg)
    (cookiestor locn) ;; client storage of authentication cookie
    (request httpreq)
    (response httpdata)
  )
  (trace
    (TLS send recv pms cr sr s spk ca) ;; establish TLS session with server
    (send (enc "login" u p (cwk pms cr sr)))
    (recv (enc "login-successful" cookie (swk pms cr sr)))
    (load cookiestor any)              ;; store authentication cookie associated
    (stor cookiestor (cat "client store" u s cookie)) ;; with the server s
    (send (enc cookie request (cwk pms cr sr)))
    (recv (enc response (swk pms cr sr)))
  )
)
```

Fig. 7. CPSA specification for an authenticating *client* role, which carries out the session establishment phase of SBP. A role consists of variable definitions and a trace expressing terms that a strand sends and receives from the network. Variable definitions comprise s-expressions that list labels followed by a sort (type). The macro *TLS* generates client terms to establish a TLS session with the server. To model alternative versions, we substitute the TLS macro to generate terms for TLS 1.2 or TLS 1.3, including the mutual authentication variations of each.

```
(defrole servera ;; Role where server authenticates user with password and
                 ;; creates authentication cookie used to authenticate
                 ;; requests.
  (vars
   (u s ca name) ;; u - username, s - server, ca - certificate authority
   (cr sr random32) ;; cr - client random, sr - server random for TLS
   (spk akey) ;; server's public key
   (pms random48) ;; pms - premaster secret generated by client for TLS
   (p password) ;; user's password
   (cookie data) ;; authentication cookie provided by the server
   (ppk skey) ;; proxy private key
   (any mesg)
   (authstor locn) ;; server storage of clients authentication cookie
   (request httpreq)
   (response httpdata)
   )
  (trace
   (TLS recv send pms cr sr s spk ca) ;; establish TLS session with client
   (recv (enc "login" u p (cwk pms cr sr)))
   (send (enc "login-successful"
(enc cookie (hash ppk (MasterSecret pms cr sr)))
(swk pms cr sr)))
   (load authstor any)                              ;; store authentication
   (stor authstor (cat "server store" s u cookie)) ;; cookie associated with u
   (recv (enc (enc cookie (hash ppk (MasterSecret pms cr sr)))
      request (cwk pms cr sr)))
   (send (enc response (swk pms cr sr)))
   )
  (facts (neq u s))
  (non-orig ppk) ;; Proxy private key is only known by the proxy or the server
                 ;; in this case as the proxy and server are implemented
                 ;; together.
  (uniq-orig cookie) ;; The unique origination assumption for the cookie is
  ;; included in the role where it is generated to illustrate cookie stealing.
  ;; If the cookie is not uniquely generated, the results are uninteresting
  ;; as the cookie is potentially known to everyone, so it is not tied to any
  ;; authentication.
  )
```

Fig. 8. CPSA specification for an authenticating server (*proxy*) role, which carries out the session establishment phase of SBP. This role, which combines the behavior of a proxy and legacy server, is *complementary* to the authenticating *client* role: each event in the trace is the complement of an event in the *client* trace in Fig. 7.

References

1. Abadi, M., Needham, R.M.: Prudent engineering practice for cryptographic protocols. IEEE Trans. Softw. Eng. **22**(1), 6–15 (1996). https://doi.org/10.1109/32.481513
2. Abou Elsaad, K.N.: A formal methods analysis of the session binding proxy protocol, Master's thesis, University of Maryland, Baltimore County (2022). http://proxy-bc.researchport.umd.edu/login?url=https://www.proquest.com/

dissertations-theses/formal-methods-analysis-session-binding-proxy/docview/
2720939643/se-2

3. Altman, J.E., Zhu, L., Williams, N.: Channel Bindings for TLS. RFC 5929 (2010). https://doi.org/10.17487/RFC5929

4. Barbosa, M., Boldyreva, A., Chen, S., Warinschi, B.: Provable security analysis of FIDO2. In: Advances in Cryptology–CRYPTO 2021: 41st Annual International Cryptology Conference, CRYPTO 2021, Virtual Event, August 16–20, 2021, Proceedings, Part III 41, pp. 125–156. Springer (2021)

5. Bellare, M., Rogaway, P.: Entity authentication and key distribution. In: Annual International Cryptology Conference, pp. 232–249. Springer (1993)

6. Bhandary, P., Zieglar, E., Nicholas, C.: Searching for selfie in TLS 1.3 with the cryptographic protocol shapes analyzer. In: Dougherty, D., Meseguer, J., Mödersheim, S.A., Rowe, P.D. (eds.) Protocols, Strands, and Logic - Essays Dedicated to Joshua Guttman on the Occasion of his 66.66th Birthday. LNCS, vol. 13066, pp. 50–76. Springer (2021). https://doi.org/10.1007/978-3-030-91631-2_3

7. Bindel, N., Cremers, C., Zhao, M.: FIDO2, CTAP 2.1, and WebAuthn 2: provable security and post-quantum instantiation. In: 2023 IEEE Symposium on Security and Privacy (SP), pp. 1471–1490. IEEE (2023)

8. Blanchet, B.: Security protocol verification: symbolic and computational models. In: International Conference on Principles of Security and Trust, pp. 3–29. Springer (2012)

9. Blanchet, B.: Automatic verification of security protocols in the symbolic model: The verifier ProVerif. In: Aldini, A., López, J., Martinelli, F. (eds.) Foundations of Security Analysis and Design VII - FOSAD 2012/2013 Tutorial Lectures. LNCS, vol. 8604, pp. 54–87. Springer (2013). https://doi.org/10.1007/978-3-319-10082-1_3

10. Burgers, W., Verdult, R., van Eekelen, M.C.J.D.: Prevent session hijacking by binding the session to the cryptographic network credentials. In: Nielson, H.R., Gollmann, D. (eds.) Secure IT Systems - 18th Nordic Conference, NordSec 2013, Ilulissat, Greenland, October 18-21, 2013, Proceedings. LNCS, vol. 8208, pp. 33–50. Springer (2013). https://doi.org/10.1007/978-3-642-41488-6_3

11. Coker, G., et al.: Principles of remote attestation. Int. J. Inf. Sec. **10**(2), 63–81 (2011). https://doi.org/10.1007/S10207-011-0124-7

12. Cremers, C., Horvat, M., Hoyland, J., Scott, S., van der Merwe, T.: A comprehensive symbolic analysis of TLS 1.3. In: Proceedings of the 2017 ACM SIGSAC Conference on Computer and Communications Security, pp. 1773–1788 (2017)

13. Dolev, D., Yao, A.: On the security of public key protocols. IEEE Trans. Inf. Theory **29**(2), 198–208 (1983). https://doi.org/10.1109/TIT.1983.1056650

14. van Eekelen, M., Moussa, R.B., Hubbers, E., Verdult, R.: Blackboard security assessment, Technical report, Nijmegen: Institute for Computing and Information Sciences (2013)

15. Elsaad, K.A.: SBP tailgating attack implementation (2022). https://github.com/kmanayer/sbp_impl

16. Escobar, S., Meadows, C., Meseguer, J.: Maude-NPA: cryptographic protocol analysis modulo equational properties. In: Aldini, A., Barthe, G., Gorrieri, R. (eds.) Foundations of Security Analysis and Design V, FOSAD 2007/2008/2009 Tutorial Lectures. LNCS, vol. 5705, pp. 1–50. Springer (2007). https://doi.org/10.1007/978-3-642-03829-7_1

17. Fuchs, J., Hamer, S., Liu, D.: A man-in-the-middle attack on the FIDO UAF registration protocol. CSEE Dept, UMBC, CMSC 491/691 report (2022)

18. Golaszewski, E., Sherman, A.T., Zieglar, E.: Cryptographic binding should not be optional: a formal-methods analysis of FIDO UAF authentication. unpublished manuscript, CSEE Dept, UMBC (2023)
19. Goldwasser, S., Micali, S., Rackoff, C.: The knowledge complexity of interactive proof-systems. In: Goldreich, O. (ed.) Providing Sound Foundations for Cryptography: On the Work of Shafi Goldwasser and Silvio Micali, pp. 203–225. ACM (2019). https://doi.org/10.1145/3335741.3335750
20. Guttman, J., Liskov, M., Ramsdell, J., Rowe, P.: The cryptographic protocol shapes analyzer (CPSA). https://github.com/mitre/cpsa
21. Guttman, J.D.: Security goals: packet trajectories and strand spaces. In: Focardi, R., Gorrieri, R. (eds.) Foundations of Security Analysis and Design, Tutorial Lectures [revised versions of lectures given during the IFIP WG 1.7 International School on Foundations of Security Analysis and Design, FOSAD 2000, Bertinoro, Italy, September 2000]. LNCS, vol. 2171, pp. 197–261. Springer (2000). https://doi.org/10.1007/3-540-45608-2_4
22. Guttman, J.D.: Establishing and preserving protocol security goals. J. Comput. Secur. **22**(2), 203–267 (2014). https://doi.org/10.3233/JCS-140499
23. Jagpal, N., et al.: Trends and lessons from three years fighting malicious extensions. In: Jung, J., Holz, T. (eds.) 24th USENIX Security Symposium, USENIX Security 15, Washington, D.C., USA, August 12-14, 2015, pp. 579–593. USENIX Association (2015). https://www.usenix.org/conference/usenixsecurity15/technical-sessions/presentation/jagpal
24. Kapravelos, A., Grier, C., Chachra, N., Kruegel, C., Vigna, G., Paxson, V.: Hulk: eliciting malicious behavior in browser extensions. In: 23rd USENIX Security Symposium (USENIX Security 14), pp. 641–654. USENIX Association, San Diego, CA (2014). https://www.usenix.org/conference/usenixsecurity14/technical-sessions/presentation/kapravelos
25. Kasturi, R.P., et al.: Mistrust plugins you must: a large-scale study of malicious plugins in WordPress marketplaces. In: Butler, K.R.B., Thomas, K. (eds.) 31st USENIX Security Symposium, USENIX Security 2022, Boston, MA, USA, August 10-12, 2022, pp. 161–178. USENIX Association (2022). https://www.usenix.org/conference/usenixsecurity22/presentation/kasturi
26. Kelsey, J., Schneier, B., Wagner, D.A.: Protocol interactions and the chosen protocol attack. In: Christianson, B., Crispo, B., Lomas, T.M.A., Roe, M. (eds.) Security Protocols, 5th International Workshop, Paris, France, April 7-9, 1997, Proceedings. LNCS, vol. 1361, pp. 91–104. Springer (1997). https://doi.org/10.1007/BFB0028162
27. Lanus, E., Zieglar, E.: Analysis of a forced-latency defense against man-in-the-middle attacks. J. Inf. Warfare **16**(2), 66–78 (2017)
28. Leischner, G., Tews, C.: Security through VLAN segmentation: isolating and securing critical assets without loss of usability. In: Proceedings of the 9th Annual Western Power Delivery and Automation Conference, Spokane, WA (2007)
29. Liskov, M., Rowe, P., Thayer, J.: Completeness of CPSA, Technical report, MITRE (2011). https://www.mitre.org/sites/default/files/pdf/12_0038.pdf
30. Liskov, M.D., Ramsdell, J.D., Guttman, J.D., Rowe, P.D.: The Cryptographic Protocol Shapes Analyzer: A Manual. The MITRE Corporation (2016)
31. Lowe, G.: An attack on the Needham-Schroeder public-key authentication protocol. Inf. Process. Lett. **56**(3), 131–133 (1995). https://doi.org/10.1016/0020-0190(95)00144-2
32. Lowe, G.: A hierarchy of authentication specifications. In: 10th Computer Security Foundations Workshop Proceedings, pp. 31–43. IEEE CS Press (1997)

33. Luotonen, A.: Web Proxy Servers. Prentice-Hall, Inc. (1998)
34. Meier, S., Schmidt, B., Cremers, C., Basin, D.A.: The TAMARIN prover for the symbolic analysis of security protocols. In: Sharygina, N., Veith, H. (eds.) Computer Aided Verification - 25th International Conference, CAV 2013, Saint Petersburg, Russia, July 13-19, 2013. Proceedings. LNCS, vol. 8044, pp. 696–701. Springer (2013). https://doi.org/10.1007/978-3-642-39799-8_48
35. Needham, R.M., Schroeder, M.D.: Using encryption for authentication in large networks of computers. Commun. ACM **21**(12), 993–999 (1978). https://doi.org/10.1145/359657.359659
36. Nikiforakis, N., Meert, W., Younan, Y., Johns, M., Joosen, W.: SessionShield: lightweight protection against session hijacking. In: Erlingsson, Ú., Wieringa, R.J., Zannone, N. (eds.) Engineering Secure Software and Systems - Third International Symposium, ESSoS 2011, Madrid, Spain, February 9-10, 2011. Proceedings. LNCS, vol. 6542, pp. 87–100. Springer (2011). https://doi.org/10.1007/978-3-642-19125-1_7
37. Pang, M.S., Tanriverdi, H.: Security breaches in the US federal government. In: Workshop on the Economics of Information Security (2017)
38. Paulson, L.C.: Inductive analysis of the internet protocol TLS. In: Christianson, B., Crispo, B., Harbison, W.S., Roe, M. (eds.) Security Protocols, 6th International Workshop, Cambridge, UK, April 15-17, 1998, Proceedings. LNCS, vol. 1550, pp. 13–23. Springer (1998). https://doi.org/10.1007/3-540-49135-X_2
39. Pournaghshband, V., Sarrafzadeh, M., Reiher, P.L.: Securing legacy mobile medical devices. In: Godara, B., Nikita, K.S. (eds.) Wireless Mobile Communication and Healthcare - Third International Conference, MobiHealth 2012, Paris, France, November 21-23, 2012, Revised Selected Papers. LNCS, Social Informatics and Telecommunications Engineering, vol. 61, pp. 163–172. Springer (2012). https://doi.org/10.1007/978-3-642-37893-5_19
40. Ramsdell, J.D.: CPSA and formal security goals. The MITRE Corporation (2015)
41. Rescorla, E.: SSL and TLS: Designing and Building Secure Systems. Addison-Wesley (2001)
42. Rescorla, E.: The Transport Layer Security (TLS) Protocol Version 1.3. RFC 8446 (2018). https://doi.org/10.17487/RFC8446
43. Rescorla, E., Dierks, T.: The Transport Layer Security (TLS) Protocol Version 1.2. RFC 5246 (2008). https://doi.org/10.17487/RFC5246
44. Rivest, R.L., Shamir, A., Adleman, L.: A method for obtaining digital signatures and public-key cryptosystems. Commun. ACM **21**(2), 120–126 (1978)
45. Rodríguez, G.E., Torres, J.G., Flores, P., Benavides, D.E.: Cross-site scripting (XSS) attacks and mitigation: a survey. Comput. Netw. **166**, 106960 (2020). https://doi.org/10.1016/j.comnet.2019.106960
46. Rowe, P.D., Guttman, J.D., Liskov, M.D.: Measuring protocol strength with security goals. Int. J. Inf. Sec. **15**(6), 575–596 (2016). https://doi.org/10.1007/S10207-016-0319-Z
47. Saleem, H., Naveed, M.: SoK: anatomy of data breaches. Proc. Priv. Enhancing Technol. **2020**(4), 153–174 (2020). https://doi.org/10.2478/POPETS-2020-0067
48. Schmandt, J., Sherman, A.T., Banerjee, N.: Mini-MAC: raising the bar for vehicular security with a lightweight message authentication protocol. Veh. Commun. **9**, 188–196 (2017)
49. Sherman, A.T., et al.: Formal methods analysis of the secure remote password protocol. In: Nigam, V., Kirigin, T.B., Talcott, C.L., Guttman, J.D., Kuznetsov, S.L., Loo, B.T., Okada, M. (eds.) Logic, Language, and Security - Essays Dedicated

to Andre Scedrov on the Occasion of His 65th Birthday. LNCS, vol. 12300, pp. 103–126. Springer (2020). https://doi.org/10.1007/978-3-030-62077-6_9

50. Thayer, F.J., Herzog, J.C., Guttman, J.D.: Strand spaces: proving security protocols correct. J. Comput. Secur. **7**(1), 191–230 (1999). https://doi.org/10.3233/JCS-1999-72-304

51. UMBC Protocol Analysis Lab: PAL GitHub repository (2023). https://tinyurl.com/3d2wnhuf

52. Wang, Q., Sawhney, S.: Vecure: a practical security framework to protect the CAN bus of vehicles. In: 4th International Conference on the Internet of Things, IOT 2014, Cambridge, MA, USA, October 6-8, 2014, pp. 13–18. IEEE (2014). https://doi.org/10.1109/IOT.2014.7030108

53. Weaver, N., Kreibich, C., Dam, M., Paxson, V.: Here be web proxies. In: Faloutsos, M., Kuzmanovic, A. (eds.) Passive and Active Measurement - 15th International Conference, PAM 2014, Los Angeles, CA, USA, March 10-11, 2014, Proceedings. LNCS, vol. 8362, pp. 183–192. Springer (2014). https://doi.org/10.1007/978-3-319-04918-2_18

54. Whited, S.: Channel Bindings for TLS 1.3. RFC 9266 (2022). https://doi.org/10.17487/RFC9266

55. Zhou, Y., Evans, D.: Why aren't HTTP-only cookies more widely deployed? In: Proceedings of 4th Web, vol. 2 (2010)

SoK: Post-Quantum Key Encapsulation Mechanisms—Security Definitions, Constructions, and Applications

Biming Zhou[1]($\boxtimes$), Yiting Liu[2], Haodong Jiang[2], and Yunlei Zhao[1]

[1] College of Computer Science and Technology, Fudan University,
Shanghai 200433, China
bmzhou22@m.fudan.edu.cn, ylzhao@fudan.edu.cn
[2] Henan Key Laboratory of Network Cryptography Technology,
Zhengzhou 450001, Henan, China
lyt9156@outlook.com, hdjiang13@163.com

Abstract. The Key Encapsulation Mechanism (KEM) is one of the most important foundational cryptographic primitives. It can be used to construct Public Key Encryption (PKE), Key Exchange, and Authenticated Key Exchange. With the continuing advances in quantum computing (e.g., Shor's algorithm), traditional KEMs based on RSA and ECC will eventually become insecure. As the NIST Post-Quantum Cryptography (PQC) Standardization progresses, exploring the construction of post-quantum secure KEMs has become a highly relevant topic.

This paper presents a comprehensive survey of general constructions of post-quantum secure KEMs in both the random oracle model (ROM) and quantum random oracle model (QROM), focusing on their security definitions, general constructions, and practical applications. We examine key security notions for KEMs, such as OW-CPA, IND-CPA, IND-1CCA, and IND-CCA, as well as their general construction from CPA-secure PKE schemes alongside applications in real-world protocols, including TLS 1.3, KEMTLS, Signal, and Noise. Specifically, we examine the FO and modular variants for IND-CCA KEMs, three distinct T-transforms for IND-1CCA KEMs, and the CPA transform for CPA-secure KEMs derived from CPA-secure PKEs. We further discuss the security requirements of KEMs within various protocols and highlight that IND-1CCA KEMs can be used to construct practical protocols such as KEMTLS, Signal, and Noise. In particular, CPA-secure KEMs can be employed in constructing post-quantum TLS 1.3.

Keywords: QROM · KEM · CCA · 1CCA · CPA

1 Introduction

With the development of quantum computing, traditional cryptographic systems such as RSA, which relies on the factorization problem, and ECC (Elliptic Curve Cryptography), which is based on discrete logarithm problems, are rendered vulnerable to quantum adversaries, as demonstrated by Shor's algorithm

© The Author(s), under exclusive license to Springer Nature Switzerland AG 2025
X. Lu and C. J. Mitchell (Eds.): SSR 2024, LNCS 15559, pp. 120–146, 2025.
https://doi.org/10.1007/978-3-031-87541-0_6

[48]. To address this vulnerability, the National Institute of Standards and Technology (NIST) initiated a competition aimed at standardizing post-quantum cryptographic (PQC) algorithms, including digital signatures (SIG), public key encryption (PKE), and key encapsulation mechanisms (KEM) (or key exchange) with security against quantum adversaries. By August 2024, NIST had published three standard documents: ML-KEM [40], ML-DSA [39], and ML-SLH [41], renamed from CRYSTALS. Kyber, CRYSTALS.Dilithium and SPHINCS+ respectively.

The Key Encapsulation Mechanism (KEM), as a foundational cryptographic primitive, is both efficient and versatile. It can be used to construct Public Key Encryption (PKE) in a black-box manner based on the KEM/DEM paradigm [16], as well as to facilitate key exchanges [12] and authenticated key exchanges [23]. When constructing a post-quantum secure KEM, the most basic requirement is OW-CPA/IND-CPA security, which ensures that no probabilistic polynomial time (PPT) adversary can compute the legitimately generated key (or distinguish between a legitimately generated key and a random key) given the ciphertext. In some other protocols, such as KEMTLS [46], Signal [13], and Noise [6], it has been demonstrated that IND-1CCA security is required for the replaced KEMs, as seen in PQ TLS [22, 29, 46, 47], PQ Signal [13], and PQ Noise [6]. Simply put, IND-1CCA security ensures that no PPT adversary can distinguish between a legitimately generated key and a random key with at most one decapsulation query. Moreover, in many cryptographic applications, a more stringent security standard, IND-CCA security [44], is often required. Unlike IND-1CCA, IND-CCA security allows an adversary to make polynomial times decapsulation queries, making it a broader more robust security guarantee, especially against reuse attacks.

This paper presents a comprehensive survey of the general construction of KEMs with the aforementioned security properties and the security requirements necessary for practical applications. The structure is as follows: Sect. 2 covers the fundamental preliminaries, Sect. 3 examines the construction of CCA-secure schemes based on the Fujisaki-Okamoto (FO) transform and its modular variants, Sect. 4 presents results related to IND-1CCA security and its applications, and Sect. 5 discusses standard CPA constructions and their application in post-quantum TLS 1.3.

2 Preliminaries

2.1 Notation

The security parameter is denoted by λ. We use the standard O-notations: O, ω. PPT is denoted to represent probabilistic polynomial time. A function $f(\lambda)$ is said to be negligible if $f(\lambda) = \lambda^{-\omega(1)}$. We denote a set of negligible functions by $\mathrm{negl}(\lambda)$. $\mathcal{K}$, $\mathcal{M}$ and $\mathcal{C}$ denote the key space, message space, and ciphertext space, respectively. For a finite set X, $x \leftarrow_\$ X$ represents the sampling of a uniformly random element from X. $\Pr[P : G]$ indicates the probability that the predicate holds true when free variables in P are assigned according to the program in

G. The sampling from some distribution D is represented by $x \leftarrow_\$ D$. For a quantum or randomized classical algorithm (resp. deterministic) A, $y \leftarrow_\$ A(x)$ (resp. $y \leftarrow A(x)$) denotes that A outputs y on input x. $x =?y$ is denoted by an integer that is 1 if $x = y$, and 0 otherwise. $|X|$ denotes the cardinality of set X. A^H (resp. $A^{|H\rangle}$) denotes that algorithm A gains classical (resp. quantum) access to the oracle H.

2.2   Cryptographic Primitives

Definition 1 (Public-Key Encryption). *A PKE scheme over $\mathcal{M}$ is a tuple of three algorithms* gen, enc, dec. *(1)* $(\mathsf{pk}, \mathsf{sk}) \leftarrow_\$ \mathsf{gen}(1^\lambda)$*: The key generation algorithm* gen *takes as inputs the security parameter and outputs a key pair* $(\mathsf{pk}, \mathsf{sk})$. *Usually, we will omit the input of* gen *for brevity. (2)* $\mathsf{ct} \leftarrow_\$ \mathsf{enc}(\mathsf{pk}, m)$*: The encryption algorithm takes as inputs the public key* pk *and a message* $m \in \mathcal{M}$ *and outputs a ciphertext* ct. *(3)* $m' \leftarrow \mathsf{dec}(\mathsf{sk}, \mathsf{ct})$*: The decryption algorithm, on input the secret key* sk *and the ciphertext* ct, *deterministically outputs a message* $m' \in \mathcal{M} \cup \{\perp\}$.

Correctness.   A   Public-Key   Encryption   (DPKE)   is δ-correct   if $E[\max_{m \in M} \Pr[\mathsf{dec}(\mathsf{sk}, \mathsf{ct}) \neq m : \mathsf{ct} \leftarrow \mathsf{enc}(\mathsf{pk}, m)]] \leq \delta$, *where the expectation is taken over* $(\mathsf{pk}, \mathsf{sk}) \leftarrow \mathsf{gen}$. *We say a PKE is perfectly correct if* $\delta = 0$.

Definition 2 (γ-spreadness). *A public-key encryption scheme is γ-spread if*

$$\min_{m \in \mathcal{M}, (pk, sk)} \left(-\log \max_{c \in \mathcal{C}} \Pr[c = enc_{pk}(m)] \right) \geq \gamma.$$

where the probability is over the randomness of the encryption, and the minimum is over all key pairs that have positive probability of being produced by gen.

We also define deterministic PKE (DPKE) where the enc algorithm is deterministic. Furthermore, we define the *Rigidity* property for DPKE as follows.

Definition 3 (Rigidity[1]). *A DPKE is rigid if for all key pairs* $(\mathsf{pk}, \mathsf{sk}) \leftarrow_\$ \mathsf{gen}$, *and all ciphertexts* ct, *it holds that either* $dec(\mathsf{sk}, \mathsf{ct}) = \perp$ *or* $\mathsf{enc}(\mathsf{pk}, dec(\mathsf{sk}, \mathsf{ct})) = \mathsf{ct}$.

Definition 4 (OW-ATK-secure PKE). *Let* PKE = (gen, enc, dec) *be a public-key encryption scheme with message space* $\mathcal{M}$. *For* ATK $\in$ {CPA, VA, qPCA, qPVCA}, *we define OW-ATK games as in Fig. 1, where*

$$O_{ATK} := \begin{cases} \perp & \text{ATK = CPA} \\ \text{CVO}(\cdot) & \text{ATK = VA} \\ \text{Pco}(\cdot, \cdot) & \text{ATK = qPCA} \\ \text{Pco}(\cdot, \cdot), \text{CVO}(\cdot) & \text{ATK = qPVCA.} \end{cases}$$

---

[1] The NIST-PQC Round-3 Finalist NTRU [17] and NIST-PQC Round-4 Candidate Classic McEliece [2], are based on rigid one-way secure deterministic PKEs. For a general deterministic PKE, the rigid property can be achieved through a re-encryption transform.

Define the OW-ATK advantage function of an adversary $\mathcal{A}$ against PKE as $\mathrm{Adv}_{\mathrm{PKE}}^{\mathrm{OW\text{-}ATK}}(\mathcal{A}) := \Pr[\mathrm{OW\text{-}ATK}_{\mathrm{PKE}}^{\mathcal{A}} = 1]$. A PKE scheme is OW-ATK secure if for any PPT adversary $\mathcal{A}$ we have $\mathrm{Adv}_{\mathrm{PKE}}^{\mathrm{OW\text{-}ATK}}(\mathcal{A}) = negl(\lambda)$.

Game OW-ATK	Pco(m,c)	CVO(c)
1: $(\mathsf{pk}, \mathsf{sk}) \leftarrow\!\!\$\ \mathsf{gen}$	1: **if** $m \notin \mathcal{M}$	1: $m := \mathsf{dec}(\mathsf{sk}, c)$
2: $m^* \xleftarrow{\$} \mathcal{M}$	2: **return** $\perp$	2: **if** $m \in \mathcal{M}$
3: $c^* \leftarrow\!\!\$\ \mathsf{enc}(\mathsf{pk}, m^*)$	3: **else return**	3: **return** 1
4: $m' \leftarrow \mathcal{A}^{O_{\mathrm{ATK}}}(\mathsf{pk}, c^*)$	4: $\mathsf{dec}(sk, c) =?m$	4: **else return** 0
5: **return** $m' =?m^*$		

Fig. 1. Games OW-ATK (ATK $\in$ {CPA, VA, qPCA, qPVCA}) for PKE, where O_{ATK} is defined in Definition 4. In games qPCA and qPVCA, the adversary $\mathcal{A}$ can query the Pco oracle with quantum state.

Remark. We note that the security game OW-qPCA (OW-qPVCA) is the same as OW-PCA (OW-PVCA) except the adversary $\mathcal{A}$'s queries to the Pco oracle. In the OW-qPCA (OW-qPVCA) game, $\mathcal{A}$ can make quantum queries to the Pco oracle, while in the OW-PCA (OW-PVCA) game, only the classical queries are allowed.

Definition 5 (IND-CPA-secure PKE). *We define the* IND-CPA *game for PKE as in Fig. 3. A PKE scheme* PKE $=$ (Gen, Enc, Dec) *is IND-CPA if for any PPT adversary* $\mathcal{A}$ *we have* $\mathrm{Adv}_{\mathrm{PKE}}^{\mathrm{IND\text{-}CPA}}(\mathcal{A}) := \left| \Pr[\mathrm{IND\text{-}CPA}_{\mathrm{PKE}}^{\mathcal{A}} = 1] - \frac{1}{2} \right| = negl(\lambda)$.

Definition 6 (Key Encapsulation Mechanism). *A KEM over* $\mathcal{K}$ *is a tuple of three algorithms* Gen, Encaps, Decaps. *(1)* $(\mathsf{pk}, \mathsf{sk}) \leftarrow\!\!\$\ \mathrm{Gen}(1^\lambda)$: *The key generation algorithm* gen *takes as input the security parameter and outputs a key pair* $(\mathsf{pk}, \mathsf{sk})$. *Usually, we will omit the input of* gen *for brevity. (2)* $(\mathsf{ct}, K) \leftarrow\!\!\$\ \mathrm{Encaps}(\mathsf{pk})$: *The encapsulation algorithm takes as input the public key* pk *and it outputs a tuple* (ct, K), *where* $K \in \mathcal{K}$ *and* $\mathsf{ct} \in \mathcal{C}$. *(3)* $K' \leftarrow \mathrm{Decaps}(\mathsf{sk}, \mathsf{ct})$: *The decapsulation procedure, on input the secret key* sk *and the ciphertext* ct, *outputs a key* K'. *If the KEM allows explicit rejection, the output is a key* $K' \in \mathcal{K}$ *or the rejection symbol* $\perp$.

Definition 7 (OW-CPA-secure KEM). *A KEM scheme* KEM $=$ (Gen, Encaps, Decaps) *is OW-CPA if for any PPT adversary* $\mathcal{A}$ *we have*

$$\mathrm{Adv}_{\mathrm{KEM}}^{\mathrm{OW\text{-}CPA}}(\mathcal{A}) = \Pr\left[\mathcal{A}(\mathsf{pk}, \mathsf{ct}^*) \Rightarrow K^* : \begin{array}{l} (\mathsf{pk}, \mathsf{sk}) \leftarrow\!\!\$\ \mathrm{Gen}; \\ (K^*, \mathsf{ct}^*) \leftarrow\!\!\$\ \mathrm{Encaps}(\mathsf{pk})] \end{array} \right]$$
$$= negl(\lambda),$$

where the probability is taken over the randomness of the public-key generation, encapsulation, and the adversary $\mathcal{A}$.

Definition 8 (IND-CPA-secure KEM). *We define the* IND-CPA *game for KEM as in Fig. 2. A KEM scheme* KEM $=$ (Gen, Encaps, Decaps) *is* IND-CPA *if for any PPT adversary $\mathcal{A}$ we have* $\mathrm{Adv}_{\mathrm{KEM}}^{\mathrm{IND\text{-}CPA}}(\mathcal{A}) :=$ $\left| \Pr[\mathrm{IND\text{-}CPA}_{\mathrm{KEM}}^{\mathcal{A}} = 1] - \frac{1}{2} \right| = negl(\lambda).$

We now define a security notion for KEM: indistinguishability against one-time chosen ciphertext attacks (IND-1CCA). In this security game, the adversary is restricted to a single query to the decapsulation oracle.

Definition 9 (IND-1CCA-secure KEM). *We define the* IND-1CCA *game as in Fig. 2. A KEM scheme* KEM $=$ (Gen, Encaps, Decaps) *is* IND-1CCA *if for any PPT adversary $\mathcal{A}$ we have* $\mathrm{Adv}_{\mathrm{KEM}}^{\mathrm{IND\text{-}1CCA}}(\mathcal{A}) :=$ $\left| \Pr[\mathrm{IND\text{-}1CCA}_{\mathrm{KEM}}^{\mathcal{A}} = 1] - \frac{1}{2} \right| = negl(\lambda).$

Game IND-1CCA/IND-CPA	DECAPS(sk, c)
1: $(\mathsf{pk}, \mathsf{sk}) \leftarrow\!\!{\scriptstyle\$}\ \mathrm{Gen}$	1: **if more than 1 query :**
2: $b \overset{\$}{\leftarrow} \{0,1\}$	2: **return** $\perp$
3: $(K_0^*, c^*) \leftarrow\!\!{\scriptstyle\$}\ \mathrm{Encaps(pk)}$	3: **if** $c = c^*$
4: $K_1^* \overset{\$}{\leftarrow} \mathcal{K}$	4: **return** $\perp$
5: $b' \leftarrow \mathcal{A}^{\mathrm{Decaps}}(\mathsf{pk}, c^*, K_b^*)$ //IND-1CCA	5: **else return**
6: $b' \leftarrow \mathcal{A}(\mathsf{pk}, c^*, K_b^*)$ //IND-CPA	6: $K := \mathrm{Decaps(sk}, c)$
7: **return** $b' =?b$	

Fig. 2. IND-CPA and IND-1CCA games for KEM.

We now define a security notion for KEM: indistinguishability against chosen ciphertext attacks (IND-CCA). IND-CCA security is the standard security requirement for KEM in the NIST PQC Standardization.

Definition 10 (IND-CCA-secure KEM). *We define the* IND-CCA *game as in Fig. 3. A KEM scheme* KEM $=$ (Gen, Encaps, Decaps) *is* IND-CCA *if for any PPT adversary $\mathcal{A}$ we have* $\mathrm{Adv}_{\mathrm{KEM}}^{\mathrm{IND\text{-}CCA}}(\mathcal{A}) := \left| \Pr[\mathrm{IND\text{-}CCA}_{\mathrm{KEM}}^{\mathcal{A}} = 1] - \frac{1}{2} \right| = negl(\lambda).$

Game IND-CPA for PKE	Game IND-CCA for KEM	$\text{DECAPS}(sk, c)$
1 : $(\text{pk}, \text{sk}) \leftarrow\!\!\$ \text{ Gen}$	1 : $(\text{pk}, \text{sk}) \leftarrow\!\!\$ \text{ Gen}$	1 : **if** $c = c^*$
2 : $b \xleftarrow{\$} \{0,1\}$	2 : $b \xleftarrow{\$} \{0,1\}$	2 : **return** $\perp$
3 : $(m_0, m_1) \leftarrow \mathcal{A}(\text{pk})$	3 : $(K_0^*, c^*) \leftarrow \text{Encaps(pk)}$	3 : **else return**
4 : $c^* \leftarrow \text{ENC}(\text{pk}, m_b)$	4 : $K_1^* \xleftarrow{\$} \mathcal{K}$	4 : $K := \text{Decaps(sk}, c)$
5 : $b' \leftarrow \mathcal{A}(\text{pk}, c^*)$	5 : $b' \leftarrow \mathcal{A}^{\text{DECAPS}}(pk, c^*, K_b^*)$	
6 : **return** $b' =?b$	6 : **return** $b' =?b$	

Fig. 3. IND-CPA game for PKE and IND-CCA game for KEM.

2.3 Quantum Random Oracle Model

We refer the reader to [42] for the basics of quantum computation and quantum information. The Random Oracle Model (ROM) [8] is an ideal model where a uniformly random function is selected and publicly accessible. In the quantum setting, a quantum adversary can evaluate the hash function on arbitrary superposition inputs. Therefore, in the Quantum Random Oracle Model (QROM), we model that a quantum adversary is allowed to query the random oracle with quantum states [10]. Note that to prove the post-quantum security of the cryptographic algorithm, one has to prove it in the QROM [10].

In the classical random oracle, we can use powerful techniques such as lazy sampling to make the proof simpler because the reduction can copy down the adversary's queries to learn what points the adversary is interested in. Furthermore, we can reprogram the RO (let $H(x)$ be some particular value y for some specific x), as long as it is random from the adversary's perspective. Unfortunately, in the QROM, by basic quantum computing mechanics, one cannot observe or copy such superposition queries made by the adversary without disturbing them. Also, reprogramming is usually done for an x that is queried by the adversary at a certain point, so also here we are stuck with the problem that we cannot look at the queries without disturbing them. Therefore, security proofs in the ROM cannot always be simply carried over to the QROM. It is often not obvious how to find a security proof in the QROM. The absence of proof does not imply that the schemes are insecure. Conversely, we generally expect that typical schemes will remain secure if the underlying computational hardness assumptions hold against quantum adversaries. Below we introduce some common QROM techniques, some of which can be used to overcome some of the obstacles in QROM proofs mentioned above.

Compressed Oracle Technique: Zhandry [56] proposed a QROM proof technique called *compressed oracle technique* to record the adversary's queries in a way that the adversary can never detect. This technique allows to maintain *some sort* of a query transcript like lazy sampling, but in the form of a quantum state.

Later, Unruh [53] extended the random functions above to random permutations, and proposed a new technique called *compressed permutation oracle*.

OW2H Techniques and Its Variants: The one-way to hiding (OW2H) lemma [51] serves as an invaluable tool within the realm of security proof, facilitating the reduction of a hiding property, which is manifested as indistinguishability, to a guessing property, namely one-wayness. This reduction process plays a crucial role in establishing the foundation of security. The OW2H lemma is an essential technique in the proof of the security of KEM schemes.

Lemma 11 (One-way to hiding [51]). *Let $S \in X$ be random. Let G, H be oracles such that $\forall x \notin S$, $G(x) = H(x)$. Let z be a random random bitstring. (S, G, H, z may have arbitrary joint distribution.) Let A be a quantum oracle algorithm that makes at most q queries (not necessarily unitary). Let $B^{|H\rangle}$ be an oracle algorithm that on input z does the following: pick $i \in [q-1]$, run $A^{|H\rangle}(z)$ until (just before) the $(i+1)$-th query, measure all query input registers in the computational basis, output the set T of measurement outcomes. Then*

$$\left| \Pr\left[1 \leftarrow A^{|H\rangle}(Z) \right] - \Pr\left[1 \leftarrow A^{|G\rangle}(Z) \right] \right| \leq 2q\sqrt{\Pr\left[S \cap T \neq \emptyset : T \leftarrow B^{|H\rangle}(z) \right]}.$$

Bindel et al. [9] provided a tighter bound for the O2H lemma using compressed oracle technique [56], when the simulator has the ability to simulate both G and H. Moreover, in this particular case, S is also required to be a single element.

Lemma 12 ((Adapted) Double-sided O2H [9]). *Let $G, H : \mathcal{X} \to \mathcal{Y}$ be oracles such that $\forall x \neq x^*. G(x) = H(x)$. Let z be a random bitstring. $(x^*, G, H, z$ may have arbitrary joint distribution.) Let A be quantum oracle algorithm that makes at most q queries (not necessarily unitary). Then, there is another double-sided oracle algorithm $B^{|G\rangle, |H\rangle}(z)$ such that B runs in about the same amount of time as A, and*

$$\left| \Pr\left[1 \leftarrow A^{|H\rangle}(z) \right] - \Pr\left[1 \leftarrow A^{|G\rangle}(z) \right] \right| \leq 2\sqrt{\Pr\left[x^* = x' : x' \leftarrow B^{|G\rangle, |H\rangle}(z) \right]}$$

In particular, the double-sided oracle algorithm $B^{|G\rangle, |H\rangle}(z)$ runs $A^{|H\rangle}(z)$ and $A^{|G\rangle}(z)$ in superposition, and the probability $\Pr\left[x^* = x' : x' \leftarrow B^{|G\rangle, |H\rangle}(z) \right]$ is exactly $\| |\psi_H^q\rangle - |\psi_G^q\rangle \|^2/4$, where $|\psi_H^q\rangle$ ($\psi_G^q\rangle$, resp.) is the final state of $A^{|H\rangle}(z)$ ($A^{|G\rangle}(z)$, resp.).

Ambainis et al. [3] proposed the Semi-classical oracle O_S^{SC} technique. In this technique, only the output $|f_S(x)\rangle$ is measured, while the input $|x\rangle$ is not. Here, f_S represents the indicator function, such that $f_S(x) = 1$ when $x \in S$, and 0 otherwise. Formally, for a query to O_S^{SC} with $\sum_{x,z} a_{x,z}|x\rangle|z\rangle$, O_S^{SC} operates as follows:

1. initialize a single qubit L with $|0\rangle$,
2. transform $\sum_{x,z} a_{x,z}|x\rangle|z\rangle|0\rangle$ into $\sum_{x,z} a_{x,z}|x\rangle|z\rangle|f_S(x)\rangle$,
3. measure L.

Then, after performing this semi-classical measurement, the query state will become $\sum_{x,z:f_S(x)=y} a_{x,z}|x\rangle|z\rangle$ (non-normalized) if the measurement outputs y $(y \in 0, 1)$.

Lemma 13 (Semi-classical OW2H [3]). *Let $S \subseteq X$ be random. Let $\mathcal{O}_1, \mathcal{O}_2$ be oracles with domain X and codomain Y such that $\mathcal{O}_1(x) = \mathcal{O}_2(x)$ for any $x \notin S$. Let z be a random bitstring. $(\mathcal{O}_1, \mathcal{O}_2, S$ and z may have arbitrary joint distribution D.) Let $\mathcal{O}_S^{SC}$ be an oracle that performs the semi-classical measurements corresponding to the projectors M_y, where $M_y := \sum_{x \in X:f_S(x)=y} |x\rangle\langle x|$ $(y \in 0, 1)$. Let $\mathcal{O}_2 \backslash S$ ("$\mathcal{O}_2$ punctured on S") be an oracle that first queries $\mathcal{O}_S^{SC}$ and then $\mathcal{O}_2$. Let $A^{\mathcal{O}_1}(z)$ be an oracle algorithm with query number at most q. Denote Find as the event that in the execution of $A^{\mathcal{O}_2 \backslash S}(z)$, $\mathcal{O}_S^{SC}$ ever outputs 1 during semi-classical measurements. Let*

$$P_{left} := \Pr[b = 1 : (\mathcal{O}_1, \mathcal{O}_2, S, z) \leftarrow D, b \leftarrow A^{\mathcal{O}_1}(z)]$$

$$P_{right} := \Pr[b = 1 : (\mathcal{O}_1, \mathcal{O}_2, S, z) \leftarrow D, b \leftarrow A^{\mathcal{O}_2}(z)]$$

$$P_{find} := \Pr[\textsf{Find} : (\mathcal{O}_1, \mathcal{O}_2, S, z) \leftarrow D, A^{\mathcal{O}_2 \backslash S}(z)].$$

Then $|P_{left} - P_{right}| \leq 2\sqrt{(q+1)P_{find}}$ *and* $|\sqrt{P_{left}} - \sqrt{P_{right}}| \leq 2\sqrt{(q+1)P_{find}}$. *The lemma also holds with bound $\sqrt{(q+1)P_{find}}$ for alternative definition of $P_{right} = \Pr[b = 1 \wedge \neg\textsf{Find} : (\mathcal{O}_1, \mathcal{O}_2, S, z) \leftarrow D, b \leftarrow A^{\mathcal{O}_2 \backslash S}(z)]$.*

- Kuchta et al. [36] proposed *Measure-Rewind-Measure* (MRM) technique and achieved tighter security proofs in the QROM. A reduction is called a black-box reduction if it merely uses the adversary's input-output behavior, and does not depend on the internals like the adversary's code. In contrast, a non-black-box reduction requires knowledge of the adversary's internals. Jiang et al. [32] showed that the quadratic loss is also unavoidable when one turns a search problem into a decision problem using the one-way to hiding technique in a black-box manner. MRM is the first non-black-box reduction and the upper bound provided by the MRM-OW2H theorem avoids the square-root advantage loss (see Table 1).
- Ge et al. [27] proposed a new technique named *Measure-Rewind-Extract* (MRE) by combining the MRM technique and semi-classical oracle technique. By using MRE technique, they proved the Measure-Rewind-Extract O2H (MRE-O2H) theorem, which provides the upper bound $\sqrt{d} \cdot \epsilon$.

Measure-and-Reprogram Technique: Measure-and-Reprogram, introduced in [19,20], demonstrates how to adaptively reprogram the quantum random oracle at a single input. Specifically, for any oracle algorithm $A^{|H\rangle}$ that makes

Table 1. Original OW2H and four OW2H variants. algorithm A makes parallel queries to its oracle with query depth d. The $|S|$ denotes the number of elements in set S. The 1_S denotes the indicator function of set S, i.e., $1_S(x) = 1$ if $x \in S$ and 0 otherwise.

Ow2H theorem	technique	$|S|$	$\mathrm{Adv}(A) \leq$	B'_{ow} s oracle
Original OW2H [51]	\	Arbitrary	$2d \cdot \sqrt{\mathrm{Adv}(B_{ow})}$	H
SC-OW2H [3]	semi-classical oracle technique [3]	Arbitrary	$2\sqrt{d \cdot \mathrm{Adv}(B_{ow})}$	H and 1_S
DS-OW2H [9]	compressed oracle technique [56]	one	$2\sqrt{\mathrm{Adv}(B_{ow})}$	H and G
MRM-OW2H [36]	Measure-Rewind-Measure (MRM) [36]	Arbitrary	$4d \cdot \mathrm{Adv}(B_{ow})$	H and G
MRE-OW2H [27]	Measure-Rewind-Extract (MRE) [27]	Arbitrary	$4\sqrt{d} \cdot \mathrm{Adv}(B_{ow})$	H, G and 1_S

at most q queries to H and outputs a pair (x, z) such that some predicate $V(x, H(x), z)$ holds true, the Measure-and-Reprogram technique demonstrates the existence of another algorithm S^A that emulates H, extracts x from $A^{|H\rangle}$ by randomly measuring one of A's queries to H, and subsequently reprograms $H(x)$ to a designated value Θ, ensuring that the output z from $A^{|H\rangle}$ satisfies $V(x, \Theta, z)$ with a multiplicative $O(q^2)$ loss in probability. Jiang et al. [35] proposed a variant of the Measure-and-Reprogram technique. Informally, this variant of the Measure-and-Reprogram technique states that if for any algorithm $A^{|H\rangle}$ (i^*-th query is classical query and equal to x) some predicate $V(x, H(x), z)$ holds true, one can build another algorithm S^A that does not query H on the i^*-th classical query (but uses its input instead) can satisfy $V(x, \Theta, z)$ with a multiplicative $O(q^2)$ loss in probability.

Other QROM Proof Techniques: Hülsing et al. [30] and Unruh [52] showed that finding preimages in the random oracle is hard. Boneh et al. [10] introduced the history-free reductions which basically means replacing the random oracle with a different function from the start. Zhandry [55] showed that random oracle can be simulated using $2q$-wise independent functions. Based on this, Unruh [52] introduced a *length-preserving hash* technique for extracting the preimage of the random oracle. Zhandry [55] proposed the *semi-constant distributions* technique enabling the programming of random oracles at multiple random locations with a challenge value without the adversary noticing. Zhandry [54] improved on this with the *small-range distribution* technique that allows us to simulate random oracles using random-looking functions with a small range. Don et al. [21] proposed *online-extractability* framework based on compressed oracle. They [21] show the generic result. Whenever a quantum query algorithm in the quantum random-oracle model outputs a classical value t that is guaranteed to be in some tight relation with $H(x)$ for some x, then x can be efficiently extracted with high probability. Ambainis et al. [5] demonstrated that the challenges associated with the quantum random oracle model extend beyond limitations in proof techniques; specifically, they [5] showed that certain schemes secure in the classical random oracle model may become insecure in the quantum random oracle model.

3   Post-Quantum IND-CCA-Secure KEMs from FO Transformation and Its Modularization

IND-CCA is a critical security property for KEMs in practice. The FO transformation [24,25] is an important cryptography technique that transforms PKEs from CPA security to CCA security in the ROM [8,24]. The FO transformation [25] is a combination of a symmetric and an asymmetric encryption scheme using two hash functions, where both schemes require only minimal security guarantees. Specifically, the asymmetric encryption scheme is required to be γ-spread OW-CPA secure, while the symmetric encryption scheme is required to be one-time security.[2] Cramer et al. [16] argued that it is more efficient to first construct an IND-CCA-secure KEM and then derive an IND-CCA-secure PKE scheme using the KEM/DEM paradigm [16]. Dent [18] subsequently proposed a general construction of IND-CCA-secure KEMs. Building on [18], Hofheinz, Hövelmanns and Kiltz [26] introduced several variants of the FO transformation, including $FO^{\perp}, FO^{\not\perp}, FO_m^{\perp}, FO_m^{\not\perp}, QFO_m^{\perp}$ and $QFO_m^{\not\perp}$. In these variants, m (or the absence of m) indicates $K = H(m)$ (or $K = H(m, c)$), while $\not\perp$ ($\perp$) denotes implicit (explicit) rejection. "Q" refers to the inclusion of an additional Targhi-Unruh hash [49] applied to the ciphertext. The variants of REACT/GEM transformation [31,43] presented in [26], referred to as modular FO transformations, include $U^{\not\perp}, U^{\perp}, U_m^{\not\perp}, U_m^{\perp}, QU_m^{\not\perp}$ and $QU_m^{\perp}$. Here, U represents a class of transformations that convert a PKE with non-standard security (e.g., OW-PCA, one-way against plaintext-checking attacks [31,43]) or a deterministic PKE (DPKE, where the encryption algorithm is deterministic) into an IND-CCA-secure KEM. In particular, Hülsing et al. [9] and Jiang et al. [33,34] showed that $FO^{\perp}$ (resp. $FO^{\not\perp}$) is as tightly secure as $FO_m^{\perp}$ (resp. $FO_m^{\not\perp}$) and vice versa.

3.1   FO Transformation and Its Modularization in the ROM

In [26], Hofheinz, Hövelmanns and Kiltz modularize the FO transformation into two components: the T transformation and the U transformation. The T transformation converts any OW-CPA secure encryption scheme (PKE) into an OW-PCA secure encryption scheme (PKE_1), as illustrated in Fig. 4. Subsequently, the transformations $U^{\not\perp}, U_m^{\not\perp}$ $(U^{\perp}, U_m^{\perp})$ can convert any OW-PCA (or OW-PCVA) secure encryption scheme, PKE_1, into an IND-CCA secure KEM, as shown in Table 2. The combination of the T transformation with various U transformations enables the construction of multiple FO variants.

T Transformation: from OW-CPA to OW-PCVA Security. The T transformation, as shown in Fig. 4, converts an OW-CPA secure PKE into an OW-PCA secure scheme (PKE_1). If PKE is γ-spread, then PKE_1 is also OW-PCVA secure. Note that PKE_1 is a rigid deterministic OW-CPA secure scheme. The

---

[2] A γ-spread OW-CPA secure asymmetric encryption scheme ensures sufficient entropy to resist plaintext-checking attacks, while one-time security guarantees confidentiality for the symmetric scheme.

OW-PCA security of PKE_1 non-tightly reduces to the OW-CPA security of PKE, with a loss factor of $q_G + q_P$, where q_G and q_P represent the number of queries to the random oracle G and the validity checking oracle CVO, respectively. Additionally, the OW-PCA security of PKE_1 is tightly reduced to the IND-CPA security of PKE.

$Enc_1(pk)$	$Dec_1(sk, c)$
1: $\quad m \leftarrow_\$ \mathcal{M}$	1: $\quad m' = dec(sk, c)$
2: $\quad c \leftarrow enc(pk, m; G(m))$	2: $\quad$ **if** $m' = \bot$ **or** $enc(pk, m'; G(m')) \neq c$
3: $\quad$ **return** c	3: $\qquad$ **return** $\bot$
	4: $\quad$ **else return** m'

Fig. 4. OW-PCVA-secure encryption scheme $PKE_1 = T[PKE, G]$ with deterministic encryption.

U Transformation. There are four variants of the U transformation, namely $U^{\not\perp}, U_m^{\not\perp}, U^{\perp}, U_m^{\perp}$, that convert a public-key encryption scheme PKE_1 to an IND-CCA secure KEM.

- $U^{\perp}$ transformation: $U^{\perp}$ transforms an OW-PCVA secure PKE into an IND-CCA secure KEM. The construction is depicted in Fig. 5.
- $U^{\not\perp}$ transformation: $U^{\not\perp}$ transforms an OW-PCA secure PKE into an IND-CCA secure KEM. Unlike $U^{\perp}$, $U^{\not\perp}$ is a variant with "implicit rejection" of invalid ciphertexts. For more details, refer to Fig. 6.
- $U_m^{\not\perp}, U_m^{\perp}$ transformation: $U_m^{\not\perp}, U_m^{\perp}$ transforms a rigid deterministic OW-CPA (OW-VA) secure PKE into an IND-CCA secure KEM. These transformations apply to rigid deterministic encryption schemes (e.g., PKEs obtained via the T transformation). In $U_m^{\not\perp}$, the KEM key is derived as $K = H(m)$, whereas in $U_m^{\perp}$, the key is derived as $K = H(m, c)$. The constructions for the corresponding KEMs are shown in Fig. 7.

Table 2. Four kinds of transformation U. Note that all the security reduction is tight in ROM.

Transformation	Rejection of invalid ciphertexts	KEM key	PKE_1's requirements
$U^{\not\perp}$	implicit	$K = H(m, c)$	OW-PCA
$U^{\perp}$	explicit	$K = H(m, c)$	OW-PCVA
$U_m^{\not\perp}$	implicit	$K = H(m)$	det. + OW-CPA
$U_m^{\perp}$	explicit	$K = H(m)$	det. + OW-VA

Encaps$_1$(pk)	Decaps$_1$(sk, c)
1: $m \leftarrow_\$ \mathcal{M}$	1: $m' = \text{dec}_1(\text{sk}, c)$
2: $c \leftarrow \text{enc}_1(\text{pk}, m)$	2: **if** $m' = \perp$
3: $K := H(m, c) \mathbin{/\!/} \text{U}^\perp$	3: **return** $\perp$
4: $K := H(m) \mathbin{/\!/} \text{U}_m^\perp$	4: **else**
5: **return** (K, c)	5: **return** $K := H(m', c) \mathbin{/\!/} \text{U}^\perp$
	6: **return** $K := H(m') \mathbin{/\!/} \text{U}_m^\perp$

Fig. 5. IND-CCA-secure key encapsulation mechanism $\text{KEM}^\perp = \text{U}^\perp[\text{PKE}_1, \text{H}]$ and $\text{KEM}_m^\perp = \text{U}_m^\perp[\text{PKE}_1, \text{H}]$. Note that the Gen algorithm in KEM is identical to the Gen algorithm in PKE_1 when we omit the Gen algorithm.

Gen$^{\not\perp}(1^n)$	Encaps(pk)	Decaps$^{\not\perp}$(sk, c)
1: $(\text{pk}', \text{sk}') \leftarrow_\$ \text{gen}_1$	1: $m \leftarrow_\$ \mathcal{M}$	1: Parse sk $= (sk', s)$
2: $s \leftarrow_\$ \mathcal{M}$	2: $c \leftarrow \text{enc}_1(\text{pk}, m)$	2: $m' = \text{dec}_1(\text{sk}, c)$
3: sk $:= (sk', s)$	3: $K := H(m, c)$	3: **if** $m' \neq \perp$
4: **return** (pk', sk)	4: **return** (K, c)	4: **return** $K := H(m', c)$
		5: **else return** $K := H(s, c)$

Fig. 6. IND-CCA-secure key encapsulation mechanism $\text{KEM}^{\not\perp} = \text{U}^{\not\perp}[\text{PKE}_1, \text{H}]$.

Based on the above sub-transformations, there are four variants of FO transformation $\text{FO} := \text{U}^{\not\perp} \circ \text{T}, \text{FO}^\perp := \text{U}^\perp \circ \text{T}, \text{FO}_m^{\not\perp} := \text{U}_m^{\not\perp} \circ \text{T}$, and $\text{FO}_m^\perp := \text{U}_m^\perp \circ \text{T}$. Therefore there are four kinds of FO transformations for KEM:

$$\text{KEM}^{\not\perp} = \text{FO}^{\not\perp}[\text{PKE}, \text{G}, \text{H}] := \text{U}^{\not\perp}[\text{T}[\text{PKE}, \text{G}], \text{H}] = \left(\text{Gen}^{\not\perp}, \text{Encaps}, \text{Decaps}^{\not\perp}\right)$$

$$\text{KEM}^\perp = \text{FO}^\perp[\text{PKE}, \text{G}, \text{H}] := \text{U}^\perp[\text{T}[\text{PKE}, \text{G}], \text{H}]] = \left(\text{Gen}, \text{Encaps}, \text{Decaps}^\perp\right)$$

$$\text{KEM}_m^{\not\perp} = \text{FO}_m^{\not\perp}[\text{PKE}, \text{G}, \text{H}] := \text{U}_m^{\not\perp}[\text{T}[\text{PKE}, \text{G}], \text{H}] = \left(\text{Gen}^{\not\perp}, \text{Encaps}_m, \text{Decaps}_m^{\not\perp}\right)$$

$$\text{KEM}_m^\perp = \text{FO}_m^\perp[\text{PKE}, \text{G}, \text{H}] := \text{U}_m^\perp[\text{T}[\text{PKE}, \text{G}], \text{H}] = \left(\text{Gen}, \text{Encaps}_m, \text{Decaps}_m^\perp\right).$$

The asymptotic bounds for the IND-CCA security of KEMs are presented in Table 3 [26], where $q_{RO} := q_G + q_H$ represents the total number of adversarial queries to the random oracles G, H. The parameter ϵ, shown in the left column, indicates the bounds relative to the OW-CPA advantage of the underlying PKE, while ϵ', shown in the right column, reflects the bounds relative to the IND-CPA advantage of the underlying PKE.

$\text{Gen}^{\not\perp}(1^n)$	$\text{Encaps}_m(\text{pk})$	$\text{Decaps}_m^{\not\perp}(\text{sk}, c)$
1: $(\text{pk}', \text{sk}') \leftarrow\!\!{}_\$ \text{gen}_1$	1: $m \leftarrow\!\!{}_\$ \mathcal{M}$	1: Parse $\text{sk} = (\text{sk}', s)$
2: $s \leftarrow\!\!{}_\$ \mathcal{M}$	2: $c \leftarrow \text{enc}_1(\text{pk}, m)$	2: $m' = \text{dec}_1(\text{sk}', c)$
3: $\text{sk} := (\text{sk}', s)$	3: $K := H(m)$	3: if $m' \neq \perp$
4: return (pk', sk)	4: return (K, c)	4: return $K := H(m')$
		5: else return $K := H(s, c)$

Fig. 7. IND-CCA-secure key encapsulation mechanism $\text{KEM}_m^{\not\perp} = \text{U}_m^{\not\perp}[\text{PKE}_1, \text{H}]$.

$\text{Gen}^{\not\perp}(1^n)$	$\text{Decaps}^{\perp}(\text{sk}, c)$ $\boxed{\text{Decaps}_m^{\perp}(\text{sk}, c)}$
1: $(\text{pk}, \text{sk}) \leftarrow\!\!{}_\$ \text{Gen}$	1: $m' = \text{Dec}(\text{sk}, c)$
2: $s \leftarrow\!\!{}_\$ \mathcal{M}$	2: if $m' = \perp$ or $\text{Enc}(\text{pk}, m'; G(m')) \neq c$
3: $\text{sk}' := (\text{sk}, s)$	3: return $\perp$
4: return (pk, sk')	4: else return $K := H(m', c)$ $\boxed{K := H(m')}$

$\text{Encaps}(\text{pk})$ $\boxed{\text{Encaps}_m(\text{pk})}$	$\text{Decaps}^{\not\perp}(\text{sk}', c)$ $\boxed{\text{Decaps}_m^{\not\perp}(\text{sk}, c)}$
1: $m \leftarrow\!\!{}_\$ \mathcal{M}$	1: Parse $\text{sk}' = (\text{sk}, s)$
2: $c \leftarrow \text{Enc}(\text{pk}, m; G(m))$	2: $m' = \text{Dec}(\text{sk}', c)$
3: $K := H(m, c)$ $\boxed{K := H(m)}$	3: if $m' = \perp$ or $\text{Enc}(\text{pk}, m'; G(m')) \neq c$
4: return (K, c)	4: return $K := H(s, c)$
	5: else return $K := H(m', c)$ $\boxed{K := H(m')}$

Fig. 8. IND-CCA secure Key Encapsulation Mechanism $\text{KEM}^{\not\perp} = (\text{Gen}^{\not\perp}, \text{Encaps}, \text{Decaps}^{\not\perp})$, $\text{KEM}^{\perp} = (\text{Gen}, \text{Encaps}, \text{Decaps}^{\perp})$, $\text{KEM}_m^{\not\perp} = (\text{Gen}^{\not\perp}, \text{Encaps}_m, \text{Decaps}_m^{\not\perp})$, and $\text{KEM}_m^{\perp} = (\text{Gen}, \text{Encaps}_m, \text{Decaps}_m^{\perp})$ obtained from PKE=(Gen,Enc,Dec).

3.2 FO Transformation and Its Modularization in the QROM

The post-quantum security of the FO transformation and its variants has received much attention in the NIST post-quantum cryptography standardization process. The quantum situation is much more difficult than the classical situation as some parts of the classical proof may not work in the quantum setting. So far, all the quantum proofs used the One-Way to Hiding (O2H) theorem [4] or its variants to solve the reprogramming problem in the QROM. Here we'll survey some main solutions for post-quantum IND-CCA-secure KEMs.

Boneh et al. [10] proved that a KEM variant of Bellare-Rogaway based on a one-way trapdoor function is IND-CCA-secure in the QROM. In their security proof, we get that $\epsilon' \approx \epsilon^2/q_H^2$, where q_H denotes the number of random oracle queries.

Table 3. Asymptotic security bounds for four kinds of KEMs in the ROM.

KEM	Bounds on $\mathrm{Adv}_{\mathrm{KEM}}^{\mathrm{IND\text{-}CCA}}(B) \leq$	
$\mathrm{KEM}^{\not\perp}$	$2q_{\mathrm{RO}} \cdot \epsilon$	$3 \cdot \epsilon'$
$\mathrm{KEM}^{\perp}$	$2q_{\mathrm{RO}} \cdot \epsilon$	$3 \cdot \epsilon'$
$\mathrm{KEM}_m^{\not\perp}$	$2q_{\mathrm{RO}} \cdot \epsilon$	$3 \cdot \epsilon'$
$\mathrm{KEM}_m^{\perp}$	$2q_{\mathrm{RO}} \cdot \epsilon$	$3 \cdot \epsilon'$

Among the 39 KEM submissions in the Round-1 of NIST PQC Standardization, there are 16 submissions including FrodoKEM etc., $\mathrm{QFO}^{\not\perp}$, $\mathrm{QFO}^{\perp}$, $\mathrm{QFO}_m^{\not\perp}$ and $\mathrm{QFO}_m^{\perp}$ are used, where an additional hash is appended to the ciphertext. In [49], Hofheinz et al. presented QROM security reductions for $\mathrm{QU}_m^{\not\perp}$, $\mathrm{QU}_m^{\perp}$, $\mathrm{QFO}_m^{\not\perp}$ and $\mathrm{QFO}_m^{\perp}$. Note that "Q" refers to the inclusion of an additional Targhi-Unruh hash [49] applied to the ciphertext. Thus for these transformations, there is a length-preserving hash (that has the same domain and range size) in the ciphertext, which plays an important role in their reductions.

Jiang et al. [33] first proved the security of $\mathrm{FO}_m^{\not\perp}, \mathrm{FO}^{\not\perp}$ based on an OW-CPA-secure PKE scheme with quadratic security loss. These schemes remove the additional hash parts in [49] and consider the correctness error. For modular FO transformations including $\mathrm{U}^{\not\perp}, \mathrm{U}^{\perp}, \mathrm{U}_m^{\not\perp}, \mathrm{U}_m^{\perp}$, Jiang et al. provided QROM security reductions without additional hash for any correctness error δ, concrete results show in Table 4. Subsequently, in ML-KEM [40], Classic McEliece [2], and FrodoKEM [37], the additional hash is removed following the work of Saito, Xagawa, and Yamakawa [45] and Jiang et al. [33].

Table 4. Modular FO transformations from non-standard security assumptions in [33]. Note that the bound $q\sqrt{\delta}$ in [5] for the general search problem can be improved to $q^2\delta$ in [30].

Transformation	Underlying security	Security bound	Additional hash	DPKE	Perfectly correct?
$\mathrm{U}^{\not\perp}$	OW-qPCA	$q\sqrt{\epsilon}$	N	N	N
$\mathrm{U}^{\perp}$	OW-qPVCA	$q\sqrt{\epsilon}$	N	N	N
$\mathrm{U}_m^{\not\perp}$	OW-CPA	$q\sqrt{\delta} + q\sqrt{\epsilon}$	N	Y	N
$\mathrm{U}_m^{\not\perp}$	DS	$q\sqrt{\delta} + \epsilon$	N	Y	N
$\mathrm{U}_m^{\perp}$	OW-VA	$q\sqrt{\delta} + q\sqrt{\epsilon}$	N	Y	N

In the following, we present a detailed overview of these relevant works [9, 27, 28, 33–36, 45] that improve the tightness of security proofs and reduce the security loss in the QROM for the T, U, and FO transformations.

When proving the security of a cryptographic scheme S under a hardness assumption of a problem P, we usually construct a reduction algorithm Adv against P that uses an adversary $\mathcal{B}$ against S as a subroutine. Let (T, ϵ) and

(T', ϵ') denote the running times and advantages of Adv and $\mathcal{B}$, respectively. The reduction is said to be tight if $T \approx T'$ and $\epsilon \approx \epsilon'$. Otherwise, if $T \gg T'$ or $\epsilon \ll \epsilon'$, the reduction is non-tight. Generally, the tightness gap, (informally) defined by $\frac{T\epsilon'}{T'\epsilon}$, is used to measure the quality of a reduction. Tighter reductions with smaller tightness gaps are desirable for cryptography in practice especially in large-scale scenarios, since the tightness of a reduction determines the strength of the security guarantees provided by the security proof.

All the security reductions for (modular) FO transformations in the QROM satisfy (1) T' is about T, i.e., $T' \approx T$; (2) $\epsilon' \approx \kappa\epsilon^{\frac{1}{\tau}}$, where κ and τ in the following are respectively denoted as the factor and degree of security loss. Let q be the total number of adversarial queries to various oracles. The following results mainly discuss the FO transformation with implicit rejection.

- In [28], Hofheinz et al. presented QROM security reductions for $\text{QFO}_m^{\not\perp}$ and $\text{QFO}_m^{\perp}$ with $\kappa = q^{\frac{3}{2}}$ and $\tau = 4$, for $\text{QU}_m^{\not\perp}$ and $\text{QU}_m^{\perp}$ with $\kappa = q$ and $\tau = 2$.
- In [45], Saito, Xagawa, and Yamakawa presented a tight security proof (i.e., $\kappa = 1$ and $\tau = 1$) for $\text{U}_m^{\not\perp}$ under a new (non-standard) security assumption called disjoint simulatability (DS). Moreover, two generic transformations, TPunc, and KC, were given to construct a DS-secure deterministic public-key encryption (DPKE) from standard assumptions, with security reductions $\kappa = q$ and $\tau = 2$.
- In [33], Jiang et al. first presented security reductions for $\text{FO}^{\not\perp}$ and $\text{FO}_m^{\not\perp}$ from the standard OW-CPA security of the underlying PKE with $\kappa = q$ and $\tau = 2$. Then, they presented security reductions for $\text{U}^{\not\perp}$ ($\text{U}^{\perp}$, resp.) from the OW-qPCA (OW-qPVCA, resp.) security of the underlying PKE, $\text{U}_m^{\not\perp}$ ($\text{U}_m^{\perp}$, resp.) from the OW-CPA (OW-VA, resp.) security of the underlying DPKE with with $\kappa = q$ and $\tau = 2$. , where OW-qPCA, OW-qPVCA, and OW-VA are new non-standard security notions of PKE introduced by [28,33].
- In [34], Jiang et al. improved the tightness of security reductions in [33] for $\text{FO}^{\not\perp}$, $\text{FO}_m^{\not\perp}$, $\text{U}^{\not\perp}$, $\text{U}^{\perp}$, $\text{U}_m^{\not\perp}$ and $\text{U}_m^{\perp}$ with $\kappa = \sqrt{q}$ and $\tau = 2$ by using semi-classical oracle technique introduced by Ambainis, Hamburg and Unruh [4]. For T, the quadratic security loss is reduced to be a linear one ($\kappa = \sqrt{q}$ and $\tau = 1$).
- In [9], Bindel et al. improved the reduction for the security of the $\text{U}^{\not\perp}$, $\text{U}^{\perp}$, $\text{U}_m^{\not\perp}$ and $\text{U}_m^{\perp}$ with $\kappa = \sqrt{q}$ and $\tau = 1$ by introducing double-sided oracle technique.
- In [35], Jiang et al. showed that the current quadratic loss ($\tau = 2$) for U and FO is indeed unavoidable for any measurement-based black-box reduction that runs the adversary once without rewinding.
- In [36], Kuchta et al. first gave non-black-box reductions for FO-like KEMs as shown in Table. 5 by introducing the Measure-Rewind-Measure(MRM) technique. In particular, for $\text{U}^{\not\perp}$ ($\text{FO}^{\not\perp}$, resp.) and its variants, the reduction tightness was improved to be $\kappa = q$ and $\tau = 1$ ($\kappa = q^2$ and $\tau = 1$, resp.).
- In [27], Ge et al. proposed a new technique called Measure-Rewind-Extract(MRE) by combining the MRM technique [36] with the semi-classical oracle technique [4]. In particular, they improved the tightness of security

reductions in [36] for $U^{\not\perp}$ ($FO^{\not\perp}$, resp.) and its variants, the reduction tightness was improved to be $\kappa = q^{1/2}$ and $\tau = 1$ ($\kappa = q^{3/2}$ and $\tau = 1$, resp.).

Table 5. Improvements of the factor κ and the degree τ of security loss. Here, we only list the results for the standard assumption and NBB means non-black-box reduction.

(κ, τ)	TPunc, KC	T	$U^{\not\perp}, U^{\perp}, U_m^{\not\perp}, U_m^{\perp}$	$FO_m^{\not\perp}, FO^{\not\perp}$
SXY18 [45]	$(q, 2)$	–	–	–
JZC$^+$18 [33]	–	$(q, 2)$	$(q, 2)$	$(q, 2)$
JZM19 [34]	$(\sqrt{q}, 2)$	$(q, 1)$	$(\sqrt{q}, 2)$	$(\sqrt{q}, 2)$
BHH$^+$19 [9]	–	$(q, 1)$	$(1, 2)$	$(\sqrt{q}, 2)$
KSS$^+$20 [36]	–	–	$(q, 1)$(NBB)	$(q^2, 1)$(NBB)
GLS24 [?]	–	–	$(q^{1/2}, 1)$(NBB)	$(q^{3/2}, 1)$(NBB)

For the explicitly rejected $FO_m^{\perp}$ and $FO^{\perp}$, Don et al. [21] give the first complete post-quantum security proof for γ-spreadness CPA PKEs by introducing the online-extractability framework, which is based on the compressed oracle.

4   Post-Quantum IND-1CCA-Secure KEMs

IND-1CCA secure KEMs play a pivotal role in existing protocols to achieve post-quantum security. Specifically, to ensure PQ security for parts of the protocol that use Diffie-Hellman (DH) key exchange, it is crucial to replace the existing DH key exchange with a PQ-secure KEM. The existing TLS 1.3 protocol [22], KEMTLS [46], Signal [13], and Noise [6] schemes, rely on the PRF-ODH [14] assumption to achieve security. For PQ variants of these protocols, it has been shown that IND-1CCA security is required for the replaced KEMs, see PQ TLS [22,29,46,47], PQ Signal [13], and PQ Noise [6].

4.1   The Construction of IND-1CCA Secure KEMs from PKEs

We present three general constructions of IND-1CCA secure KEMs from CPA-secure PKEs in the ROM and QROM.

Using IND-CCA Secure KEMs: Usually, IND-CCA secure KEMs are taken as IND-1CCA secure KEMs for the implementation of PQ TLS 1.3 [1,22], PQ KEMTLS [46,47], PQ Signal [13] and PQ Noise [6]. As discussed in Sect. 3, IND-CCA secure KEMs are generally constructed using an FO-like transformation. In particular, ML-KEM (CRYSTALS-Kyber) [40] and the remaining KEMs in the Round-4 submissions [38] all employ an FO-like transformation. However, the FO-like transformation in IND-CCA secure KEMs requires a re-encryption step during decapsulation, and Huguenin-Dumittan and Vaudenay

[29] show that this re-encryption step significantly degrades decapsulation efficiency. For example, they [29] demonstrate a 2.17X speedup over decapsulation in CRYSTALS-Kyber [11], and a 6.11X speedup in FrodoKEM [37] when re-encryption is removed. Moreover, re-encryption can render KEMs more vulnerable to side-channel attacks as shown in [7,50], impacting nearly all NIST-PQC Round-3 KEMs.

T_H, T_{CH} **Transfrom from CPA-secure PKEs:** Huguenin-Dumittan and Vaudenay [29] propose two general constructions of IND-1CCA secure KEMs from OW-CPA/IND-CPA PKEs. One construction is shown in Fig. 9, denoted as T_{CH}, incorporates a key-confirmation component (i.e., an additional length-preserving hash) into the original ciphertext, causing ciphertext expansion. Note that T_{CH} is basically the REACT transform [43] without the asymmetric part to get a KEM instead of a PKE. The security of T_{CH} was proved in the ROM with tightness $\epsilon_R \approx O(1/q)$, and in the QROM with tightness, $\epsilon_R \approx O(1/q^3)$, where ϵ_R (ϵ_A, resp.) is the advantage of the reduction R (adversary A, resp.) breaking the security of the underlying PKE (the resulting KEM, resp.), and q is the number of A's queries to the random oracle (RO). Unfortunately, the QROM proof of T_{CH} in [29] relies on key confirmation (a length-preserving hash that has the same domain and range size), which leads to ciphertext expansion.

Another construction is shown in Fig. 10, denoted as T_H, works without ciphertext expansion, and the key is derived by $H(m, c)$. In fact, T_H is the same as $U^\perp$ in [28]. However, Huguenin-Dumittan and Vaudenay [29] only gave the ROM proof of T_H with tightness $\epsilon_R \approx O(1/q^3)$, where ϵ_A represents the advantage. The QROM proof is left open due to the challenge that a lot of random oracle (RO) programming property is used [29]. Jiang et al. [32] provided a tighter security reduction for both T_H in the ROM compared to the proof presented in [29]. Jiang et al. [32] also established the security of T_H in the QROM by introducing a variant of the measure-and-reprogram technique [19,20]. The overall security bound is shown in Table. 6.

T_{RH} **Transfrom from CPA-secure PKEs:** Jiang et al. [32] introduced an implicit variant of T_H, denoted as T_{RH} and shown in Fig. 10. T_{RH} is the same as T_H except that in decapsulation a pseudorandom value $H(\star, c)$ is returned instead of an explicit $\perp$ for an invalid ciphertext c such that $\mathsf{dec}'(\mathsf{sk}, c) = \perp$. Here, $\star$ can be any fixed public value. Compared to secret seed, public value can reduce the secret key size and make the construction more concise. Moreover, from a high-assurance implementation (i.e., side-channel protected) point of view, public value is also preferable to secure seed. For security, [32] provided a security reduction for T_{RH} in the ROM and QROM, the overall security bound is shown in Table. 6.

For T_H and T_{CH}, Jiang et al. [32] showed that if the underlying PKE meets the malleability property, a $O(1/q)$ ($O(1/q^2)$, resp.) loss is unavoidable in the ROM (QROM, resp.). That is, their [32] ROM reduction is optimal in general. Roughly speaking, the malleability property indicates that an adversary is able to efficiently convert one ciphertext into another that decrypts to a related plaintext. In particular, such a malleability property is exhibited by real-world PKE schemes, including ElGamal, FrodoKEM.PKE [37], and ML-KEM.PKE [40], etc.

Chen et al. [15] improved the security tightness of the T_{RH}-transformation in both the ROM and QROM, for the case where the underlying PKE is rigid deterministic. In both ROM and QROM models, their reductions achieve security loss factors of $O(1)$, significantly improving upon Jiang et al.'s results, which had security loss factors of $O(q)$ in the ROM and $O(q^2)$ in the QROM, respectively. Notably, they introduce a new tool called 'reprogram-after-measure' to overcome the reduction loss posed by oracle reprogramming in QROM proofs.

IND-qCCA: In [29], they actually demonstrated that KEMs constructed using the T_{CH} and T_H transforms are IND-qCCA secure. Here, q (a constant number) refers to the number of times that the adversary can query the decapsulation oracle. The results for the T_H and T_{RH} transforms in [32] can also be readily extended to the IND-qCCA KEM case for any arbitrary constant q. However, as mentioned earlier, IND-1CCA KEM security is sufficient for practical protocols, such as TLS 1.3, KEMTLS, Signal, and Noise.

Gen(1^n)	Encaps(pk)	Decaps(sk, (c, tag))
1: $(\text{pk}, \text{sk}) \leftarrow\!\!\$ \text{ gen}$	1: $m \leftarrow\!\!\$ \mathcal{M}$	1: $m' = \text{dec}'(\text{sk}, c)$
2: **return** (pk, sk)	2: $c \leftarrow\!\!\$ \text{enc}'(\text{pk}, m)$	2: **if** $H'(m', c) \neq \text{tag}$
	3: $\text{tag} = H'(m, c)$	3: **return** $\perp$
	4: $K := H(m)$	4: **else return** $K := H(m')$
	5: **return** $(K, (c, \text{tag}))$	

Fig. 9. $\text{KEM}_{CH} = T_{CH}[\text{PKE}', H]$

Gen(1^n)	Encaps(pk)	Decaps(sk, c)
1: $(\text{pk}, \text{sk}) \leftarrow\!\!\$ \text{ gen}$	1: $m \leftarrow\!\!\$ \mathcal{M}$	1: $m' = \text{dec}'(\text{sk}, c)$
2: **return** (pk, sk)	2: $c \leftarrow\!\!\$ \text{enc}'(\text{pk}, m)$	2: **if** $m' = \perp$
	3: $K := H(m, c)$	3: **return** $\perp$ // T_H
	4: **return** (K, c)	4: **return** $K := H(\star, c)$ // T_{RH}
		5: **else return** $K := H(m', c)$

Fig. 10. $\text{KEM}_H = T_H[\text{PKE}', H]$ and $\text{KEM}_{RH} = T_{RH}[\text{PKE}', H]$

Table 6. Reduction Tightness of IND-1CCA KEMs in the ROM/QROM Based on the Standard Security Notion for PKEs.

Transformation	Reduction Tightness	Ciphertext Expansion	Re-encryption	ROM/ QROM
FO [28]	$\epsilon_R \approx \epsilon_A$	N	Y	ROM
T_{CH} [29]	$\epsilon_R \approx O(1/q)\epsilon_A$	Y	N	ROM
T_{RH} and T_H [32]	$\epsilon_R \approx O(1/q)\epsilon_A$	N	N	ROM
FO [9,34]	$\epsilon_R \approx O(1/q)\epsilon_A^2$	N	Y	QROM
T_{CH} [29]	$\epsilon_R \approx O(1/q^3)\epsilon_A^2$	Y	N	QROM
T_{RH} and T_H [32]	$\epsilon_R \approx O(1/q^2)\epsilon_A^2$	N	N	QROM

4.2 Practical Impact

IND-1-CCA KEMs are sufficient to replace Diffie-Hellman in the post-quantum migration of the widely deployed protocols, such as KEMTLS [46], Signal [13] and Noise [6]. Compared with IND-CCA secure KEMs based on FO transform such as ML-KEM [40], the IND-1CCA secure KEMs constructed from T_H, T_{RH} do not require the re-encryption in decapsulation. The re-encryption is highly vulnerable to side-channel attacks and its side-channel protection will significantly increase deployment costs. Moreover, The re-encryption step significantly degrades decapsulation efficiency. Therefore, removing the re-encryption of FO-like KEMs will improve the performance of embedded side-channel secure implementations. Therefore, one can easily transform ML-KEM [40] to an IND-1-CCA-secure KEM based on T_H, T_{RH} without re-encryption and cipher-expansion, and then establish PQ secure variants of Signal and Noise with better performance in the embedded implementation. The benchmark for ML-KEM [40] is shown in Table. 9.

Table 7. Benchmark of Encaps and Decaps for ML-KEM [40] with different transforms using liboqs (AVX2 enabled, NIST security level I) on system specs: Intel(R) Core(TM) i9-10900X CPU @ 3.7 GHz, 32.0 GB RAM, 64-bit OS.

Algorithm	T_{RH}	T_{CH}	FO
Encaps (μs)	7.255	7.682	7.666
Decaps (μs)	2.274	2.277	7.428

4.3 Risks Associated with Key-Reuse

The primary security risk associated with using an IND-1CCA KEM instead of its IND-CCA counterpart is the vulnerability to attacks exploiting key reuse or misuse. Specifically, if a protocol incorrectly implements the IND-1CCA KEM with a "static" public key rather than an ephemeral one, adversaries could potentially recover the secret key through multiple decryption queries. The risk of key recovery after several key reuses can be mitigated by employing hybrid cryptography. For example, an efficient IND-CCA KEM could be combined with an IND-1CCA KEM. This approach would enhance overall security and resistance to key reuse attacks with minimal cost. Notably, if ephemeral keys are incorrectly implemented as static ones in these systems, the forward security property would be compromised.

5   Post-Quantum CPA-Secure KEMs and Their Application to PQ-TLS 1.3

The Transport Layer Security (TLS) protocol is one of the most widely used cryptographic protocols for securing application protocols, such as web browsing, email, instant messaging, and voice-over-IP. TLS 1.3 was standardized in August 2018 is the latest version of TLS and has already been widely adopted. As the NIST standardization of post-quantum cryptography advances, the exploration of transitioning the TLS 1.3 protocol to PQ security has become a crucial topic. To ensure PQ security for components of the protocol utilizing DH key exchange, it is essential to replace the current DH key exchange with a PQ-secure KEM.

5.1   Security Analysis of PQ TLS 1.3

The existing TLS 1.3 protocol [22] relies on the PRF-ODH [14] assumption to achieve security. For PQ TLS 1.3 [22,29], it has been shown that IND-1CCA security is required for the replaced KEMs. Later, Huguenin-Dumittan and Vaudenay [29] showed that OW-CPA KEMs are sufficient for PQ TLS 1.3 in the ROM. They observed that in the TLS 1.3 key schedule, the keys are obtained by applying key-derivation functions (KDFs) to the shared secret and the hash of the transcript so far (including the ciphertext). Inspired by the proof of security of the T_H transform which is discussed in Sect. 4.1, they proved that if the underlying KEM is OW-CPA secure, then the TLS 1.3 handshake protocol is secure in the MultiStage model of Dowling et al. [22]. Specifically, they introduced a distinct intermediate IND-1CCA-MAC game to demonstrate that OW-CPA KEMs are sufficient for TLS 1.3 in the ROM. They initially demonstrated that OW-CPA KEMs ensure the security of IND-1CCA-MAC when combined with a secure MAC in the ROM. Building on this, they used the security of IND-1CCA-MAC to establish the security of TLS 1.3 in the standard model. It is important to note that the IND-1CCA-MAC game functions merely as an intermediate step in the overall proof.

However, they only proved that OW-CPA KEMs can derive IND-1CCA-MAC security with a secure MAC in the ROM [29]. They did not extend their proof to the QROM. Also, the bound of the ROM proof is very much non-tight, with $\epsilon_R \approx O(1/q^6)\epsilon_A$ for OW-CPA KEMs to prove IND-1CCA-MAC secure, where ϵ_R (resp. ϵ_A) is the advantage of the reduction R (resp. adversary A) breaking the

OW-CPA security of the underlying KEM (resp. the IND-1CCA-MAC security), and q is the number of $\mathcal{A}$'s queries to the RO.

CPA-Secure KEMs Are Sufficient for PQ TLS 1.3: Building on [29], B. Zhou, H. Jiang, and Y. Zhao [57] showed that standard CPA-secure KEMs are sufficient to guarantee the security of PQ TLS 1.3 in practice, see Table. 8. Specifically, they [57] revisit the proof in [29] implies that IND-1CCA-MAC* (a restricted version of IND-1CCA-MAC) is sufficient for the full proof. They [57] improved the ROM reduction in [29] from an $O(1/q^6)$-loss to an $O(1/q)$-loss for standard IND-CPA KEMs, which can be instantiated by ML-KEM.PKE [40]. Additionally, They [57] improved the ROM reduction in [29] from an $O(1/q^6)$-loss to $O(1)$-loss for rigid D-OW-CPA KEM that can be instantiated by Classic McEliece.PKE [2] and NTRU.PKE [17]. Here, rigid D-OW-CPA KEMs denote KEMs that are constructed by applying a simple transform to a rigid one-way secure deterministic PKE, as shown in Fig. 11). In particular, the NIST-PQC Round-3 Finalist NTRU [17] and the NIST-PQC Round-4 Candidate Classic McEliece [2] are based on rigid one-way secure deterministic PKEs, which can be transformed into the corresponding D-OW-CPA KEMs. Moreover, they [57] first prove the security of IND-1CCA-MAC* from OW-CPA/IND-CPA/D-OW-CPA KEMs in the QROM. Finally, they [57] show that if the IND-1CCA-MAC* security is satisfied, then the MultiStage [22] security of TLS 1.3 handshake protocol is satisfied in the standard model. In particular, the reduction for TLS 1.3 from IND-1CCA-MAC* exhibits the same tightness as the reduction given by [29] for TLS 1.3 from IND-1CCA-MAC or 1CCA KEM. Putting everything together, they [57] prove that if the underlying KEM is OW-CPA/IND-CPA/D-OW-CPA secure, then the TLS 1.3 handshake protocol is secure in the MultiStage model with a much tighter ROM proof and the first QROM proof.

Table 8. Reduction tightness of the intermediate game IND-1CCA-MAC*.

Underlying KEM	Reduction Tightness[a]	Model
OW-CPA [29]	$\epsilon_R \approx O(1/q^6)\epsilon_A$	ROM
OW-CPA [57]	$\epsilon_R \approx O(1/q^2)\epsilon_A$	ROM
IND-CPA [57]	$\epsilon_R \approx O(1/q)\epsilon_A$	ROM
D-OW-CPA [57]	$\epsilon_R \approx O(1)\epsilon_A$	ROM
OW-CPA [57]	$\epsilon_R \approx O(1/q^4)\epsilon_A^2$	QROM
IND-CPA [57]	$\epsilon_R \approx O(1/q^2)\epsilon_A^2$	QROM
D-OW-CPA [57]	$\epsilon_R \approx O(1/q^2)\epsilon_A^2$	QROM

In [29], they actually prove IND-1CCA-MAC, which implies the security of IND-1CCA-MAC[a]. Essentially, IND-1CCA-MAC* is sufficient for the security proof of TLS 1.3, see [57] for details.

5.2   Construction of CPA KEMs

- CPA-I: One can easily construct OW-CPA (D-OW-CPA) KEMs based on the CPA-I transform Fig. 11 from OW-CPA (rigid deterministic OW-CPA) secure PKEs in the standard model. Furthermore, one can easily construct IND-CPA KEMs based on the CPA-I transform in Fig. 11 from IND CPA secure PKEs in the standard model. In particular, one can construct the IND-CPA KEM from ML-KEM.PKE [40] and rigid D-OW-CPA KEM from Classic McEliece.PKE [2] and NTRU.PKE [17] based on the CPA-I transform.
- CPA-II: One can also construct IND-CPA KEMs based on the CPA-II transform in Fig. 11 from OW-CPA secure PKEs in the ROM/QROM model.

Encaps(pk)		Decaps(sk, c)	
1 :	$m \leftarrow\!\!\$\ \mathcal{M}$	1 :	$m' = \mathrm{dec}'(\mathsf{sk}, c)$
2 :	$c \leftarrow\!\!\$\ \mathrm{enc}'(\mathsf{pk}, m)$	2 :	**if** $m' = \bot$
3 :	$K := m$ CPA-I	3 :	**return** $\bot$
4 :	$K := H(m)$ CPA-II	4 :	**else return** $K := m'$ CPA-I
5 :	**return** (K, c)	5 :	**else return** $K := H(m')$ CPA-II

Fig. 11. The construction of CPA KEMs from PKEs

5.3   Practical Efficiency Impact for PQ TLS 1.3

As shown in Fig. 12, the most straightforward method to construct a secure TLS 1.3 is to use an OW-CPA/IND-CPA secure KEM, which does not require the redundant T (T_{CH}, T_H, T_{RH}) transformation [29,32] or FO transformation [24,28] to achieve IND-1CCA security. Directly using the CPA KEM based on ML.KEM.PKE [40] as in Fig. 11 (CPA-I) can bring a significant speed improvement, see Table 9. In particular, for decapsulation, there is a 6X speedup over using T_{CH}, T_{RH}, and a 20X speedup over using FO.

Security Loss: IND-1CCA KEMs Versus CPA KEMs. The results in [57] show that the reduction limits for IND-1CCA-MAC* of CPA KEMs exhibit the same tightness as those 1CCA KEMs of PKEs [32]. We also note that CPA KEMs in Fig. 11 can be tightly reduced to CPA PKEs. Therefore, if one considers the complete reduction from the CPA security of the underlying PKE to the MultiStage security of the resulting TLS 1.3, reduction in [57] for TLS 1.3 with CPA KEM has the same tightness as the currently tightest reduction for TLS 1.3 with 1CCA KEM given by [32].

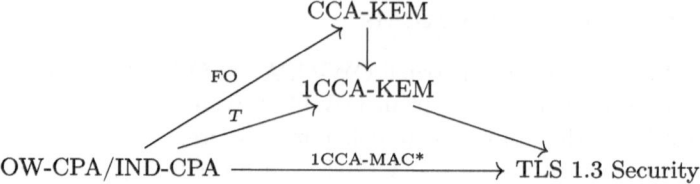

Fig. 12. Diagram of the process for constructing TLS 1.3 using KEMs based on different security assumptions.

Table 9. Benchmark of Encaps and Decaps for ML-KEM [40] with different transforms using liboqs (AVX2 enabled, NIST security level I) on system specs: Intel(R) Core(TM) i9-10900X CPU @ 3.7 GHz, 32.0 GB RAM, 64-bit OS.

Algorithm	CPA-I	T_{RH}	T_{CH}	FO
Encaps (μs)	5.35	7.255	7.682	7.666
Decaps (μs)	0.366	2.274	2.277	7.428

5.4   KEMTLS

KEMTLS [46] utilizes post-quantum KEMs to provide post-quantum authenticated key exchange (AKE) in TLS 1.3 without signing messages. The main idea of KEMTLS is based on the observation that signing messages between the client and server is sufficient but not necessary for authentication, one can use a KEM to implicitly authentication. This is done by using a KEM to prove to the client that the server knows a secret key corresponding to its public verification key. Moreover, PQ secure KEM such as ML-KEM [40] is more efficient and compact compared to PQ SIG such as ML-DSA [39]. For PQ TLS 1.3 [46], it has been shown that IND-1CCA security is required for the substituted KEMs. However, whether CPA security is sufficient for KEMTLS remains an open question. It is possible to prove a similar result for KEMTLS as in [57], but could result in a bigger security loss.

References

1. Open-quantum-safe OpenSSL (2024). https://github.com/open-quantum-safe/openssl
2. Albrecht, M.R., et al.: Classic McEliece, Technical report, National Institute of Standards and Technology (2020). https://csrc.nist.gov/Projects/post-quantum-cryptography/post-quantum-cryptography-standardization/round-3-submissions
3. Ambainis, A., Hamburg, M., Unruh, D.: Quantum security proofs using semi-classical oracles. In: Advances in Cryptology–CRYPTO 2019: 39th Annual International Cryptology Conference, Santa Barbara, CA, USA, August 18–22, 2019, Proceedings, Part II 39, pp. 269–295. Springer (2019)
4. Ambainis, A., Hamburg, M., Unruh, D.: Quantum security proofs using semi-classical oracles. In: Boldyreva, A., Micciancio, D. (eds.) Advances in Cryptology

– CRYPTO 2019, Part II. LNCS, vol. 11693, pp. 269–295. Springer, Heidelberg, Germany, Santa Barbara, CA, USA (2019)

5. Ambainis, A., Rosmanis, A., Unruh, D.: Quantum attacks on classical proof systems: The hardness of quantum rewinding. In: 55th Annual Symposium on Foundations of Computer Science, pp. 474–483. IEEE Computer Society Press, Philadelphia, PA, USA (2014)

6. Angel, Y., Dowling, B., Hülsing, A., Schwabe, P., Weber, F.J.: Post quantum noise. In: Yin, H., Stavrou, A., Cremers, C., Shi, E. (eds.) ACM CCS 2022: 29th Conference on Computer and Communications Security, pp. 97–109. ACM Press, Los Angeles, CA, USA (2022)

7. Azouaoui, M., Bronchain, O., Hoffmann, C., Kuzovkova, Y., Schneider, T., Standaert, F.X.: Systematic study of decryption and re-encryption leakage: the case of Kyber. In: Balasch, J., O'Flynn, C. (eds.) COSADE 2022: 13th International Workshop on Constructive Side-Channel Analysis and Secure Design. LNCS, vol. 13211, pp. 236–256. Springer, Heidelberg (2022)

8. Bellare, M., Rogaway, P.: Random oracles are practical: a paradigm for designing efficient protocols. In: Denning, D.E., Pyle, R., Ganesan, R., Sandhu, R.S., Ashby, V. (eds.) ACM CCS 93: 1st Conference on Computer and Communications Security, pp. 62–73. ACM Press, Fairfax, Virginia, USA (1993)

9. Bindel, N., Hamburg, M., Hövelmanns, K., Hülsing, A., Persichetti, E.: Tighter proofs of CCA security in the quantum random oracle model. In: Hofheinz, D., Rosen, A. (eds.) TCC 2019: 17th Theory of Cryptography Conference, Part II. LNCS, vol. 11892, pp. 61–90. Springer, Heidelberg (2019)

10. Boneh, D., Dagdelen, Ö., Fischlin, M., Lehmann, A., Schaffner, C., Zhandry, M.: Random oracles in a quantum world. In: Lee, D.H., Wang, X. (eds.) Advances in Cryptology – ASIACRYPT 2011. LNCS, vol. 7073, pp. 41–69. Springer, Heidelberg (2011)

11. Bos, J.W., et al.: Crystals - Kyber: a CCA-secure module-lattice-based KEM. In: 2018 IEEE European Symposium on Security and Privacy (EuroS&P), pp. 353–367 (2017)

12. Boyd, C., Cliff, Y., Nieto, J.G., Paterson, K.G.: Efficient one-round key exchange in the standard model. In: Mu, Y., Susilo, W., Seberry, J. (eds.) Information Security and Privacy, 13th Australasian Conference - ACISP 2008. LNCS, vol. 5107, pp. 69–83. Springer, Verlag (2008)

13. Brendel, J., Fiedler, R., Günther, F., Janson, C., Stebila, D.: Post-quantum asynchronous deniable key exchange and the signal handshake. In: Hanaoka, G., Shikata, J., Watanabe, Y. (eds.) PKC 2022: 25th International Conference on Theory and Practice of Public Key Cryptography, Part II. LNCS, vol. 13178, pp. 3–34. Springer, Heidelberg, Germany, Virtual Event (2022)

14. Brendel, J., Fischlin, M., Günther, F., Janson, C.: PRF-ODH: Relations, instantiations, and impossibility results. In: Katz, J., Shacham, H. (eds.) Advances in Cryptology – CRYPTO 2017, Part III. LNCS, vol. 10403, pp. 651–681. Springer, Heidelberg, Germany, Santa Barbara, CA, USA (2017)

15. Chen, J., Wang, Y., Chen, R., Huang, X., Peng, W.: Tighter proofs for PKE-to-KEM transformation in the quantum random oracle model. In: Chung, K., Sasaki, Y. (eds.) ASIACRYPT 2024. LNCS, vol. 15486, pp. 101–133. Springer, Singapore (2024)

16. Cramer, R., Shoup, V.: Design and analysis of practical public-key encryption schemes secure against adaptive chosen ciphertext attack. SIAM J. Comput. **33**(1), 167–226 (2003)

17. Danba, O., et al.: NTRU, Technical report, National Institute of Standards and Technology (2020). https://csrc.nist.gov/Projects/post-quantum-cryptography/post-quantum-cryptography-standardization/round-3-submissions

18. Dent, A.W.: A designer's guide to KEMs. In: Paterson, K.G. (ed.) 9th IMA Conference in Coding and Cryptography, pp. 133–151. LNCS, vol. 2898. Springer-Verlag (2003)

19. Don, J., Fehr, S., Majenz, C.: The measure-and-reprogram technique 2.0: multiround Fiat-Shamir and more. In: Micciancio, D., Ristenpart, T. (eds.) Advances in Cryptology – CRYPTO 2020, Part III. LNCS, vol. 12172, pp. 602–631. Springer, Heidelberg, Germany, Santa Barbara, CA, USA (2020)

20. Don, J., Fehr, S., Majenz, C., Schaffner, C.: Security of the Fiat-Shamir transformation in the quantum random-oracle model. In: Boldyreva, A., Micciancio, D. (eds.) Advances in Cryptology – CRYPTO 2019, Part II. LNCS, vol. 11693, pp. 356–383. Springer, Heidelberg, Germany, Santa Barbara, CA, USA (2019)

21. Don, J., Fehr, S., Majenz, C., Schaffner, C.: Online-extractability in the quantum random-oracle model. In: Dunkelman, O., Dziembowski, S. (eds.) Advances in Cryptology – EUROCRYPT 2022, Part III. LNCS, vol. 13277, pp. 677–706. Springer, Heidelberg, Germany, Trondheim, Norway (2022)

22. Dowling, B., Fischlin, M., Günther, F., Stebila, D.: A cryptographic analysis of the TLS 1.3 handshake protocol. J. Cryptol. **34**(4), 37 (2021)

23. Fujioka, A., Suzuki, K., Xagawa, K., Yoneyama, K.: Strongly secure authenticated key exchange from factoring, codes, and lattices. Des. Codes Crypt. **76**(3), 469–504 (2015)

24. Fujisaki, E., Okamoto, T.: Secure integration of asymmetric and symmetric encryption schemes. In: Wiener, M.J. (ed.) Advances in Cryptology – CRYPTO'99. LNCS, vol. 1666, pp. 537–554. Springer, Heidelberg, Germany, Santa Barbara, CA, USA (1999)

25. Fujisaki, E., Okamoto, T.: Secure integration of asymmetric and symmetric encryption schemes. J. Cryptol. **26**(1), 80–101 (2013)

26. Gay, R., Hofheinz, D., Kohl, L.: Kurosawa-desmedt meets tight security. In: Katz, J., Shacham, H. (eds.) Advances in Cryptology – CRYPTO 2017, Part III. LNCS, vol. 10403, pp. 133–160. Springer, Heidelberg, Germany, Santa Barbara, CA, USA (2017)

27. Ge, J., Liao, H., Xue, R.: Measure-rewind-extract: tighter proofs of one-way to hiding and CCA security in the quantum random oracle model. Cryptology ePrint Archive, Paper 2024/777 (2024). https://eprint.iacr.org/2024/777

28. Hofheinz, D., Hövelmanns, K., Kiltz, E.: A modular analysis of the Fujisaki-Okamoto transformation. In: Kalai, Y., Reyzin, L. (eds.) TCC 2017: 15th Theory of Cryptography Conference, Part I. LNCS, vol. 10677, pp. 341–371. Springer, Heidelberg, Germany, Baltimore, MD, USA (2017)

29. Huguenin-Dumittan, L., Vaudenay, S.: On IND-qCCA security in the ROM and its applications - CPA security is sufficient for TLS 1.3. In: Dunkelman, O., Dziembowski, S. (eds.) Advances in Cryptology – EUROCRYPT 2022, Part III. LNCS, vol. 13277, pp. 613–642. Springer, Heidelberg, Germany, Trondheim, Norway (2022)

30. Hülsing, A., Rijneveld, J., Song, F.: Mitigating multi-target attacks in hash-based signatures. In: Cheng, C.M., Chung, K.M., Persiano, G., Yang, B.Y. (eds.) PKC 2016: 19th International Conference on Theory and Practice of Public Key Cryptography, Part I. LNCS, vol. 9614, pp. 387–416. Springer, Heidelberg, Germany, Taipei, Taiwan (2016)

31. Jean-Sébastien, C., Handschuh, H., Joye, M., Paillier, P., Pointcheval, D., Tymen, C.: GEM: a generic chosen-ciphertext secure encryption method. In: Preneel, B. (ed.) Topics in Cryptology – CT-RSA 2002, pp. 263–276. Springer, Berlin Heidelberg, Berlin, Heidelberg (2002)

32. Jiang, H., Ma, Z., Zhang, Z.: Post-quantum security of key encapsulation mechanism against CCA attacks with a single decapsulation query. In: Guo, J., Steinfeld, R. (eds.) Advances in Cryptology – ASIACRYPT 2023, Part IV. LNCS, vol. 14441, pp. 434–468. Springer, Heidelberg, Germany, Guangzhou, China (2023)

33. Jiang, H., Zhang, Z., Chen, L., Wang, H., Ma, Z.: IND-CCA-secure key encapsulation mechanism in the quantum random oracle model, revisited. In: Shacham, H., Boldyreva, A. (eds.) Advances in Cryptology – CRYPTO 2018, Part III. LNCS, vol. 10993, pp. 96–125. Springer, Heidelberg, Germany, Santa Barbara, CA, USA (2018)

34. Jiang, H., Zhang, Z., Ma, Z.: Tighter security proofs for generic key encapsulation mechanism in the quantum random oracle model. In: Ding, J., Steinwandt, R. (eds.) Post-Quantum Cryptography - 10th International Conference, PQCrypto 2019, pp. 227–248. Springer, Heidelberg, Germany, Chongqing, China (2019)

35. Jiang, H., Zhang, Z., Ma, Z.: On the non-tightness of measurement-based reductions for key encapsulation mechanism in the quantum random oracle model. In: Tibouchi, M., Wang, H. (eds.) Advances in Cryptology – ASIACRYPT 2021, Part I. LNCS, vol. 13090, pp. 487–517. Springer, Heidelberg, Germany, Singapore (2021)

36. Kuchta, V., Sakzad, A., Stehlé, D., Steinfeld, R., Sun, S.F.: Measure-rewind-measure: tighter quantum random oracle model proofs for one-way to hiding and CCA security. In: Canteaut, A., Ishai, Y. (eds.) EUROCRYPT 2020, pp. 703–728. Springer, Cham (2020)

37. Naehrig, M., et al.: FrodoKEM learning with errors key encapsulation (2021). https://frodokem.org/files/FrodoKEM-specification-20210604.pdf

38. National Institute for Standards and Technology: Post-quantum cryptography project (2022). https://csrc.nist.gov/Projects/post-quantum-cryptography/round-4-submissions

39. National Institute of Standards and Technology: Module-lattice-based digital signature standard. FIPS 204, U.S. Department of Commerce, Gaithersburg, MD (2024)

40. National Institute of Standards and Technology: Module-lattice-based key-encapsulation mechanism standard. FIPS 203, U.S. Department of Commerce, Gaithersburg, MD (2024)

41. National Institute of Standards and Technology: Stateless hash-based digital signature standard. FIPS 205, U.S. Department of Commerce, Gaithersburg, MD (2024)

42. Nielsen, M.A., Chuang, I.L.: Quantum Computation and Quantum Information, 2nd edn. Cambridge University Press (2000)

43. Okamoto, T., Pointcheval, D.: REACT: rapid enhanced-security asymmetric cryptosystem transform. In: Naccache, D. (ed.) Topics in Cryptology – CT-RSA 2001, pp. 159–174. Springer, Berlin, Heidelberg (2001)

44. Rackoff, C., Simon, D.: Non-interactive zero-knowledge proof of knowledge and chosen ciphertext attack. In: Feigenbaum, J. (ed.) Advances in Cryptology – CRYPTO 1991. LNCS, vol. 576, pp. 433–444. Springer (1992)

45. Saito, T., Xagawa, K., Yamakawa, T.: Tightly-secure key-encapsulation mechanism in the quantum random oracle model. In: Nielsen, J.B., Rijmen, V. (eds.) Advances in Cryptology – EUROCRYPT 2018, Part III. LNCS, vol. 10822, pp. 520–551. Springer, Heidelberg, Germany, Tel Aviv, Israel (2018)

46. Schwabe, P., Stebila, D., Wiggers, T.: Post-quantum TLS without handshake signatures. In: Ligatti, J., Ou, X., Katz, J., Vigna, G. (eds.) ACM CCS 2020: 27th Conference on Computer and Communications Security, pp. 1461–1480. ACM Press, Virtual Event, USA (2020)

47. Schwabe, P., Stebila, D., Wiggers, T.: More efficient post-quantum KEMTLS with pre-distributed public keys. In: Bertino, E., Shulman, H., Waidner, M. (eds.) ESORICS 2021: 26th European Symposium on Research in Computer Security, Part I. LNCS, vol. 12972, pp. 3–22. Springer, Heidelberg, Germany, Darmstadt, Germany (2021)

48. Shor, P.W.: Algorithms for quantum computation: discrete logarithms and factoring. In: Proceedings 35th Annual Symposium on Foundations of Computer Science, pp. 124–134 (1994)

49. Targhi, E.E., Unruh, D.: Post-quantum security of the Fujisaki-Okamoto and OAEP transforms. In: Theory of Cryptography Conference (2016). https://api.semanticscholar.org/CorpusID:11686611

50. Ueno, R., Xagawa, K., Tanaka, Y., Ito, A., Takahashi, J., Homma, N.: Curse of re-encryption: a generic power/EM analysis on post-quantum KEMs. IACR Trans. Cryptogr. Hardw. Embed. Syst. **2022**, 296–322 (2021)

51. Unruh, D.: Revocable quantum timed-release encryption. In: Nguyen, P.Q., Oswald, E. (eds.) EUROCRYPT 2014, pp. 129–146. Springer, Berlin, Heidelberg (2014)

52. Unruh, D.: Non-interactive zero-knowledge proofs in the quantum random oracle model. In: Oswald, E., Fischlin, M. (eds.) Advances in Cryptology – EUROCRYPT 2015, Part II. LNCS, vol. 9057, pp. 755–784. Springer, Heidelberg, Germany, Sofia, Bulgaria (2015)

53. Unruh, D.: Towards compressed permutation oracles. In: Guo, J., Steinfeld, R. (eds.) Advances in Cryptology – ASIACRYPT 2023, Part IV. LNCS, vol. 14441, pp. 369–400. Springer, Heidelberg, Germany, Guangzhou, China (2023)

54. Zhandry, M.: How to construct quantum random functions. In: 53rd Annual Symposium on Foundations of Computer Science, pp. 679–687. IEEE Computer Society Press, New Brunswick, NJ, USA (2012)

55. Zhandry, M.: Secure identity-based encryption in the quantum random oracle model. In: Safavi-Naini, R., Canetti, R. (eds.) Advances in Cryptology – CRYPTO 2012. LNCS, vol. 7417, pp. 758–775. Springer, Heidelberg, Germany, Santa Barbara, CA, USA (2012)

56. Zhandry, M.: How to record quantum queries, and applications to quantum indifferentiability. In: Boldyreva, A., Micciancio, D. (eds.) Advances in Cryptology – CRYPTO 2019, Part II. LNCS, vol. 11693, pp. 239–268. Springer, Heidelberg, Germany, Santa Barbara, CA, USA (2019)

57. Zhou, B., Jiang, H., Zhao, Y.: CPA-secure KEMs are also sufficient for post-quantum TLS 1.3. In: Chung, K., Sasaki, Y. (eds.) 30th International Conference on the Theory and Application of Cryptology and Information Security, Kolkata, India, December 9–13, 2024, Proceedings, Part III. LNCS, vol. 15486, pp. 433–464. Springer, Singapore (2024)

Scloud$^+$: An Efficient LWE-Based KEM Without Ring/Module Structure

Anyu Wang[1,6,7], Zhongxiang Zheng[2], Chunhuan Zhao[3], Zhiyuan Qiu[4],
Guang Zeng[3], Ye Yuan[3], Changchun Mu[5], and Xiaoyun Wang[1,4,5,7,8](✉)

[1] Institute for Advanced Study, BNRist, Tsinghua University, Beijing, China
{anyuwang,xiaoyunwang}@tsinghua.edu.cn
[2] School of Computer and Cyber Sciences, Communication University of China,
Beijing, China
zhengzx@cuc.edu.cn
[3] Shield Lab, Huawei Technologies, Beijing, China
{zhaochunhuan,zengguang13,yuanye44}@huawei.com
[4] Shandong Institute of Blockchain, Jinan, China
qiuzhiyuan@sdibc.cn
[5] Digital Currency Institute, the People's Bank of China, Hong Kong, China
mchangchun@pbc.gov.cn
[6] Zhongguancun Laboratory, Beijing, China
[7] National Financial Cryptography Research Center, Beijing, China
[8] Key Laboratory of Cryptologic Technology and Information Security, School of
Cyber Science and Technology, Shandong University, Qingdao, China

Abstract. We present Scloud$^+$, an LWE-based key encapsulation mechanism (KEM). The key feature of Scloud$^+$ is its use of the unstructured-LWE problem (i.e., without algebraic structures such as rings or modules) and its incorporation of ternary secrets and lattice coding to enhance performance. A notable advantage of the unstructured-LWE problem is its resistance to potential attacks exploiting algebraic structures, making it a conservative choice for constructing high-security schemes. However, a key disadvantage of such schemes is their limited computational and communication efficiency. Scloud$^+$ utilizes ternary secrets and BW$_{32}$ lattice codes to enhance noise control and ensure robust error correction during decryption, enabling smaller parameters while maintaining low decryption failure probabilities. Equipped with these techniques, Scloud$^+$ exhibits a significant improvement in efficiency. When compared with FrodoKEM for parameter sets targeting 128, 192, and 256 bits of security respectively, Scloud$^+$ achieves practical performance with a public key size approximately $0.71 \sim 0.87$x and a ciphertext size approximately $0.56 \sim 0.78$x that of FrodoKEM. The encapsulation plus decapsulation time is approximately $0.74 \sim 0.84$x that of FrodoKEM.

Keywords: post-quantum cryptography · key encapsulation mechanism · learning with errors · lattice code · Barnes-Wall lattice

A. Wang and Z. Zheng—These authors contributed equally to this work.

X. Lu and C. J. Mitchell (Eds.): SSR 2024, LNCS 15559, pp. 147–174, 2025.
https://doi.org/10.1007/978-3-031-87541-0_7

1   Introduction

Shor's quantum algorithm [1] makes the migration to post-quantum public key cryptography inevitable. Among the post-quantum public key schemes, those based on the *learning with errors* (LWE) problem have gained particularly prevalent. The LWE problem was first introduced by Regev in 2005 [2], which roughly requires to solve a noisy linear equations modulo a known positive integer. Concretely, the goal of LWE is to find the secret vector $\mathbf{s} \in \mathbb{Z}_q^n$, given the instance $(\mathbf{A}, \mathbf{b} = \mathbf{As} + \mathbf{e})$ where $\mathbf{A} \in \mathbb{Z}_q^{m \times n}$ is an uniformly-random matrix and $\mathbf{e}$ is an error vector with small components sampled from some probability distributions over $\mathbb{Z}$. It has been proven that the LWE problem is at least as hard as the approximate *shortest vector problem* (SVP) and the *shortest independent vectors problem* (SIVP) on lattices, which remain difficult even in the sense of quantum computing. This reduction also establishes the average-case hardness of LWE, making it a strong candidate for cryptographic constructions.

Since Regev proposed the first LWE-based public key encryption algorithm [2], various schemes have been developed based on the hardness of LWE. These schemes can be broadly divided into two categories, depending on whether they introduce algebraic structure into the LWE problem. The first category includes schemes that base their security purely on the hardness of the LWE problem without any additional algebraic structure (referred to as *unstructured-LWE*), such as FrodoKEM [3]. The second category includes schemes built on variants of the LWE problem that incorporate algebraic structures (referred to as *structured-LWE*), such as the Ring-LWE problem [4,5] and the Module-LWE problem [6]. Examples of schemes in this category include CRYSTALS-Kyber [7], Saber [8], LAC [9], Aigis [10], and etc.

The primary benefit of introducing algebraic structure is that it enables the construction of LWE-based schemes that are more 'compact', i.e., more efficient in terms of computation and communication complexity. However, the algebraic structure also complicates the ability to reduce the hardness of the structured-LWE problems to the hardness of random lattice problems (which lack such structure), such as the approximate SVP and SIVP. Instead, it is known that these LWE variants can be reduced to hard problems on algebraically structured lattices. Specifically, the Ring-LWE problem has been shown to be at least as hard as the approximate Ideal-SVP [4], and the Module-LWE problem is known to be at least as hard as the approximate Module-SVP [6]. Unlike the approximate SVP and SIVP, the hardness of the approximate Ideal-SVP and approximate Module-SVP under quantum computation remains a topic of debate. In fact, several efficient quantum algorithms for the approximate Ideal-SVP have been discovered in recent years. In 2016, Cramer et al. demonstrated that the approximate Ideal-SVP for specific cyclotomic fields with an approximation factor of $2^{\tilde{O}(\sqrt{n})}$ can be solved in quantum polynomial time [11], whereas the best-known algorithm for the approximate SVP with the same approximation factor is still sub-exponential [12]. This result has been extended to general cyclotomic fields [13,15–17], and arbitrary number fields [17,18]. Although it seems unlikely that these approaches can be directly extended to address the approximate Module-SVP or the Ring-LWE/Module-LWE problems, the impact of algebraic structure on security remains unclear.

As a result, schemes based on the unstructured LWE problem, such as FrodoKEM, are often regarded as conservative choices for high-security applications [19], and are considered suitable for ensuring long-term confidentiality [20]. However, a key disadvantage of such schemes is that their computation and communication efficiency is much worse than that of structured-LWE-based schemes, posing a major obstacle to their deployment in practical systems. Thus, a natural question arises regarding how the performance of unstructured-LWE-based schemes can be improved.

Two primary approaches have been explored for improving the performance of LWE-based schemes. The first approach focuses on modifying the distribution of the secret in LWE for easier sampling. In the original LWE problem, the secret is uniformly distributed over $\mathbb{Z}_q^n$. Applebaum et al. [21] demonstrated that the LWE problem remains hard if both $\mathbf{s}$ and $\mathbf{e}$ follow a Gaussian distribution, and this idea was refined in Kyber and Aigis, where $\mathbf{s}$ and $\mathbf{e}$ are set to follow a binomial distribution. LAC [9] showed that using a ternary secret, where each entry is in $\{0, \pm 1\}$, can significantly reduce parameter sizes and improve the scheme's efficiency. It is worth noting that ternary secrets are also widely adopted in homomorphic encryption schemes such as BGV [22], BFV [23], and CKKS [24]. The second approach leverages error-correction methods for improved communication efficiency. One line of such work involves using linear error-correcting codes, such as BCH codes [9,25], LDPC codes [26], and others [27–29]. Another line of work involves lattice coding, such as the D_4 lattice [30], the E_8 lattice [31,32], the Leech lattice [33], and others [34]. Although these methods have proven effective in boosting the efficiency of LWE-based schemes, the challenge of how to achieve performance approaching optimal for unstructured LWE-based schemes persists as a significant and unresolved problem.

1.1 Our Contributions

We present Scloud$^+$, a key encapsulation mechanism (KEM) based on the unstructured-LWE problem. In a nutshell, Scloud$^+$ leverages ternary secrets and lattice coding to significantly enhance both computational and communication efficiency. Our detailed contributions are as follows.

Ternary Secret. For all parameters, Scloud$^+$ employs a ternary secret with a Hamming weight equal to half its length. We observe that in unstructured-LWE-based schemes, two of the most time-consuming operations are the generation of the matrix $\mathbf{A}$ and the matrix-vector multiplication, i.e., the computation of $\mathbf{As}$. Employing a ternary secret in Scloud$^+$ improves noise control during decryption, enabling the use of a smaller ciphertext modulus to ensure correct decryption. This provides an opportunity to reduce matrix sizes while maintaining the same security level, thereby facilitating faster matrix sampling and more efficient matrix-vector multiplication for implementation. Furthermore, fixing the

Hamming weight of the secret to half its length prevents it from becoming overly sparse, addressing potential security concerns for sparse-secret LWE.

Lattice Coding. Scloud$^+$ designs a robust error correction method based on BW$_{32}$ lattice codes, ensuring a smaller choice of parameters while maintaining the appropriate decryption failure probability. While the use of lattice coding is common in LWE-based constructions, previous schemes often involve lattice codes with dimensions 4 to 16. Although larger-dimensional lattice codes generally offer better signal-to-noise ratios and thus stronger error correction capabilities, they require specially designed labeling and delabeling processes to efficiently map the message to the lattice code or vice versa, which poses a challenge for high-dimensional lattice codes. For example, the 24-dimensional Leech lattice-based PKE proposed in [33] suffers from a lack of a labeling technique, making it impractical [34]. Scloud$^+$ overcomes this by designing efficient labeling and delabeling for Barnes-Wall lattice codes, enabling the use of 32-dimensional lattice codes for error correction without compromising the scheme's performance.

Security and Parameters. Scloud$^+$ provides three sets of parameters, targeting 128, 192, and 256 bits of security. Benefiting from the aforementioned techniques, we can achieve a very flexible parameter selection for Scloud$^+$, making it possible to maintain a moderate security margin (about 8 bits) for all sets of parameters while ensuring the conformed decryption failure probability. The security is comprehensively analyzed using potentially the most effective attacks for LWE, including primal attack, dual attack, and hybrid attack.

Combining the above, Scloud$^+$ achieves a remarkable improvement in its performance. Compared with FrodoKEM, Scloud$^+$ achieves a public key size approximately 0.71 – 0.87x, and a ciphertext size approximately 0.56 – 0.78x that of FrodoKEM, and achieves an encapsulation + decapsulation time approximately 0.74 – 0.84x that of FrodoKEM.

Table 1. Summary of the performance of Scloud$^+$.KEM.

Scheme	Scloud$^+$-128	Scloud$^+$-192	Scloud$^+$-256
Classical Security (bits)	136.07	200.42	263.11
Decryption Failure Rates	$2^{-134.21}$	$2^{-200.64}$	$2^{-265.74}$
Public Key Size (bytes)	7200	11136	18744
Cipertext Size (bytes)	5456	10832	16916
Shared Secret Size (bytes)	16	24	32
KeyGen (10^3cycles)	998	2226	3454
Encaps (10^3cycles)	1125	2418	2417
Decaps (10^3cycles)	1127	2417	3826

1.2   Related Works

FrodoKEM. FrodoKEM is the first Key Encapsulation Mechanism (KEM) based on the unstructured-LWE problem. One of its distinguishing features is that both the secret and error terms follow a rounded Gaussian distribution, closely resembling the discrete Gaussian distribution from the original LWE formulation. A key modification in Scloud$^+$ is the adoption of ternary secrets. We note that ternary secrets are commonly used in homomorphic encryption and NTRU schemes, and they are generally not believed to significantly weaken the hardness of the underlying problem. To ensure the security of our parameter choices, we perform a thorough security analysis of Scloud$^+$, incorporating potentially effective LWE attacks.

Lattice Coding for Unstructured-LWE-Based Schemes. Several efforts have been made to leverage lattice coding to reduce the communication cost of unstructured-LWE-based schemes. As previously mentioned, a theoretical analysis of applying the Leech lattice to unstructured-LWE-based schemes is provided in [33], but it suffers from a lack of a labeling technique. In [32], it is demonstrated that using the E_8 lattice can reduce the communication cost of FrodoKEM by 7%. Similarly, in [34], the authors analyze the impact of applying various lattice codes up to dimension 64 on FrodoKEM, achieving a communication cost reduction of approximately 7%. However, both [32] and [34] lack computational performance evaluations, leaving it uncertain whether these improvements can be practically implemented in real-world schemes.

1.3   Outline

Section 2 lays out the preliminaries. Section 3 delves into lattice coding and our tailored approach for Scloud$^+$. The PKE and KEM are detailed in Sect. 4 and Sect. 5, respectively. Section 6 discusses the parameters and security analysis. Finally, Sect. 7 assesses the performance of Scloud$^+$.

2   Preliminaries

2.1   Notations

- Vectors are denoted by bold lower-case letters, such as $\mathbf{v}$, while matrices are represented by bold upper-case letters, such as $\mathbf{A}$.
- The Hamming weight of a vector $\mathbf{v}$ is denoted as $w_H(\mathbf{v})$. For any integer $0 \leq n < 2^k$, we define $\mathrm{Bit}(n,k) = (b_0, \ldots, b_{k-1}) \in \{0,1\}^k$ as the base-2 expansion of n, where $n = \sum_{i=0}^{k-1} b_i \cdot 2^i$. The Hamming weight of the vector $\mathrm{Bit}(n,k)$ is denoted by $w_H(n)$.
- The inner product of vectors $\mathbf{u}, \mathbf{v} \in \mathbb{R}^n$ is expressed as $\langle \mathbf{u}, \mathbf{v} \rangle$, and the Euclidean norm of a vector $\mathbf{v}$ is expressed as $\|\mathbf{v}\| = \langle \mathbf{v}, \mathbf{v} \rangle$. The distance between a vector $\mathbf{v}$ and a set $\mathcal{S} \subseteq \mathbb{R}^n$ is defined by $\mathrm{dist}(\mathbf{v}, \mathcal{S}) := \min_{t \in \mathcal{S}} \|\mathbf{t} - \mathbf{v}\|$.

- For any real number $x \in \mathbb{R}$, we use $\lfloor x \rfloor$ to denote the greatest integer less than or equal to x, and $\lfloor x \rceil = \lfloor x + 1/2 \rfloor$ to denote the integer closest to x. Additionally, $\lfloor x \rceil_{\text{odd}}$ denotes the nearest integer to x, where any half-integer $n + 1/2$ is rounded to the closest odd integer. For integers n and $q > 0$, we denote by $[n]_q$ the integer such that $q \mid (n - [n]_q)$ and $0 \leq [n]_q < q$. These notations extend to vectors by applying the operations component-wise.
- Sampling from a distribution χ is denoted by $x \leftarrow \chi$. The uniform discrete distribution over a finite set $\mathcal{S}$ is denoted by $U(\mathcal{S})$.

2.2   Lattices and Related Problems

A lattice $\mathcal{L}$ of rank m and dimension n (with $m \leq n$) is a discrete subset of $\mathbb{R}^n$ defined as

$$\mathcal{L} = \{c_1 \mathbf{b}_1 + \cdots + c_m \mathbf{b}_m \mid c_i \in \mathbb{Z} \text{ for } 1 \leq i \leq m\}, \tag{1}$$

where $\mathbf{b}_1, \ldots, \mathbf{b}_m$ are linearly independent vectors in $\mathbb{R}^n$. The matrix $\mathbf{B} = (\mathbf{b}_1, \ldots, \mathbf{b}_m)$ is called a *basis* for $\mathcal{L}$, and we denote the lattice generated by $\mathbf{B}$ as $\mathcal{L}(\mathbf{B})$. A lattice $\mathcal{L}$ is said to be of *full rank* if $m = n$. We use $\lambda_1(\mathcal{L})$ to denote the norm of shortest non-zero lattice vector in $\mathcal{L}$.

The *fundamental parallelepiped* of a basis $\mathbf{B}$ is defined as

$$\mathcal{P}(\mathbf{B}) = \{a_1 \mathbf{b}_1 + \cdots + a_m \mathbf{b}_m \mid a_i \in [0, 1) \text{ for } 1 \leq i \leq m\}.$$

The *Voronoi cell* $\mathcal{V}(\mathcal{L})$ of a lattice $\mathcal{L}$ is the set of all points in $\mathbb{R}^n$ for which the closest lattice point is the origin $\mathbf{0}$.

Definition 1 (CVP). *Given a lattice $\mathcal{L}$ and a target vector $\mathbf{t} \in \mathbb{R}^n$, the Closest Vector Problem (CVP) asks to find a lattice point $\mathbf{v} \in \mathcal{L}$ that is closest to $\mathbf{t}$, i.e., $\|\mathbf{v} - \mathbf{t}\| \leq \|\mathbf{v}' - \mathbf{t}\|$ for all $\mathbf{v}' \in \mathcal{L}$.*

Definition 2 (BDD). *Given a lattice $\mathcal{L}$ and a target vector $\mathbf{t} \in \mathbb{R}^n$ such that $\text{dist}(\mathbf{t}, \mathcal{L}) \leq r$ for some radius r, the Bounded Distance Decoding (BDD) problem asks to find a lattice point $\mathbf{v} \in \mathcal{L}$ that is closest to $\mathbf{t}$, i.e., $\|\mathbf{v} - \mathbf{t}\| \leq \|\mathbf{v}' - \mathbf{t}\|$ for all $\mathbf{v}' \in \mathcal{L}$.*

Algorithms solve the above two problems are typically referred as Maximum Likelihood Decoding (MLD) algorithm and BDD algorithm (with decoding radius r) respectively.

2.3   Cryptographic Definitions

Definition 3 (PKE). *A public-key encryption (PKE) scheme is a tuple of algorithms (KeyGen, Enc, Dec) along with a message space $\mathcal{M}$.*

- *The probabilistic key generation algorithm KeyGen outputs a pair of public key and secret key (pk, sk).*
- *The probabilistic encryption algorithm Enc takes as input pk and a message $m \in \mathcal{M}$, and outputs a ciphertext c.*

– *The deterministic decryption algorithm* Dec *takes as input sk and c, and outputs either a message* $m' \in \mathcal{M}$ *or a special error symbol* $\perp \notin \mathcal{M}$.

A PKE scheme is δ-*correct* if $\mathbb{E}\left[\max_{m \in \mathcal{M}} \Pr[\text{Dec}(sk, \text{Enc}(pk, m)) \neq m]\right] \leq \delta$, where the expectation is taken over $(pk, sk) \leftarrow \text{KeyGen}()$, and the probability is taken over the randomness of Enc. The PKE scheme in our construction is considered to satisfy IND-CPA security *(indistinguishability under chosen plaintext attack)*. Specifically, the advantage of an adversary A is defined as

$$\mathbf{Adv}_{\text{PKE}}^{\text{CPA}}(\mathsf{A}) = \left| \Pr\left[b = b' \mid \begin{array}{l} (pk, sk) \leftarrow \text{KeyGen}(), (m_0, m_1, s) \leftarrow \mathsf{A}(pk) \\ b \leftarrow \{0,1\}, c^* \leftarrow \text{Enc}(pk, m_b), b' \leftarrow \mathsf{A}(pk, c^*, s) \end{array} \right] - \frac{1}{2} \right|.$$

Definition 4 (KEM). *A key encapsulation mechanism* (KEM) *is a tuple of algorithms* (KeyGen, Encaps, Decaps) *along with a key space* $\mathcal{K}$.

– *The probabilistic key generation algorithm* KeyGen *outputs a pair of public key and secret key* (pk, sk).
– *The probabilistic encapsulation algorithm* Encaps *takes as input pk and outputs an ciphertext c and a shared secret* $\mathbf{ss} \in \mathcal{K}$.
– *The deterministic decapsulation algorithm* Decaps *takes as input sk and c, and outputs a shared secret* $\mathbf{ss}' \in \mathcal{K}$.

A KEM is δ-*correct* if $\Pr[\text{Decaps}(sk, c) \neq \mathbf{ss} \mid (c, \mathbf{ss}) \leftarrow \text{Encaps}(pk)] \leq \delta$, where the probability is taken over $(pk, sk) \leftarrow \text{KeyGen}()$ and the randomness of *Encaps*. The KEM in our construction is considered to satisfy IND-CCA security *(indistinguishability under chosen ciphertext attack, or IND-CCA2)*. Specifically, the advantage of an adversary A is defined as

$$\mathbf{Adv}_{\text{KEM}}^{\text{CCA}}(\mathsf{A}) = \left| \Pr\left[b = b' \mid \begin{array}{l} (pk, sk) \leftarrow \text{KeyGen}(), b \leftarrow \{0,1\} \\ (c^*, \mathbf{ss}_0) \leftarrow \text{Encaps}(), \mathbf{ss}_1 \leftarrow U(\mathcal{K}) \\ b' \leftarrow \mathsf{A}^{\text{DECAPS}(\cdot)}(pk, \mathbf{ss}_b, c^*) \end{array} \right] - \frac{1}{2} \right|,$$

where the DECAPS oracle is defined as $\text{DECAPS}(\cdot) := \text{Decaps}(sk, \cdot)$, and the adversary A is not allowed to make queries with input c^*.

3 Lattice Coding and Barnes-Wall Lattices

In this section, we first introduce fundamental concepts related to lattice codes and Barnes-Wall lattices. We then present the specific lattice codes used in Scloud$^+$, along with our proposed efficient labeling and delabeling methods.

3.1 Lattice Codes

Definition 5 (Lattice Code). *Let* $\mathcal{L}_s, \mathcal{L}_c \subseteq \mathbb{R}^n$ *be two full-rank lattices such that* $\mathcal{L}_s \subseteq \mathcal{L}_c$. *A lattice code* $\mathcal{C}$ *(based on the nested lattices* $\mathcal{L}_s \subseteq \mathcal{L}_c$*) is defined as a subset of* $\mathcal{L}_c$ *that forms a complete set of representatives for the quotient group* $\mathcal{L}_c/\mathcal{L}_s$.

Given a basis $\mathbf{B}_s$ for $\mathcal{L}_s$, the set $\mathcal{C}$ is typically chosen to lie within the fundamental parallelepiped $\mathcal{P}(\mathbf{B}_s)$. The lattices $\mathcal{L}_s$ and $\mathcal{L}_c$ are commonly referred to as the *shaping lattice* and *coding lattice*, respectively.[1]

When a lattice code $\mathcal{C}$ is employed for message transmission over a noisy channel, the following steps are typically involved:

- *Labeling*: Each message $\mathbf{m} \in \mathcal{M}$ is mapped to a lattice vector $\mathbf{x} \in \mathcal{C}$, where $\mathcal{M}$ is the message space.
- *Lattice Decoding*: Given a noisy received vector $\mathbf{y} = \mathbf{x} + \mathbf{e} \in \mathbb{R}^n$, where $\mathbf{e}$ represents noise, this step employs an MLD or BDD algorithm. The algorithm takes $\mathbf{y}$ as the target vector and $\mathcal{L}_c$ as the lattice, producing a lattice vector $\mathbf{x}' \in \mathcal{C}$.
- *Delabeling*: The decoded lattice vector $\mathbf{x}' \in \mathcal{L}_c$ is mapped back to a message $\mathbf{m}' \in \mathcal{M}$, essentially reversing the labeling step.

Note that in the lattice decoding step, the output $\mathbf{x}'$ of the MLD or BDD algorithm may not initially fall within the lattice code $\mathcal{C}$. In such cases, an additional operation is required to reduce $\mathbf{x}'$ modulo $\mathcal{L}_s$ to ensure it belongs to $\mathcal{C}$. If $\mathcal{C}$ is chosen to lie within the fundamental parallelepiped $\mathcal{P}(\mathbf{B}_s)$, this reduction can be achieved by expressing $\mathbf{x}'$ in terms of the basis $\mathbf{B}_s$ and reducing it to lie within $\mathcal{P}(\mathbf{B}_s)$.

A sufficient condition for correct decoding (i.e., $\mathbf{m} = \mathbf{m}'$) is that the labeling function is injective, and the noise vector $\mathbf{e}$ lies either within the Voronoi cell of $\mathcal{L}_c$ (if an MLD algorithm is employed) or within a decoding radius r (if a BDD algorithm with radius r is employed). To guarantee injectivity of the labeling map, we require that $|\mathcal{M}| \leq |\mathcal{C}| = \frac{\det(\mathcal{L}_s)}{\det(\mathcal{L}_c)}$. In this work, we focus on the message space $\mathcal{M}$ consisting of all bit strings of length μ, which necessitates $\mu = \log_2(|\mathcal{M}|) \leq \log_2\left(\frac{\det(\mathcal{L}_s)}{\det(\mathcal{L}_c)}\right)$. The quantity $\frac{1}{n} \log_2\left(\frac{\det(\mathcal{L}_s)}{\det(\mathcal{L}_c)}\right)$ is referred to as the *code rate* of $\mathcal{C}$, representing the average number of encoded bits per dimension.

3.2   Barnes-Wall Lattices

The Barnes-Wall lattices form a sequence of lattices defined for dimensions n that are powers of 2. In addition to their lattice structure, it is known that Barnes-Wall lattices can be viewed as $\mathbb{Z}[\mathtt{i}]$-submodules of $\mathbb{Z}[\mathtt{i}]^{n/2}$, i.e., lattices over the Gaussian integers $\mathbb{Z}[\mathtt{i}]$ [35]. In this paper, we adopt this construction of Barnes-Wall lattices, which simplifies the labeling and delabeling processes we propose later. These lattices can be easily converted to lattices over the integers via a mapping from $\mathbb{C}^{n/2}$ to $\mathbb{R}^n$, as follows:

$$(a_1 + b_1\mathtt{i}, a_2 + b_2\mathtt{i}, \ldots, a_{n/2} + b_{n/2}\mathtt{i}) \mapsto (a_1, \ldots, a_{n/2}, b_1, \ldots, b_{n/2}), \quad (2)$$

where $a_i, b_i \in \mathbb{R}$ for $1 \leq i \leq n/2$. Under this mapping, we naturally extend the norm and distance notations, defined in Sect. 2 for real vectors, to complex vectors.

---

[1] In some literature, these are also called the *coarse lattice* and *fine lattice*.

Throughout the remainder of this section, we denote $\phi = 1 + i$, so that $\phi^{-1} = \frac{1}{2}(1 - i) = \frac{1}{2}\bar{\phi}$. The Barnes-Wall lattices can be defined recursively as follows.

Definition 6 (Barnes-Wall lattice). *For any positive integer $n = 2^k \geq 4$, the n-dimensional Barnes-Wall lattice BW_n is defined as*

$$\mathrm{BW}_n = \{[\mathbf{u}, \mathbf{u} + \phi\mathbf{v}] \mid \mathbf{u}, \mathbf{v} \in \mathrm{BW}_{n/2}\}, \tag{3}$$

with the initial case $\mathrm{BW}_2 = \mathbb{Z}[i]$.

Alternatively, it can be deduced that the Barnes-Wall lattices can also be expressed as

$$\mathrm{BW}_n = \{\mathbf{W}_n \cdot \mathbf{v} \mid \mathbf{v} \in \mathbb{Z}[i]^{\frac{n}{2}}\}, \text{ where } \mathbf{W}_n = \begin{pmatrix} 1 & 0 \\ 1 & \phi \end{pmatrix}^{\otimes(k-1)} \in \mathbb{C}^{\frac{n}{2} \times \frac{n}{2}} \tag{4}$$

is the Kronecker product of $(k-1)$ matrices $\begin{pmatrix} 1 & 0 \\ 1 & \phi \end{pmatrix}$.

For $n = 2, 4, 8$, the Barnes-Wall lattices correspond, under the mapping defined in (2), to $\mathbb{Z}^2$, D_4, and E_8, respectively. These are known to be the densest packings in their respective dimensions.

Lemma 1 ([36]). *For the Barnes-Wall lattice BW_n, where $n = 2^k \geq 2$, the following properties hold:*

(1) The minimum distance $\lambda_1 = \sqrt{\frac{n}{2}}$, and the packing radius $\rho = \frac{1}{2}\lambda_1 = \sqrt{\frac{n}{8}}$.
(2) The determinant $\det(\mathrm{BW}_n) = 2^{\frac{n}{4}(k-1)}$.
(3) $2^{\lfloor \frac{k}{2} \rfloor} \cdot \mathbb{Z}[i]^{\frac{n}{2}} \subseteq \mathrm{BW}_n$.

Decoding Algorithms for Barnes-Wall Lattices. Several algorithms have been proposed to decode Barnes-Wall lattices, which can be broadly categorized into three main types. The first category focuses on MLD. Efficient MLD algorithms are known for Barnes-Wall lattices of specific low dimensions, such as BW_4 and BW_8 [37,38]. The only known MLD algorithm for arbitrary Barnes-Wall lattices was proposed by Forney in 1988, utilizing the trellis representation of BW_n [36]. However, the computational complexity of this algorithm is exponential in n, making it impractical for dimensions $n \geq 32$, particularly in the context of constructing efficient cryptographic schemes. The second category addresses BDD for Barnes-Wall lattices. Micciancio and Nicolosi first demonstrated that BDD can be performed in polynomial time for Barnes-Wall lattices [35]. Further improvements to this approach have been made in subsequent works [39,40]. The third category focuses on list decoding for Barnes-Wall lattices, which seeks to output all lattice vectors within a ball of radius r around a given target vector $\mathbf{t}$. A comprehensive analysis of this approach has been provided by Grigorescu and Peikert [41].

Algorithm 1: BDD Algorithm for Barnes-Wall lattices

Input: A target vector $\mathbf{t} \in \mathbb{C}^{n/2}$ and the lattice BW_n
Output: A lattice vector $\mathbf{y} \in \mathrm{BW}_n$
1: **if** $n = 2$ **then**
2:    **return** $\lfloor \mathbf{t} \rceil$
3: **else**
4:    Write $\mathbf{t} = (\mathbf{t_1}, \mathbf{t_2})$ such that $\mathbf{t_1}, \mathbf{t_2} \in \mathbb{C}^{n/4}$
5:    Compute $\mathbf{y}_1 = \mathrm{BDD}(\mathbf{t_1}, \mathrm{BW}_{n/2})$, $\mathbf{y}_2 = \mathrm{BDD}(\mathbf{t_2}, \mathrm{BW}_{n/2})$
6:    Compute $\mathbf{z}_1 = \mathrm{BDD}(\phi^{-1}(\mathbf{t_2} - \mathbf{y}_1), \mathrm{BW}_{n/2})$, $\mathbf{z}_2 = \mathrm{BDD}(\phi^{-1}(\mathbf{t_1} - \mathbf{y}_2), \mathrm{BW}_{n/2})$
7:    Compute $\mathbf{x} = (\mathbf{y}_1, \mathbf{y}_1 + \phi\mathbf{z}_1)$, $\mathbf{x}' = (\mathbf{y}_2 + \phi\mathbf{z}_2, \mathbf{y}_2)$
8:    **if** $\|\mathbf{x} - \mathbf{t}\| < \|\mathbf{x}' - \mathbf{t}\|$ **then**
9:       **return** $\mathbf{x}$
10:   **else**
11:      **return** $\mathbf{x}'$
12:   **end if**
13: **end if**

In this paper, we focus on BDD for Barnes-Wall lattices, specifically using a variant of the BDD algorithm proposed in [39]. The decoding procedure is recursive, and its details are presented in Algorithm 1. Given an input target vector $\mathbf{t}$ such that $\mathrm{dist}(\mathbf{t}, \mathrm{BW}_n) \leq r = \sqrt{\frac{n}{8}}$, Algorithm 1 guarantees to return a lattice vector $\mathbf{y}$ satisfying $\|\mathbf{t} - \mathbf{y}\| \leq r$.

3.3   Lattice Coding Based on Barnes-Wall Lattices

In this subsection, we focus on the message space $\mathcal{M} = \{0,1\}^{\mu}$, and present lattice codes using Barnes-Wall Lattices.

For dimension $n = 2^k \geq 4$, let the coding lattice $\mathcal{L}_c = \mathrm{BW}_n$ and the shaping lattice $\mathcal{L}_s = 2^{\tau} \cdot \mathbb{Z}[\mathrm{i}]^{n/2}$, where $\tau \geq \lfloor \frac{k}{2} \rfloor$ is a positive integer. Then by Lemma 1, it has $\mathcal{L}_s \subseteq 2^{\lfloor \frac{k}{2} \rfloor} \cdot \mathbb{Z}[\mathrm{i}]^{n/2} \subseteq \mathcal{L}_c$. Denote $\mathcal{C}$ to be the lattice code defined based on the nested lattices $\mathcal{L}_s \subseteq \mathcal{L}_c$, where each vector of $\mathcal{C}$ is required to be within the region $\mathcal{P} = \{(a_1 + b_1\mathrm{i}, a_2 + b_2\mathrm{i}, \dots, a_{n/2} + b_{n/2}\mathrm{i}) \mid 0 \leq a_j, b_j < 2^{\tau} \text{ for all } 1 \leq j \leq n/2\}$, i.e., the fundamental parallelepiped with respect to the standard basis of $\mathcal{L}_s = 2^{\tau} \cdot \mathbb{Z}[\mathrm{i}]^{n/2}$. By Lemma 1 it has

$$|\mathcal{C}| = \frac{\det(\mathcal{L}_s)}{\det(\mathcal{L}_c)} = \frac{2^{\tau n}}{2^{\frac{n}{4}(k-1)}} = 2^{\tau n - \frac{n}{4}(k-1)}. \tag{5}$$

Next we assume that $\mu \leq \tau n - \frac{n}{4}(k-1)$ and present the explicit labeling and delabeling methods between $\mathcal{M}$ and $\mathcal{C}$.

Labeling. Firstly, we pad the message $\mathbf{m}$ by appending 0's to obtain a vector

$$\mathbf{m}' \in \{0,1\}^{\tau n - \frac{n}{4}(k-1)}. \tag{6}$$

Algorithm 2: The Labeling Method

Input: A message vector $\mathbf{m} \in \{0,1\}^\mu$
Input: Positive integers n, τ such that $n = 2^k \geq 4$, $\lfloor \frac{k}{2} \rfloor \leq \tau$, and $\mu \leq \tau n - \frac{n}{4}(k-1)$
Output: A lattice vector $\mathbf{x} \in \mathcal{C}$, where $\mathcal{C}$ is the lattice code defined based on the nested
    lattices $2^\tau \cdot \mathbb{Z}[\mathrm{i}]^{n/2} \subseteq \mathrm{BW}_n$
1: Pad $\mathbf{m}$ with 0's to obtain a vector $\mathbf{m}'$ of length $\tau n - \frac{n}{4}(k-1)$
2: Write $\mathbf{m}' = (\mathbf{u}_0, \mathbf{u}_1, \ldots, \mathbf{u}_{\frac{n}{2}-1})$ such that $\mathbf{u}_j \in \{0,1\}^{2\tau - w_H(j)}$
3: Compute $\mathbf{v} = (v_0, \ldots, v_{\frac{n}{2}-1})$, where $v_j = f_{2\tau - w_H(j)}(\mathbf{u}_j)$ for $0 \leq j < n/2$
4: **for** l from 1 to $k-1$ **do**
5:     Write $\mathbf{v} = (\mathbf{w}_1, \mathbf{w}_2, \ldots, \mathbf{w}_{\frac{n}{2^l}})$, where $\mathbf{w}_j \in \mathbb{Z}[\mathrm{i}]^{2^{l-1}}$
6:     Update $\mathbf{v} \leftarrow (\mathbf{w}_1, \mathbf{w}_1 + \phi\mathbf{w}_2, \mathbf{w}_3, \mathbf{w}_3 + \phi\mathbf{w}_4, \ldots, \mathbf{w}_{\frac{n}{2^l}-1}, \mathbf{w}_{\frac{n}{2^l}-1} + \phi\mathbf{w}_{\frac{n}{2^l}})$
7: **end for**
8: Compute $\mathbf{w} = [\mathbf{v}]_{2^\tau}$
9: **return** $\mathbf{w}$

Next, we consider the mapping of $\mathbf{m}'$ to a vector in the lattice $\mathcal{C}$, which is a two-step process. The first step maps $\mathbf{m}'$ to a vector $\mathbf{v} \in \mathbb{Z}[\mathrm{i}]^{n/2}$, while the second step maps $\mathbf{v}$ to a lattice vector $\mathbf{x} \in \mathcal{C}$. The detailed algorithm for this labeling method is outlined in Algorithm 2.

Step 1. Define a map $f_l : \{0,1\}^l \to \mathbb{Z}[\mathrm{i}]$ such that $f_l(\mathbf{u}) = a + b\mathrm{i}$, where $0 \leq a < 2^{\lceil \frac{l}{2} \rceil}, 0 \leq b < 2^{\lfloor \frac{l}{2} \rfloor}$. The first $\lceil \frac{l}{2} \rceil$ bits of $\mathbf{u}$ encode a, while the remaining $\lfloor \frac{l}{2} \rfloor$ bits encode b. Specifically, $a = \sum_{j=0}^{\lceil \frac{l}{2} \rceil - 1} u_j \cdot 2^j$ and $b = \sum_{j=\lceil \frac{l}{2} \rceil}^{l-1} u_j \cdot 2^j$, where $\mathbf{u} = (u_0, \ldots, u_{l-1})$.

Next, divide $\mathbf{m}'$ into $\frac{n}{2}$ sub-vectors, $\mathbf{m}' = (\mathbf{u}_0, \mathbf{u}_1, \ldots, \mathbf{u}_{\frac{n}{2}-1})$, where $\mathbf{u}_j \in \{0,1\}^{2\tau - w_H(j)}$. It can be verified that the sum of the lengths of $\mathbf{u}_j$ is

$$\sum_{0 \leq j < n/2} (2\tau - w_H(j)) = \tau n - \frac{n}{4}(k-1). \tag{7}$$

Finally, we map $\mathbf{m}'$ to $\mathbf{v} = (v_0, \ldots, v_{\frac{n}{2}-1}) \in \mathbb{Z}[\mathrm{i}]^{n/2}$, where $v_j = f_{2\tau - w_H(j)}(\mathbf{u}_j)$.

Step 2. This step computes $\mathbf{x}' = \mathbf{W}_n \cdot \mathbf{v}$, where $\mathbf{W}_n$ is defined in (4). Due to the tensor product structure of $\mathbf{W}_n$, this computation is performed iteratively as shown in Algorithm 2 (line 4 to line 7). Finally, we compute $\mathbf{x} = [\mathbf{x}']_{2^\tau}$, producing a lattice vector in $\mathcal{C}$.

Lemma 2. *The labeling in Algorithm 2 defines an injective map from the message space $\mathcal{M}$ to the lattice code $\mathcal{C}$.*

Proof. Let $\mathcal{S}_l$ denote the image space of the map f_l, i.e., $\mathcal{S}_l = \{a + b\mathrm{i} \mid a, b \in \mathbb{Z}, 0 \leq a < 2^{\lceil \frac{l}{2} \rceil}, 0 \leq b < 2^{\lfloor \frac{l}{2} \rfloor}\}$. It is evident that the first three lines of Algorithm 2 define an injective map from the message space $\mathcal{M}$ to the product space $\prod_{0 \leq j < n/2} \mathcal{S}_{2\tau - w_H(j)}$.

Next, we show that, for $\mathbf{v} \in \prod_{0 \leq j < n/2} \mathcal{S}_{2\tau - w_H(j)}$, the map $\mathbf{v} \mapsto [\mathbf{W}_n \cdot \mathbf{v}]_{2^\tau}$ is injective. Suppose there exist vectors $\mathbf{v}, \mathbf{v}' \in \prod_{0 \leq j < n/2} \mathcal{S}_{2\tau - w_H(j)}$ such that

---

Algorithm 3: The Delabeling Method

Input: Positive integers n, τ, μ such that $n = 2^k \geq 4$, $\lfloor \frac{k}{2} \rfloor \leq \tau$, $\mu \leq \tau n - \frac{n}{4}(k-1)$

Input: A lattice vector $\mathbf{w} \in \mathcal{C}$, where $\mathcal{C}$ is the lattice code defined based on the nested lattices $2^\tau \cdot \mathbb{Z}[\mathtt{i}]^{n/2} \subseteq \mathrm{BW}_n$

Output: A message vector $\mathbf{m} \in \{0,1\}^\mu$

1: **for** l from $k-1$ to 1 **do**
2:     Write $\mathbf{w} = (\mathbf{w}_1, \mathbf{w}_2, \ldots, \mathbf{w}_{n/2^l})$, where $\mathbf{w}_j \in \mathbb{Z}[\mathtt{i}]^{2^{l-1}}$ for $1 \leq j \leq n/2^l$
3:     Update $\mathbf{w} \leftarrow (\mathbf{w}_1, \phi^{-1}(\mathbf{w}_2 - \mathbf{w}_1), \mathbf{w}_3, \phi^{-1}(\mathbf{w}_4 - \mathbf{w}_3), \ldots)$
4: **end for**
5: Write $\mathbf{w} = (v_0, \ldots, v_{\frac{n}{2}-1})$
6: **for** j from 0 to $\frac{n}{2} - 1$ **do**
7:     Write $v_j = a + b\mathtt{i}$
8:     Compute $b' = [b]_{2^{\tau - \lceil w_H(j)/2 \rceil}}$, $a' = [a - (b - b')]_{2^{\tau - \lfloor w_H(j)/2 \rfloor}}$
9:     Set $v'_j = a' + b'\mathtt{i}$
10: **end for**
11: Compute $\mathbf{u}_j = f^{-1}_{2^{\tau - w_H(j)}}(v'_j)$ for $0 \leq j < n/2$
12: Set $\mathbf{m}' = (\mathbf{u}_0, \mathbf{u}_1, \ldots, \mathbf{u}_{\frac{n}{2}-1})$ and define $\mathbf{m}$ as the first μ bits of $\mathbf{m}'$
13: **return** $\mathbf{m}$

$\mathbf{W}_n \cdot \mathbf{v} = \mathbf{W}_n \cdot \mathbf{v}' \bmod 2^\tau$, i.e., $\mathbf{W}_n \cdot (\mathbf{v} - \mathbf{v}') = 0 \bmod 2^\tau$. Let $\mathbf{v} - \mathbf{v}' = (w_0, w_1, \ldots, w_{\frac{n}{2}-1})$. We will prove by induction that $w_j = 0$ for all $0 \leq j < \frac{n}{2}$.

Note that $\mathbf{W}_n$ is a lower triangular matrix, with the j-th diagonal entry given by $\phi^{w_H(j)}$. For $j = 0$, the condition $\mathbf{W}_n \cdot (\mathbf{v} - \mathbf{v}') = 0 \bmod 2^\tau$ implies $w_0 = 0 \bmod 2^\tau$. Writing $w_0 = a + b\mathtt{i}$, with $-2^\tau < a, b < 2^\tau$ (since $\mathbf{v}, \mathbf{v}' \in \prod_{0 \leq j < n/2} \mathcal{S}_{2^{\tau - w_H(j)}}$), it follows that $a = b = 0$. Now, assume that $w_0 = \cdots = w_{j-1} = 0$. We will show that $w_j = 0$. Since $\mathbf{W}_n$ is lower triangular, the condition $\mathbf{W}_n \cdot (\mathbf{v} - \mathbf{v}') = 0 \bmod 2^\tau$ implies $w_j \cdot \phi^{w_H(j)} = 0 \bmod 2^\tau$. If $w_H(j)$ is even, we have $\phi^{w_H(j)} = (\phi^2)^{w_H(j)/2} = (-2\mathtt{i})^{w_H(j)/2}$, so $w_j \cdot \phi^{w_H(j)} = 0 \bmod 2^\tau$ implies $w_j \cdot 2^{w_H(j)/2} = 0 \bmod 2^\tau$. Writing $w_j = a + b\mathtt{i}$, with $-2^{\tau - w_H(j)/2} < a, b < 2^{\tau - w_H(j)/2}$, it follows that $a = b = 0 \bmod 2^{\tau - w_H(j)/2}$, and hence $a = b = 0$. If $w_H(j)$ is odd, a similar argument shows that $w_j \cdot \phi \cdot 2^{(w_H(j)-1)/2} = 0 \bmod 2^\tau$. Writing $w_j = a + b\mathtt{i}$, where $|a| < 2^{\tau - (w_H(j)-1)/2}$ and $|b| < 2^{\tau - (w_H(j)+1)/2}$, we get $a - b = a + b = 0 \bmod 2^{\tau - (w_H(j)-1)/2}$. From $b = \frac{1}{2}((a + b) - (a - b))$, it follows that $b = 0 \bmod 2^{\tau - (w_H(j)-1)/2-1}$, and thus $b = 0$. Consequently, $a = 0 \bmod 2^{\tau - (w_H(j)-1)/2}$, implying $a = 0$.

Putting all these deductions together, we conclude that the labeling is injective, completing the proof. □

Delabeling. The delabeling is the reverse of the labeling, as described in Algorithm 3. It is important to note that the computation in line 8 of Algorithm 2 cannot be completely reversed due to the modulo operation. To address this, in the delabeling, we adjust the entries of the vector $\mathbf{w} = (v_0, \ldots, v_{\frac{n}{2}-1})$ so that each v_j belongs to $\mathcal{S}_{2^{\tau - w_H(j)}}$ (lines 6 to 10), where $\mathcal{S}_{2^{\tau - w_H(j)}}$ is defined in the proof of Lemma 2. In fact, this ensures that $\phi^{2\tau - w_H(j)}$ divides $(v_j - v'_j)$ and thus leads the following lemma.

Lemma 3. *The delabeling in Algorithm 3 is the inverse of the labeling in Algorithm 2.*

Proof. First, we show that the computation in lines 6 to 10 ensures that $\phi^{2\tau - w_H(j)}$ divides $(v_j - v'_j)$. Observe that $v_j - v'_j = (a + bi) - (a' + b'i) = (a - a' - (b - b')) + (b - b')\phi$. Then by $\phi^2 \mid 2$ and the definitions of a' and b' we can deduce that $\phi^{2\tau - w_H(j)} \mid (v_j - v'_j)$.

For any $\mathbf{v} \in \prod_{0 \leq j < n/2} \mathcal{S}_{2\tau - w_H(j)}$, let $\mathbf{w} = [\mathbf{W}_n \cdot \mathbf{v}]_{2^\tau}$ (corresponding to lines 4 to 8 in Algorithm 2). Let $\mathbf{W}_n^{-1} \cdot \mathbf{w} = (v_0, \ldots, v_{\frac{n}{2}-1})$ and $\mathbf{v}' = (v'_0, \ldots, v'_{\frac{n}{2}-1})$ such that $\mathbf{v}' \in \prod_{0 \leq j < n/2} \mathcal{S}_{2\tau - w_H(j)}$ and $\phi^{2\tau - w_H(j)} \mid (v_j - v'_j)$ (corresponding to lines 1 to 10 in Algorithm 3). It suffices to show that $\mathbf{v} = \mathbf{v}'$ to complete the proof.

Let $\boldsymbol{\delta} = (\delta_0, \ldots, \delta_{\frac{n}{2}-1}) = \mathbf{W}_n^{-1}\mathbf{w} - \mathbf{v}'$. Then $\phi^{2\tau - w_H(j)} \mid \delta_j$ and

$$\mathbf{W}_n \cdot (\boldsymbol{\delta} + \mathbf{v}') = \mathbf{W}_n \cdot \mathbf{v} \bmod 2^\tau. \tag{8}$$

Since each entry of the j-th column of $\mathbf{W}_n$ is divisible by $\phi^{w_H(j)}$, it follows that each entry of $\mathbf{W}_n \cdot \boldsymbol{\delta}$ is divisible by $\phi^{2\tau}$. Therefore, $\mathbf{W}_n \cdot \boldsymbol{\delta} = 0 \bmod 2^\tau$, and (8) implies that $\mathbf{W}_n \cdot \mathbf{v}' = \mathbf{W}_n \cdot \mathbf{v} \bmod 2^\tau$. By the same reasoning used in Lemma 2, we conclude that $\mathbf{v} = \mathbf{v}'$, which completes the proof. □

4   The IND-CPA-Secure PKE

Scloud$^+$.PKE consists of three algorithms: key generation, encryption, and decryption, which are outlined in Algorithm 4 to Algorithm 6. The algorithms utilize the following parameters:

- Moduli: powers of 2 integers $q > q_1, q_2$;
- Matrix size parameters: positive integers $m, n, \bar{m}, \bar{n}$;
- Secret weight parameters: h_1, h_2;
- Error parameters: η_1, η_2;
- Message length: $l_m \in \{128, 192, 256\}$.

Distributions and Sub-functions. Scloud$^+$.PKE involves the use of the central binomial distribution and the constant Hamming distribution.

Central Binomial Distribution. Let $\rho(\eta)$ denote the central binomial distribution with parameter η. For a random variable $X \leftarrow \rho(\eta)$, it can be expressed as $X = \sum_{i=1}^{\eta}(x_i - y_i)$, where $x_i, y_i \leftarrow U(\{0, 1\})$. In this scheme, we are interested in sampling a matrix $\mathbf{E} \leftarrow \rho(\eta)^{m \times n}$, generated by the sampling function CenBinom. This function takes random bits $\mathbf{r} \in \{0, 1\}^{256}$ and parameters (m, n) and η as

---

Algorithm 4: $\text{Scloud}^+.\text{PKE.KeyGen}()$

Output: Public key $pk \in \mathbb{Z}_q^{m \times \bar{n}} \times \{0,1\}^{128}$
Output: Secret key $sk \in \mathbb{Z}_q^{n \times \bar{n}}$
1: $\alpha \leftarrow \{0,1\}^{256}$
2: $(\text{seed}_\mathbf{A}, \mathbf{r}_1, \mathbf{r}_2) = F(\alpha) \in \{0,1\}^{128} \times \{0,1\}^{256} \times \{0,1\}^{256}$
3: $\mathbf{A} = \text{gen}(\text{seed}_\mathbf{A}) \in \mathbb{Z}_q^{m \times n}$
4: $\mathbf{S} = \Psi(\mathbf{r}_1, (n, \bar{n}), h_1) \in \mathbb{Z}^{n \times \bar{n}}$, $\mathbf{E} = \text{CenBinom}(\mathbf{r}_2, (m, \bar{n}), \eta_1) \in \mathbb{Z}^{m \times \bar{n}}$
5: $\mathbf{B} = \mathbf{A} \cdot \mathbf{S} + \mathbf{E} \in \mathbb{Z}_q^{m \times \bar{n}}$
6: **return** $pk = (\mathbf{B}, \text{seed}_\mathbf{A})$, $sk = \mathbf{S}$

Algorithm 5: $\text{Scloud}^+.\text{PKE.Enc}(pk, \mathbf{m}, \mathbf{r})$

Input: Public key $pk = (\mathbf{B}, \text{seed}_\mathbf{A}) \in \mathbb{Z}_q^{m \times \bar{n}} \times \{0,1\}^{128}$
Input: Message $\mathbf{m} \in \{0,1\}^l$
Input: Random coins $\mathbf{r} \in \{0,1\}^{256}$
Output: Ciphertext $\mathbf{C} \in \mathbb{Z}_{q_1}^{\bar{m} \times n} \times \mathbb{Z}_{q_2}^{\bar{m} \times \bar{n}}$
1: $\mathbf{A} = \text{gen}(\text{seed}_\mathbf{A})$
2: $(\mathbf{r}_1', \mathbf{r}_2') = F(\mathbf{r}) \in \{0,1\}^{256 \times 2}$
3: $\mathbf{S}' = \Phi(\mathbf{r}_1', (\bar{m}, m), h_2) \in \mathbb{Z}^{\bar{m} \times m}$
4: $\mathbf{E}' = (\mathbf{E}_1, \mathbf{E}_2) = \text{CenBinom}(\mathbf{r}_2', (\bar{m}, n + \bar{n}), \eta_2)$, where $\mathbf{E}_1 \in \mathbb{Z}^{\bar{m} \times n}$, $\mathbf{E}_2 \in \mathbb{Z}^{\bar{m} \times \bar{n}}$
5: $\mathbf{M} = \text{MsgEnc}(\mathbf{m}) \in \mathbb{Z}_q^{\bar{m} \times \bar{n}}$
6: $\mathbf{C}_1 = \mathbf{S}' \cdot \mathbf{A} + \mathbf{E}_1$, $\mathbf{C}_2 = \mathbf{S}' \cdot \mathbf{B} + \mathbf{E}_2 + \mathbf{M}$
7: $\bar{\mathbf{C}}_1 = \lfloor \frac{q_1}{q} \cdot \mathbf{C}_1 \rceil$, $\bar{\mathbf{C}}_2 = \lfloor \frac{q_2}{q} \cdot \mathbf{C}_2 \rceil_{\text{odd}}$
8: **return** $\mathbf{C} = (\bar{\mathbf{C}}_1, \bar{\mathbf{C}}_2)$

---

input, and outputs a matrix $\mathbf{E}$ drawn from $\rho(\eta)^{m \times n}$. Details of CenBinom are provided in Sect. 7.

Constant Hamming Distribution. Let $\mathcal{H}^{(m,n,h)}$ be the set of $m \times n$ matrices where each row contains exactly $(n - 2h)$ zeros, h ones, and h negative ones. Similarly, let $\mathcal{L}^{(m,n,h)}$ be the set of $m \times n$ matrices where each column contains exactly $(m - 2h)$ zeros, h ones, and h negative ones. In this scheme, we are interested in sampling matrices $\mathbf{S}' \leftarrow U(\mathcal{H}^{(m,n,h)})$ and $\mathbf{S} \leftarrow U(\mathcal{L}^{(m,n,h)})$. We define Φ and Ψ as two sampling functions that take random bits $\mathbf{r} \in \{0,1\}^*$ and parameters

---

Algorithm 6: $\text{Scloud}^+.\text{PKE.Dec}(sk, \mathbf{C})$

Input: Secret key $sk = \mathbf{S} \in \mathbb{Z}_q^{n \times \bar{n}}$
Input: Ciphertext $\mathbf{C} \in \mathbb{Z}_{q_1}^{\bar{m} \times n} \times \mathbb{Z}_{q_2}^{\bar{m} \times \bar{n}}$
Output: Message $\mathbf{m} \in \{0,1\}^l$
1: $\mathbf{C}_1' = \frac{q}{q_1} \cdot \bar{\mathbf{C}}_1$, $\mathbf{C}_2' = \frac{q}{q_2} \cdot \bar{\mathbf{C}}_2$
2: $\mathbf{D} = \mathbf{C}_2' - \mathbf{C}_1'\mathbf{S} \in \mathbb{Z}_q^{\bar{m} \times \bar{n}}$
3: **return** $\mathbf{m} = \text{MsgDec}(\mathbf{D}) \in \{0,1\}^l$

(m, n), h as input, and output matrices uniformly drawn from $\mathcal{H}^{(m,n,h)}$ and $\mathcal{L}^{(m,n,h)}$, respectively. Details of Φ and Ψ are provided in Sect. 7.

Sub-functions. Scloud$^+$.PKE employs a hash function $\mathbf{F} : \{0,1\}^{256} \rightarrow \{0,1\}^*$, and a function **gen** which generates a random $m \times n$ matrix $\mathbf{A}$ over $\mathbb{Z}_q$ using a seed $\mathbf{seed_A}$ as input. Additionally, the encoding and decoding functions MsgEnc and MsgDec are described below.

Algorithm 7: The MsgEnc Function

Input: Message $\mathbf{m} \in \{0,1\}^{l_m}$
Input: Parameters μ, τ and $q, \bar{m}, \bar{n}$ such that $32 \cdot \frac{l_m}{\mu} \leq \bar{m} \cdot \bar{n}$
Output: Matrix $\mathbf{M} \in \mathbb{Z}_q^{\bar{m} \times \bar{n}}$
1: Divide the message $\mathbf{m}$ into $\frac{l_m}{\mu}$ sub-vectors, $\mathbf{m}_j \in \{0,1\}^\mu$, where $1 \leq j \leq \frac{l_m}{\mu}$
2: **for** $j = 1$ to $\frac{l_m}{\mu}$ **do**
3:     Invoke Algorithm 2 (labeling) with input $\mathbf{m}_j$ and parameters $(2^k = 32, \tau)$ to obtain a vector $\mathbf{w}_j \in \mathcal{C}$
4:     Decompose $\mathbf{w}_j$ into $\mathbf{w}_j = \mathbf{u}_j + \mathbf{v}_j \mathrm{i}$, where $\mathbf{u}_j, \mathbf{v}_j \in \mathbb{Z}^{16}$
5: **end for**
6: Construct the vector $\mathbf{x} = (\mathbf{u}_1, \mathbf{v}_1, \mathbf{u}_2, \mathbf{v}_2, \dots) \in \mathbb{Z}^{32 \cdot \frac{l_m}{\mu}}$
7: Pad $\mathbf{x}$ with zeros to extend its length to $\bar{m}\bar{n}$
8: Compute the scaled vector $\mathbf{y} = (y_1, \dots, y_{\bar{m}\bar{n}}) = \frac{q}{2^\tau} \cdot \mathbf{x}$
9: Construct matrix $\mathbf{M}$ by setting the (i,j)-th element as $y_{\bar{n}(i-1)+j}$ for $1 \leq i \leq \bar{m}$
10: **return** $\mathbf{M}$

The MsgEnc and MsgDec Functions. The functions MsgEnc and MsgDec are constructed using the labeling, BDD, and delabeling algorithms outlined in Sect. 3. Specifically, we set the coding lattice to BW$_{32}$ (i.e., $2^k = 32$). The labeling and delabeling parameters, μ and τ, are chosen as $\mu = 64, 96, 64$ and $\tau = 3, 4, 3$ for message lengths $l_m = 128, 192, 256$, respectively. Note that for these choices of μ and τ, the relation $\mu = \tau \cdot 2^k - \frac{2^k}{4}(k-1)$ holds, implying that no padding is required during the labeling process. The detailed constructions of MsgEnc and MsgDec are provided in Algorithm 7 and Algorithm 8.

Correctness of the PKE Scheme. Let $\mathbf{F}_1 := \mathbf{C}'_1 - \mathbf{C}_1$ and $\mathbf{F}_2 := \mathbf{C}'_2 - \mathbf{C}_2$. Then during decryption, we have

$$\mathbf{D} = \mathbf{C}'_2 - \mathbf{C}'_1 \mathbf{S} = (\mathbf{C}_2 + \mathbf{F}_2) - (\mathbf{C}_1 + \mathbf{F}_1)\mathbf{S}$$
$$= \mathbf{S}'\mathbf{E} + (\mathbf{E}_2 + \mathbf{F}_2) - (\mathbf{E}_1 + \mathbf{F}_1)\mathbf{S} + \mathrm{MsgEnc}(\mathbf{m}).$$

Define $\mathbf{E}_{\mathrm{total}} := \mathbf{S}'\mathbf{E} + (\mathbf{E}_2 + \mathbf{F}_2) - (\mathbf{E}_1 + \mathbf{F}_1)\mathbf{S}$, then decryption is correct if $\mathrm{MsgDec}(\mathrm{MsgEnc}(\mathbf{m}) + \mathbf{E}_{\mathrm{total}}) = \mathbf{m}$.

According to Algorithm 8, $\mathrm{MsgEnc}(\mathbf{m}) + \mathbf{E}_{\mathrm{total}}$ can be truncated and partitioned into vectors $\boldsymbol{\omega}_j + \boldsymbol{\epsilon}_j$, where $1 \leq j \leq \frac{l_m}{\mu}$. The real and imaginary parts of

Algorithm 8: The `MsgDec` Function

Input: Matrix $\mathbf{M} \in \mathbb{Z}_q^{\bar{m} \times \bar{n}}$

Input: Parameters μ, τ, q, and l_m, such that $32 \cdot \frac{l_m}{\mu} \leq \bar{m} \cdot \bar{n}$

Output: Message $\mathbf{m} \in \{0,1\}^{l_m}$

1: Construct vector $\mathbf{y} = (y_1, \ldots, y_{\bar{m}\bar{n}})$ where $y_{\bar{n}(i-1)+j}$ is the (i,j)-th element of $\mathbf{M}$

2: Truncate $\mathbf{y}$ to form vector $\mathbf{x} \in \mathbb{Z}^{32 \cdot \frac{l_m}{\mu}}$

3: Update $\mathbf{x} \leftarrow \frac{2^\tau}{q} \cdot \mathbf{x}$

4: Partition $\mathbf{x}$ as $\mathbf{x} = (\mathbf{u}_1, \mathbf{v}_1, \mathbf{u}_2, \mathbf{v}_2, \ldots)$ such that $\mathbf{u}_j, \mathbf{v}_j \in \mathbb{Z}^{32}$

5: **for** $j = 1$ to $\frac{l_m}{\mu}$ **do**

6:     Compute $\mathbf{w}'_j = \mathbf{u}_j + \mathbf{v}_j \mathbf{i}$

7:     Invoke Algorithm 1 (BDD) on input $\mathbf{w}'_j$ to obtain lattice vector $\mathbf{w}_j \in \mathrm{BW}_{32}$

8:     Invoke Algorithm 3 (delabeling) with input $[\mathbf{w}_j]_{2^\tau}$ and parameters $(2^k = 32, \tau, \mu)$ to obtain $\mathbf{m}_j \in \{0,1\}^\mu$

9: **end for**

10: **return** $\mathbf{m} = (\mathbf{m}_1, \ldots, \mathbf{m}_{l_m/\mu})$

$\epsilon_j \in \mathbb{Z}[\mathbf{i}]^{16}$ correspond to components of $\mathbf{E}_{\text{total}}$, while those of $\omega_j \in \frac{q}{2^\tau} \cdot \mathrm{BW}_{32}$ correspond to components of $\mathtt{MsgEnc}(\mathbf{m})$. Thus, $\mathtt{MsgDec}(\mathtt{MsgEnc}(\mathbf{m}) + \mathbf{E}_{\text{total}}) = \mathbf{m}$ holds if $\left\| \frac{2^\tau}{q} \cdot \epsilon_j \right\| \leq r$ for all j, where $r = \sqrt{\frac{32}{8}} = 2$ is the decoding radius. It follows that

$$\Pr\left[\mathtt{MsgDec}(\mathtt{MsgEnc}(\mathbf{m}) + \mathbf{E}_{\text{total}}) = \mathbf{m}\right] = \Pr\left[\|\epsilon_j\| \leq \frac{2q}{2^\tau} \text{ for all } j\right]. \quad (9)$$

Next, we analyze the distribution of the error matrix $\mathbf{E}_{\text{total}}$ to approximate (9). Since $\mathbf{F}_1 = \frac{q}{q_1} \cdot \left\lceil \frac{q_1}{q} \cdot \mathbf{C}_1 \right\rceil - \mathbf{C}_1$ and $\mathbf{C}_1$ is pseudo-random based on the hardness of LWE, we assume that each component of $\mathbf{F}_1$ follows the distribution $\Omega_{\mathbf{F}_1} := U\left(\left\{-\frac{q}{2q_1} + 1, \cdots, \frac{q}{2q_1}\right\}\right)$. Similarly, we assume that each component of $\mathbf{F}_2$ follows the distribution $\Omega_{\mathbf{F}_2}$, which equals $\pm \frac{q}{2q_2}$ with probability $\frac{q_2}{2q}$, and equals each $j \in \left\{-\frac{q}{2q_2} + 1, \cdots, \frac{q}{2q_2} - 1\right\}$ with probability $\frac{q_2}{q}$. The variance of $\Omega_{\mathbf{F}_1}$ is $\frac{1}{12}\left(\frac{q^2}{q_1^2} - 1\right)$, and the variance of $\Omega_{\mathbf{F}_2}$ is $\frac{1}{12}\left(\frac{q^2}{q_2^2} + 2\right)$. Considering that $\mathbf{S} \leftarrow U(\mathcal{H}^{(m,n,h_1)})$, $\mathbf{S}' \leftarrow U(\mathcal{L}^{(m,n,h_2)})$, $\mathbf{E} \leftarrow \rho(\eta_1)^{m \times \bar{n}}$, and $(\mathbf{E}_1, \mathbf{E}_2) \leftarrow \rho(\eta_2)^{\bar{m} \times (n+\bar{n})}$, we deduce that each component of $\mathbf{E}_{\text{total}}$ follows a distribution χ_{total} with mean 0 and variance

$$\sigma_{\text{total}}^2 = 2h_2 \cdot \frac{\eta_1}{2} + \left(\frac{\eta_2}{2} + \frac{1}{12}\left(\frac{q^2}{q_2^2} + 2\right)\right) + 2h_1 \cdot \left(\frac{\eta_2}{2} + \frac{1}{12}\left(\frac{q^2}{q_1^2} - 1\right)\right). \quad (10)$$

As adopted in other schemes, we approximate the right-hand side of (9) using the discrete Gaussian distribution $\mathcal{D}_{\mathbb{Z}, \sigma_{\text{total}}}$. Assuming each component of $\mathbf{E}_{\text{total}}$

is independent, it follows that, for each j,

$$\Pr\left[\|\epsilon_j\| \leq \frac{2q}{2^\tau}\right] \approx \sum_{\mathbf{z}\in\mathbb{Z}^{32}, \frac{2^\tau}{q}\cdot\|\mathbf{z}\|\leq 2} \prod_{j=1}^{32} \frac{g_{\sigma_\text{total}}(z_i)}{g_{\sigma_\text{total}}(\mathbb{Z})}$$

$$\approx \int_{\mathbf{x}\in\mathbb{R}^{32}, \|\mathbf{x}\|\leq\frac{2q}{2^\tau}} \frac{1}{(2\pi\sigma_\text{total}^2)^{16}} \cdot e^{-\|\mathbf{x}\|^2/(2\sigma_\text{total}^2)} \, d\mathbf{x}$$

$$= 1 - \Gamma\left(16, \left(2q/(2^\tau\sqrt{2}\sigma_\text{total})\right)^2\right)/\Gamma(16,0),$$

where $g_\sigma(z) = \frac{1}{\sqrt{2\pi}\sigma}e^{-z^2/(2\sigma^2)}$ is the Gaussian function. The second approximation comes from treating the discrete Gaussian distribution as continuous. Thus, it follows that the PKE scheme is δ-correct for

$$\delta = 1 - \Pr\left[\|\epsilon_j\| \leq \frac{2q}{2^\tau} \text{ for all } j\right] \approx \frac{l_m}{\mu}\cdot\left(1 - \Pr\left[\|\epsilon_j\| \leq \frac{2q}{2^\tau}\right]\right)$$

$$\approx \frac{l_m}{\mu}\cdot\Gamma\left(16, \left(2q/(2^\tau\sqrt{2}\sigma_\text{total})\right)^2\right)/\Gamma(16,0). \tag{11}$$

In Sect. 6, we select parameters such that the right-hand side of (11) is less than $2^{-128}, 2^{-192}, 2^{-256}$ for security levels targeting $128, 192, 256$ bits respectively.

Security of the PKE Scheme. The security of the proposed scheme relies on the LWE problem, which is defined as follows.

Definition 7 (LWE Distribution). *Let n, q be positive integers, and let χ_e be a distribution over $\mathbb{Z}$. Given $\mathbf{s} \in \mathbb{Z}_q^n$, the LWE distribution $\mathcal{A}_{\mathbf{s},\chi_e}$ outputs $(\mathbf{a}, \langle\mathbf{a},\mathbf{s}\rangle + e \mod q) \in \mathbb{Z}_q^n \times \mathbb{Z}_q$, where $\mathbf{a} \leftarrow U(\mathbb{Z}_q^n)$ and $e \leftarrow \chi_e$.*

Definition 8 (LWE Problem). *Let n, m, q be positive integers, and let χ_e, χ_s be distributions over $\mathbb{Z}$ and $\mathbb{Z}^n$ respectively. The LWE problem is to distinguish between m samples $(\mathbf{a}_i, b_i) \leftarrow U(\mathbb{Z}_q^n \times \mathbb{Z}_q)$ and m samples $(\mathbf{a}_i, b_i) \leftarrow \mathcal{A}_{\mathbf{s},\chi_e}$, where the secret vector $\mathbf{s} \leftarrow \chi_s$ is common to all samples. More formally, for an adversary A, we define*

$$\mathbf{Adv}_{n,m,q,\chi_e,\chi_s}^\text{LWE}(\mathsf{A}) = \left|\Pr\left[\mathcal{A}(\mathbf{A},\mathbf{b}) = 1 \mid \begin{array}{l} \mathbf{A} \leftarrow U(\mathbb{Z}_q^{m\times n}), \mathbf{e} \leftarrow \chi_e^m \\ \mathbf{s} \leftarrow \chi_s, \mathbf{b} = \mathbf{As} + \mathbf{e} \end{array}\right]\right.$$
$$\left. - \Pr[\mathcal{A}(\mathbf{A},\mathbf{b}) = 1 \mid \mathbf{A} \leftarrow U(\mathbb{Z}_q^{m\times n}), \mathbf{b} \leftarrow U(\mathbb{Z}_q^m)]\right|.$$

In our scheme we choose χ_e to be the binomial distribution $\rho(\eta)$, and χ_s to be the constant Hamming distribution, i.e., $\mathbf{s}$ is uniformly sampled from the set of vectors in $\mathbb{Z}^n$ with exactly $(n-2h)$ zeros, h ones, and h negative ones. We denote the corresponding LWE problem to be $\mathbf{Adv}_{n,m,q,\eta,h}^\text{LWE}(\mathsf{A})$. It is important to note that while the original LWE problem was established using the discrete Gaussian distribution [5,42], the hardness of the LWE problem does not seem to be affected by the exact shape of the error distribution. Moreover, an analysis based on Rényi divergence demonstrates that $\rho(\eta)$ can be substituted with a discrete Gaussian distribution of variance $\eta/2$ without compromising security [43]. The following theorem establishes the security of Scloud$^+$.PKE.

Theorem 1. Scloud$^+$.PKE *is IND-CPA secure, assuming that the LWE problem is hard and that the matrix* $\mathbf{A}$ *generated by* gen *is uniformly distributed over* $\mathbb{Z}_q^{m \times n}$. *Specifically, for any adversary* C *against the IND-CPA security of* Scloud$^+$.PKE, *there exist adversaries* B$_1$, B$_2$ *with running times approximately equal to that of* C, *such that*

$$\mathbf{Adv}_{\mathrm{Scloud}^+.\mathrm{PKE}}^{\mathrm{CPA}}(\mathsf{C}) \leq \bar{n} \cdot \mathbf{Adv}_{n,m,q,\eta_1,h_1}^{\mathrm{LWE}}(\mathsf{B}_1) + \bar{m} \cdot \mathbf{Adv}_{m+\bar{m},n,q,\eta_2,h_2}^{\mathrm{LWE}}(\mathsf{B}_2).$$

Proof. We begin by considering the matrix-LWE problem where the secret and errors are also matrices (as in our PKE scheme). For an adversary A, we define

$$\mathbf{Adv}_{n,m,\bar{n},q,\eta,h}^{\mathrm{matrix\text{-}LWE}}(\mathsf{A}) = \left| \Pr\left[\mathsf{A}(\mathbf{A},\mathbf{B}) = 1 \mid \begin{matrix} \mathbf{A} \leftarrow U(\mathbb{Z}_q^{m \times n}), \mathbf{E} \leftarrow \rho(\eta)^{m \times \bar{n}} \\ \mathbf{S} \leftarrow U(\mathcal{L}^{(\bar{n},h)}), \mathbf{B} = \mathbf{AS} + \mathbf{E} \end{matrix}\right] \right.$$
$$\left. - \Pr[\mathsf{A}(\mathbf{A},\mathbf{B}) = 1 \mid \mathbf{A} \leftarrow U(\mathbb{Z}_q^{m \times n}), \mathbf{B} \leftarrow U(\mathbb{Z}_q^{m \times \bar{n}})] \right|.$$

Using a standard hybrid argument [44], it can be shown that there exists an adversary A$'$ with approximately the same running time as A, such that:

$$\mathbf{Adv}_{n,m,q,\eta,h}^{\mathrm{LWE}}(\mathsf{A}') \geq \frac{1}{\bar{n}}\mathbf{Adv}_{n,m,\bar{n},q,\eta,h}^{\mathrm{matrix\text{-}LWE}}(\mathsf{A}). \tag{12}$$

Now, let C be executed in the IND-CPA security game G_0, where

$$\mathbf{Adv}_{\mathrm{Scloud}^+.\mathrm{PKE}}^{\mathrm{CPA}}(\mathsf{C}) = |\Pr[b = b' \text{ in game } G_0] - 1/2|.$$

Define G_1 as the game where the matrix $\mathbf{B}$ in key generation is drawn from $U(\mathbb{Z}_q^{m \times \bar{n}})$ rather than generated via $\mathbf{B} = \mathbf{A} \cdot \mathbf{S} + \mathbf{E}$. Then, there exists an adversary B$_1'$ with a running time comparable to that of C such that $|\Pr[b = b' \text{ in game } G_0] - \Pr[b = b' \text{ in game } G_1]| \leq \mathbf{Adv}_{n,m,\bar{n},q,\eta_1,h_1}^{\mathrm{matrix\text{-}LWE}}(\mathsf{B}_1')$. Define game G_2 where the matrix $(\mathbf{C}_1 = \mathbf{S}' \cdot \mathbf{A} + \mathbf{E}_1, \mathbf{C}_2' = \mathbf{S}' \cdot \mathbf{B} + \mathbf{E}_2)$ used to generate the challenge ciphertext is drawn from $U(\mathbb{Z}_q^{\bar{m} \times n} \times \mathbb{Z}_q^{\bar{m} \times \bar{n}})$. Similarly, there exists an adversary B$_2'$ with a running time similar to that of C such that $|\Pr[b = b' \text{ in game } G_1] - \Pr[b = b' \text{ in game } G_2]| \leq \mathbf{Adv}_{m+\bar{m},n,\bar{m},q,\eta_2,h_2}^{\mathrm{matrix\text{-}LWE}}(\mathsf{B}_2')$. In game G_2, the ciphertext $\mathbf{C}_2 = \mathbf{C}_2' + \mathbf{M}$ is uniformly distributed over $\mathbb{Z}_q^{\bar{m} \times \bar{n}}$ and is independent of the message $\mathbf{m}$, implying that $\Pr[b = b' \text{ in game } G_2] = 1/2$. Thus, from the above analysis, we obtain

$$\mathbf{Adv}_{\mathrm{Scloud}^+.\mathrm{PKE}}^{\mathrm{CPA}}(\mathsf{C}) \leq \mathbf{Adv}_{n,m,\bar{n},q,\eta_1,h_1}^{\mathrm{matrix\text{-}LWE}}(\mathsf{B}_1') + \mathbf{Adv}_{m+\bar{m},n,\bar{m},q,\eta_2,h_2}^{\mathrm{matrix\text{-}LWE}}(\mathsf{B}_2').$$

The theorem follows directly by combining this result with (12). □

5   The IND-CCA-Secure KEM

Scloud$^+$.KEM is derived from Scloud$^+$.PKE by applying the Fujisaki-Okamoto transformation with implicit rejection [45,46]. Scloud$^+$.KEM consists of three algorithms: key generation, encapsulation, and decapsulation, which are described in Algorithm 9 to Algorithm 11. These algorithms utilize three hash functions: $H : \{0,1\}^* \to \{0,1\}^{256}$, $G : \{0,1\}^* \to \{0,1\}^{256 \times 2}$, and $K : \{0,1\}^* \to \{0,1\}^{l_{ss}}$, where l_{ss} is the length of the shared secret ss, which we set to be equal to l_m.

Algorithm 9: Scloud$^+$.KEM.KeyGen()

Output: Public key $pk \in \mathbb{Z}_q^{m \times \bar{n}} \times \{0,1\}^{128}$
Output: Secret key $sk \in \mathbb{Z}_q^{n \times \bar{n}} \times \mathbb{Z}_q^{m \times \bar{n}} \times \{0,1\}^{128+256 \times 2}$
1: $(pk, sk') = $ Scloud$^+$.PKE.KeyGen()
2: $\mathbf{hpk} = H(pk) \in \{0,1\}^{256}$
3: $\mathbf{z} \leftarrow U(\{0,1\}^{256})$
4: $sk = (sk', pk, \mathbf{hpk}, \mathbf{z})$
5: **return** (pk, sk)

Algorithm 10: Scloud$^+$.KEM.Encaps(pk)

Input: Public key $pk \in \mathbb{Z}_q^{m \times \bar{n}} \times \{0,1\}^{128}$
Output: Ciphertext $\mathbf{C} \in \mathbb{Z}_{q_1}^{\bar{m} \times n} \times \mathbb{Z}_{q_2}^{\bar{m} \times \bar{n}}$
Output: Shared session key $ss \in \{0,1\}^{l_{ss}}$
1: $\mathbf{m} \leftarrow U(\{0,1\}^{l_m})$
2: $(\mathbf{r}, \mathbf{k}) = G(\mathbf{m}\|H(pk)) \in \{0,1\}^{256 \times 2}$
3: $\mathbf{C} = $ Scloud$^+$.PKE.Enc($pk, \mathbf{m}, \mathbf{r}$)
4: $ss = K(\mathbf{k}\|\mathbf{C})$
5: **return** $(\mathbf{C}, ss)$

Correctness and Security of the KEM. It is evident that the failure probability δ of Scloud$^+$.KEM is equal to the failure probability of Scloud$^+$.PKE computed in Sect. 4. Following the approach in [45], when the hash functions H, G, and K are modeled as independent random oracles, we can derive the following security bounds, for which the proof is omitted in this work.

Theorem 2. *Suppose that Scloud$^+$.PKE is a δ-correct PKE with message space* $\mathcal{M}$. *Then for any classical adversary A against Scloud$^+$.KEM that makes at most q_{RO} random oracle queries, there exists a classical adversary B against*

Algorithm 11: Scloud$^+$.KEM.Decaps()

Input: Ciphertext $\mathbf{C} \in \mathbb{Z}_{q_1}^{\bar{m} \times n} \times \mathbb{Z}_{q_2}^{\bar{m} \times \bar{n}}$
Input: Secret key $sk = (sk', pk, \mathbf{hpk}, \mathbf{z}) \in \mathbb{Z}_q^{n \times \bar{n}} \times \mathbb{Z}_q^{m \times \bar{n}} \times \{0,1\}^{128+256 \times 2}$
Output: Shared session key $\mathbf{ss} \in \{0,1\}^{l_{ss}}$
1: $\mathbf{m}' = $ Scloud$^+$.PKE.Dec($sk', \mathbf{C}$)
2: $(\mathbf{r}', \mathbf{k}') = $ G($\mathbf{m}'\|\mathbf{hpk}$)
3: $\mathbf{C}' = $ Scloud$^+$.PKE.Enc($pk, \mathbf{m}', \mathbf{r}'$)
4: **if** $\mathbf{C} = \mathbf{C}'$ **then**
5:     **return** $\mathbf{ss} = $ K($\mathbf{k}', \mathbf{C}$)
6: **else**
7:     **return** $\mathbf{ss} = $ K($\mathbf{z}, \mathbf{C}$)
8: **end if**

Scloud$^+$.PKE, whose running time is approximately the same as that of A, such that

$$\mathbf{Adv}_{\text{Scloud+.KEM}}^{\text{CCA}}(\mathsf{A}) \leq 3 \cdot \mathbf{Adv}_{\text{Scloud+.PKE}}^{\text{CPA}}(\mathsf{B}) + \frac{3q_{RO}}{|\mathcal{M}|} + q_{RO} \cdot \delta.$$

For security in the *quantum* random oracle model, the approach proposed in [47,48] can be applied to obtain the following bound.

Theorem 3. *Suppose that Scloud$^+$.PKE is a δ-correct PKE with message space $\mathcal{M}$. Then for any quantum adversary A against Scloud$^+$.KEM, making at most q_F quantum oracle queries to K and at most q_G quantum oracle queries to G, there exists a quantum adversary B against Scloud$^+$.PKE, whose running time is approximately the same as that of A, such that*

$$\mathbf{Adv}_{\text{Scloud+.KEM}}^{\text{CCA}}(\mathsf{A}) \leq 2\sqrt{q_{RO} \cdot \mathbf{Adv}_{\text{Scloud+.PKE}}^{\text{CPA}}(\mathsf{B}) + \frac{2(q_{RO}+1)^2}{|\mathcal{M}|}} + \frac{2q_F}{\sqrt{|\mathcal{M}|}} + 4q_G \cdot \sqrt{\delta},$$

where $q_{RO} = q_F + q_G$.

6   Parameters and Security Analysis

We provide three parameter sets for Scloud$^+$, targeting classical security levels of 128, 192, and 256 bits respectively. The parameter sets are listed in Table 2, where the modulus q is fixed to be 2^{12} for all sets of parameters, and h_1, h_2 are fixed to be $\frac{1}{4}m, \frac{1}{4}n$ respectively. Additionally, the parameters for MsgEnc and MsgDec are provided in Table 3. We note that Scloud$^+$-256 selects $(\bar{m}, \bar{n}) = (12, 11)$ to accommodate 256 message bits. In this case, the encoded message has a length of 128, which is smaller than $\bar{m} \times \bar{n} = 132$. This implies that there are 4 positions in the message matrix $\mathbf{M} \in \mathbb{Z}^{\bar{m} \times \bar{n}}$ that are filled with 0.

According to the reductions established in Sect. 4 and Sect. 5, it suffices to consider the LWE instances with parameters (n, m, q, η_1, h_1) and $(m + \bar{m}, n, q, \eta_2, h_2)$ to evaluate the security of the scheme.

Table 2. Parameters for Scloud$^+$.PKE and Scloud$^+$.KEM.

	$l_{ss} = l_m$	(q, q_1, q_2)	(m, n)	$(\bar{m}, \bar{n})$	(h_1, h_2)	(η_1, η_2)
Scloud$^+$-128	128	$(2^{12}, 2^9, 2^7)$	$(600, 600)$	$(8, 8)$	$(150, 150)$	$(7, 7)$
Scloud$^+$-192	192	$(2^{12}, 2^{12}, 2^{10})$	$(928, 896)$	$(8, 8)$	$(224, 232)$	$(2, 1)$
Scloud$^+$-256	256	$(2^{12}, 2^{10}, 2^7)$	$(1136, 1120)$	$(12, 11)$	$(280, 284)$	$(3, 2)$

Table 3. Parameters for `MsgEnc` and `MsgDec`.

	μ	τ	Coding lattice	Shaping lattice
Scloud$^+$-128	64	3	BW$_{32}$	$8 \cdot \mathbb{Z}[\mathtt{i}]^{16}$
Scloud$^+$-192	96	4	BW$_{32}$	$16 \cdot \mathbb{Z}[\mathtt{i}]^{16}$
Scloud$^+$-256	64	3	BW$_{32}$	$8 \cdot \mathbb{Z}[\mathtt{i}]^{16}$

Core-SVP Hardness. For most known attacks on LWE problems, algorithms designed for solving approximate SVP are inevitably invoked as subroutines. Among these, the BKZ lattice reduction algorithm has the best known computational complexity [49]. The overall complexity of the BKZ algorithm is primarily determined by its crucial component, which involves solving SVP in lower-dimensional lattices. Specifically, the BKZ algorithm with block size b invokes a b-dimensional SVP algorithm polynomially many times, and its cost can be described as $\text{poly}(b) \cdot 2^{cb+o(b)}$, where the factor $2^{cb+o(b)}$ represents the complexity of solving the b-dimensional SVP. The *core-SVP* model is typically used to obtain a conservative estimate of the BKZ algorithm's complexity, where $o(b)$ and $\text{poly}(b)$ factors are ignored, and only the core 2^{cb} complexity is considered. The best known constant c for classical algorithms is $c = \log_2(\sqrt{3/2}) \approx 0.292$, as derived from the sieve algorithm [50]. For quantum algorithms, the constant c is usually taken to be $c = \log_2(\sqrt{13/9}) \approx 0.265$ [30,51]. Although a quantum random walk approach has been shown to provide an improved quantum algorithm for solving SVP with $c \approx 0.257$ [52], this method has not been widely adopted in the analysis of LWE-based schemes. Therefore, in the analysis of quantum security, we adhere to the common choice of $c \approx 0.265$.

Primal Attack. For a given LWE instance $(\mathbf{A} \in \mathbb{Z}_q^{m \times n}, \mathbf{b} = \mathbf{As} + \mathbf{e} \in \mathbb{Z}_q^m)$, the primal attack first constructs a lattice $\Lambda = \{\mathbf{x} \in \mathbb{Z}^{m+n+1} \mid (\mathbf{A} \mid \mathbf{I}_m \mid -\mathbf{b})\mathbf{x} = 0 \bmod q\}$, and then finds the unique shortest vector $\mathbf{x} = (\mathbf{s}, \mathbf{e}, 1) \in \Lambda$ using the BKZ algorithm. We refer to [30,53] for a detailed analysis of the primal attack.

Dual Attack. For a given LWE instance $(\mathbf{A} \in \mathbb{Z}_q^{m \times n}, \mathbf{b} = \mathbf{As} + \mathbf{e} \in \mathbb{Z}_q^m)$, the dual attack first finds short vectors $\{\mathbf{x}_j, \mathbf{y}_j\}_{1 \le j \le N}$ in the lattice $\Lambda' = \{(\mathbf{x}, \mathbf{y}) \in \mathbb{Z}^{n+m} \mid \mathbf{x}^\top \mathbf{A} = \mathbf{y}^\top \bmod q\}$, and then tries to distinguish the samples $\{\mathbf{x}_j^\top \mathbf{b}\}_{1 \le j \le N}$ from samples drawn from $\mathbb{Z}_q$. We refer to [53] for a detailed analysis of the dual attack. Although some recent works report improvements to the dual attack using a Fast Fourier Transform (FFT) method [54,55], Ducas and Pulles have shown that the underlying statistical assumptions are not solid [56]. Therefore, we still adopt the commonly used dual attack as in [53].

Hybrid Dual Attack. Our scheme adopts a ternary secret for LWE, for which the hybrid attack approach is typically effective. A hybrid attack guesses part of the secret key and then seeks a trade-off between the cost of guessing and the cost of the dual attack. The guessing techniques mainly include enumeration [53,57] and meet-in-the-middle (MITM) [58]. Recently, [59] proposes a combinatorial MITM attack technique, which is further explored in [60] for hybrid dual attacks, demonstrating better performance for extremely sparse instances.

Estimator. We provide a concrete security analysis of our scheme using the primal, dual, and hybrid attacks. The results are summarized in Table 4.

Table 4. The estimated bits of security of Scloud$^+$ under the primal, dual and hybrid attacks. The decryption failure rates (DFRs) are calculated based on (11).

	Model	Classical	Quantum	DFR
Scloud$^+$-128	Primal	136.07	**123.49**	$2^{-134.21}$
	Dual	142.20	129.06	
	Hybrid	**136.07**	125.55	
Scloud$^+$-192	Primal	202.36	**183.65**	$2^{-200.64}$
	Dual	209.66	190.27	
	Hybrid	**200.42**	184.76	
Scloud$^+$-256	Primal	266.89	**242.21**	$2^{-265.74}$
	Dual	275.94	250.43	
	Hybrid	**263.11**	242.71	

7   Implementation

In this section, we provide the remaining implementation details for Scloud$^+$ and present the performance results of Scloud$^+$.KEM. The experimental results are summarized in Table 5. All experiments are conducted on a machine running Fedora 33 (Workstation Edition), equipped with an Intel Core-i9 10980XE @3.00GHz, with hyperthreading and TurboBoost disabled. For compilation, we used GNU GCC version 7.2.0 with the command 'gcc -O3 -march=native -lm'.

Table 5. The performance of Scloud$^+$.KEM measured in 10^3 cycles, with each data representing the median count over 1000 measurements.

Scheme	KeyGen	Encaps	Decaps	Encaps + Decaps
Scloud$^+$.KEM-128	998	1125	1127	2273
Scloud$^+$.KEM-192	2226	2418	2417	4859
Scloud$^+$.KEM-256	3454	3671	3826	7539

Cryptographic Primitives. Scloud$^+$ makes use of four hash functions F : $\{0,1\}^{256} \rightarrow \{0,1\}^*$, H : $\{0,1\}^* \rightarrow \{0,1\}^{256}$, G : $\{0,1\}^* \rightarrow \{0,1\}^{2\times256}$, and K : $\{0,1\}^* \rightarrow \{0,1\}^{l_{ss}}$. In our implementation, F and K are instantiated using SHAKE-256, H is instantiated using SHA3-256, and G is instantiated using SHA3-512.

Matrix Generation and Multiplication. Matrix $\mathbf{E}$ is generated by first extending the random coin $\mathbf{r}_2$ to a sequence of random bits

$$(x_1, x_2, \ldots, x_{\eta_1 mn}, y_1, y_2, \ldots, y_{\eta_1 mn})$$

using SHAKE-256. Then $\mathbf{E}$ is constructed by setting its (i,j)-th element as $e_{i,j} = \sum_{k=1}^{\eta_1}(x_{\eta_1 l+k} - y_{\eta_1 l+k})$, where $l = n(i-1)+j-1$. Matrix $\mathbf{E}'$ is generated in a similar manner.

Matrix $\mathbf{S}$ is generated by first extending the random coin $\mathbf{r}_2$ into a sequence of random bits using SHAKE-256. These bits are then used to generate a constant weight distribution column by column. For each column of $\mathbf{S}$, we randomly select $2h_1$ indices from the n coordinates, setting h_1 of them to 1 and the other h_1 to -1. For Scloud$^+$-128, where $n = 600$, the simplest method to generate a random index is to use 10 bits of randomness to generate a random integer in $[0, 2^{10} - 1]$, then reject any values outside $[0, n-1]$. A well-known optimization is to generate multiple indices at once to reduce random bit consumption. Specifically, since n^3 is slightly less than 2^{28}, we can sample a random integer $x \in [0, 2^{28} - 1]$ and apply rejecting to obtain a random integer $y \in [0, n^3 - 1]$, and then output three indices $i_1 = [y]_n$, $i_2 = [\frac{y-i_1}{n}]_n$, $i_3 = [\frac{y-i_1-i_2 n}{n^2}]_n$. A similar approach applies to Scloud$^+$-256, where $n = 1120$, and 51 bits are used to generate 5 indices at once. Matrix $\mathbf{S}'$ is generated in a similar manner.

Matrix $\mathbf{A}$ is generated by extending the 128-bit random seed $\mathbf{seed_A}$ using AES-128 in CTR mode. Specifically, for any $0 \le i < m$ and $0 \le j < n/8$, we generate 8 elements $a_{i,8j}, a_{i,8j+1}, \ldots, a_{i,8j+7}$ from the 128-bit ciphertext AES-128$_{\mathbf{seed_A}}$(Bit($i \cdot n/8 + j, 32$)$||\mathbf{0}_{96}$), using $\mathbf{seed_A}$ as the key, and then set the corresponding element of $\mathbf{A}$ to $a_{i,j}$.

In our implementation, matrix-vector multiplications are performed in a conventional manner, similar to FrodoKEM. Specifically, we use the '-O3' optimization in GCC, which automatically uses SIMD (Single Instruction Multiple Data) capabilities on our platform, significantly accelerating matrix multiplication. An alternative approach for matrix multiplication in Scloud$^+$ involves storing only the nonzero indices of each column of $\mathbf{S}$ (or each row of $\mathbf{S}'$) and replacing the matrix-vector multiplications in $\mathbf{AS}$ with direct summation (or subtraction) of the columns corresponding to these nonzero indices. However, given the efficiency of SIMD, this alternative offers no practical advantage so far.

Table 6. The size of the public key, ciphertext, and shared secret in Scloud$^+$.KEM (measured in bytes), with packing and unpacking functions applied.

Scheme	Public key pk	Ciphertext C	Shared secret ss
Scloud$^+$.KEM-128	7200	5456	16
Scloud$^+$.KEM-192	11136	10832	24
Scloud$^+$.KEM-256	18744	16916	32

Packing and Unpacking. We note that the public key pk and ciphertext $\mathbf{C}$ should be packed for transmission. For instance, given the ciphertext $\mathbf{C} = (\bar{\mathbf{C}}_1, \bar{\mathbf{C}}_2) \in \mathbb{Z}_{q_1}^{\bar{m} \times n} \times \mathbb{Z}_{q_2}^{\bar{m} \times \bar{n}}$, we denote the elements of $\bar{\mathbf{C}}_1$ and $\bar{\mathbf{C}}_2$ as $c_{i,j}^{(1)}$ and $c_{i,j}^{(2)}$, respectively. Then, $\mathsf{Pack}(\mathbf{C})$ returns the bit string

$$\left(\mathrm{Bit}(c_{i,j}^{(1)}, \log_2(q_1)) \right)_{\substack{0 \leq i < \bar{m} \\ 0 \leq j < n}} || \left(\mathrm{Bit}(c_{i,j}^{(2)}, \log_2(q_2)) \right)_{\substack{0 \leq i < \bar{m} \\ 0 \leq j < \bar{n}}} || \; \mathbf{0},$$

where 0's are padded to the end to ensure the length is a multiple of 8. The function Unpack is the inverse of Pack. In Table 6, we present the sizes of the public key, and ciphertext for Scloud$^+$.KEM with the packing method applied.

Comparison of Scloud$^+$.KEM and FrodoKEM. We compare Scloud$^+$. KEM with FrodoKEM in terms of performance, as well as the sizes of the public key and ciphertext. For FrodoKEM, the performance data is based on the optimized implementation developed by the FrodoKEM team and Microsoft Research [61], tested on the same platform used to evaluate Scloud$^+$.KEM. The performance metrics, along with the public key and ciphertext sizes for FrodoKEM, are provided in Tables 7 and 8 in the Appendix.

Note that FrodoKEM-640, FrodoKEM-976, and FrodoKEM-1344 target security levels of 128-bit, 192-bit, and 256-bit, respectively. Their concrete bits of security are comparable to those of Scloud$^+$.KEM-128, Scloud$^+$.KEM-192, and Scloud$^+$.KEM-256, allowing for meaningful comparisons between them. In terms of public key and ciphertext sizes, Scloud$^+$.KEM achieves a public key size approximately $0.71 \sim 0.87$x, and a ciphertext size approximately $0.56 \sim 0.78$x that of FrodoKEM. Regarding performance, Scloud$^+$.KEM demonstrates a key generation time approximately $0.70 \sim 0.80$x, and an encapsulation + decapsulation time approximately $0.74 \sim 0.84$x that of FrodoKEM.

Acknowledgments. We thank Matt Henricksen for valuable discussions. This work is supported by the National Key R&D Program of China (2018YFA0704701), the Major Program of Guangdong Basic and Applied Research (2019B030302008), Shandong Key Research and Development Program (2020ZLYS09), and Tsinghua University Dushi Program.

Appendix

This appendix presents the performance metrics (on the same platform detailed in Sect. 7), along with the public key and ciphertext sizes for FrodoKEM.

Table 7. The performance of FrodoKEM measured in 10^3 cycles, with each data representing the median count over 1000 measurements.

Scheme	KeyGen	Encaps	Decaps	Encaps + Decaps
FrodoKEM-640	1375	1541	1474	3015
FrodoKEM-976	2786	2993	2814	5807
FrodoKEM-1344	4906	5183	4992	10174

Table 8. The size of the public key, ciphertext, and shared secret in FrodoKEM (measured in bytes).

Scheme	Public key pk	Ciphertext C	Shared secret ss
FrodoKEM-640	9616	9720	16
FrodoKEM-976	15632	15744	24
FrodoKEM-1344	21520	21632	32

References

1. Shor, P.W.: Algorithms for quantum computation: discrete logarithms and factoring, pp. 124–134 (1994)
2. Regev, O.: On lattices, learning with errors, random linear codes, and cryptography, pp. 84–93 (2005)
3. Naehrig, M., et al.: FrodoKEM, Technical report, National Institute of Standards and Technology (2020)
4. Lyubashevsky, V., Peikert, C., Regev, O.: On ideal lattices and learning with errors over rings, pp. 1–23 (2010)
5. Peikert, C., Regev, O., Stephens-Davidowitz, N.: Pseudorandomness of ring-LWE for any ring and modulus, pp. 461–473 (2017)

6. Langlois, A., Stehlé, D.: Worst-case to average-case reductions for module lattices. Des. Codes Cryptogr. **75**(3), 565–599 (2015)
7. Schwabe, P., et al.: CRYSTALS-KYBER, Technical report, National Institute of Standards and Technology (2022)
8. D'Anvers, J.-P., et al.: SABER, Technical report, National Institute of Standards and Technology (2020)
9. Xianhui, L., et al.: LAC, Technical report, National Institute of Standards and Technology (2019)
10. Zhang, J., Yu, Y., Fan, S., Zhang, Z., Yang, K.: Tweaking the asymmetry of asymmetric-key cryptography on lattices: KEMs and signatures of smaller sizes, pp. 37–65 (2020)
11. Cramer, R., Ducas, L., Peikert, C. and Regev, O.: Recovering short generators of principal ideals in cyclotomic rings, pp. 559–585 (2016)
12. Schnorr, C.-P.: A hierarchy of polynomial time lattice basis reduction algorithms. Theor. Comput. Sci. **53**, 201–224 (1987)
13. Cramer, R., Ducas, L., Wesolowski, B.: Short stickelberger class relations and application to ideal-SVP, pp. 324–348 (2017)
14. Ducas, L., Plançon, M., Wesolowski, B.: On the shortness of vectors to be found by the ideal-SVP quantum algorithm, pp. 322–351 (2019)
15. Cramer, R., Ducas, L., Wesolowski, B.: Mildly short vectors in cyclotomic ideal lattices in quantum polynomial time. J. ACM **68**(2), 8:1–8:26 (2021)
16. Pan, Y., Xu, J., Wadleigh, N., Cheng, Q.: On the ideal shortest vector problem over random rational primes. In: Canteaut, A., Standaert, F.-X. (eds.) EUROCRYPT 2021. LNCS, vol. 12696, pp. 559–583. Springer, Cham (2021). https://doi.org/10.1007/978-3-030-77870-5_20
17. Pellet-Mary, A., Hanrot, G., Stehlé, D.: Approx-SVP in ideal lattices with pre-processing, pp. 685–716 (2019)
18. Bernard, O., Roux-Langlois, A.: Twisted-PHS: using the product formula to solve Approx-SVP in ideal lattices, pp. 349–380 (2020)
19. ANSSI (2022). https://cyber.gouv.fr/en/publications/anssi-views-post-quantum-cryptography-transition
20. BSI–Technical Guideline. Cryptographic Mechanisms: Recommendations and Key Lengths (2024)
21. Applebaum, B., Cash, D., Peikert, C., Sahai, A.: Fast cryptographic primitives and circular-secure encryption based on hard learning problems. In: Halevi, S. (ed.) CRYPTO 2009. LNCS, vol. 5677, pp. 595–618. Springer, Heidelberg (2009). https://doi.org/10.1007/978-3-642-03356-8_35
22. Brakerski, Z., Gentry, C., Vaikuntanathan, V.: (Leveled) fully homomorphic encryption without bootstrapping, pp. 309–325 (2012)
23. Fan, J., Vercauteren, F.: Somewhat practical fully homomorphic encryption. Cryptology ePrint Archive Report 2012/144 (2012)
24. Cheon, J.H., Kim, A., Kim, M., Song, Y.: Homomorphic encryption for arithmetic of approximate numbers, pp. 409–437 (2017)
25. Zheng, Z., et al.: SCloud: public key encryption and key encapsulation mechanism based on learning with errors. Cryptology ePrint Archive, Report 2020/095 (2020)
26. Fritzmann, T., Pöppelmann, T., Sepúlveda, J.: Analysis of error-correcting codes for lattice-based key exchange, pp. 369–390 (2019)
27. Saarinen, M.J.O.: HILA5: on reliability, reconciliation, and error correction for ring-LWE encryption, pp. 192–212 (2017)
28. Zhao, Y., Jin, Z., Gong, B., Sui, G.: KCL (pka OKCN/AKCN/CNKE), Technical report, National Institute of Standards and Technology (2017)

29. Hamburg, M.: Three Bears, Technical report, National Institute of Standards and Technology (2017)
30. Alkim, E., Ducas, L., Pöppelmann, T., Schwabe, P.: Post-quantum key {Exchange–A} new hope. In: 25th USENIX Security Symposium (USENIX Security 16), pp. 327–343 (2016)
31. Jin, Z., Zhao, Y.: AKCN-E8: compact and flexible KEM from ideal lattice. Cryptology ePrint Archive, Report 2020/056 (2020)
32. Saliba, C., Luzzi, L., Ling, C.: Error correction for Frodokem using the Gosset lattice. arXiv preprint arXiv:2110.01740 (2021)
33. van Poppelen, A.: Cryptographic decoding of the leech lattice. Cryptology ePrint Archive, Report 2016/1050 (2016). https://eprint.iacr.org/2016/1050
34. Lyu, S., Liu, L., Lai, J., Ling, C., Chen, H.: Lattice codes for lattice-based PKE. Cryptology ePrint Archive, Report 2022/874 (2022)
35. Micciancio, D., Nicolosi, A.: Efficient bounded distance decoders for Barnes-wall lattices. In: ISIT 2008, Toronto, ON, Canada, July 6-11, 2008, pp. 2484–2488. IEEE (2008)
36. Forney, G.D., Jr.: Coset codes-ii: binary lattices and related codes. IEEE Trans. Inf. Theory **34**(5), 1152–1187 (1988)
37. Ran, M., Snyders, J.: Efficient decoding of the Gosset, Coxeter-Todd and the Barnes-wall lattices. In: Proceedings of the 1998 IEEE International Symposium on Information Theory (Cat. No. 98CH36252), p. 92. IEEE (1998)
38. Wang, C., Shen, B., Tzeng, K.K.: Generalised minimum distance decoding of Reed-Muller codes and Barnes-wall lattices. In: Proceedings of 1995 IEEE International Symposium on Information Theory, p. 186. IEEE (1995)
39. Corlay, V., Boutros, J.J., Ciblat, P., Brunel, L.: On the decoding of Barnes-Wall lattices. In: 2020 IEEE International Symposium on Information Theory (ISIT), pp. 519–524. IEEE (2020)
40. Corlay, V.: Decoding algorithms for Lattices. (Algorithmes de décodage pour les réseaux de points), PhD thesis, Polytechnic Institute of Paris, France (2020)
41. Grigorescu, E., Peikert, C.: List decoding Barnes-Wall lattices. In: 2012 IEEE 27th Conference on Computational Complexity, pp. 316–325. IEEE (2012)
42. Regev, O.: On lattices, learning with errors, random linear codes, and cryptography. JACM **56**(6), 1–40 (2009)
43. Bai, S., Lepoint, T., Roux-Langlois, A., Sakzad, A., Stehlé, D., Steinfeld, R.: Improved security proofs in lattice-based cryptography: using the Rényi divergence rather than the statistical distance, pp. 3–24 (2015)
44. Bos, J.W., et al.: Frodo: take off the ring! Practical, quantum-secure key exchange from LWE, pp. 1006–1018 (2016)
45. Hofheinz, D., Hövelmanns, K., Kiltz, E.: A modular analysis of the Fujisaki-Okamoto transformation, pp. 341–371 (2017)
46. Zheng, Z., Wang, A., Fan, H., Zhao, C., Liu, C., Zhang, X.: Scloud: public key encryption and key encapsulation mechanism based on learning with errors. IACR Cryptology ePrint Archive, p. 95 (2020)
47. Jiang, H., Zhang, Z., Chen, L., Wang, H., Ma, Z.: IND-CCA-secure key encapsulation mechanism in the quantum random oracle model, pp. 96–125 (2018)
48. Jiang, H., Zhang, Z., Ma, Z.: Tighter security proofs for generic key encapsulation mechanism in the quantum random oracle model, pp. 227–248 (2019)
49. Chen, Y., Nguyen, P.Q.: BKZ 2.0: better lattice security estimates, pp. 1–20 (2011)
50. Becker, A., Ducas, L., Gama, N., Laarhoven, T.: New directions in nearest neighbor searching with applications to lattice sieving, pp. 10–24 (2016)

51. Laarhoven, T.: Search problems in cryptography: from fingerprinting to lattice sieving (2016)
52. Chailloux, A., Loyer, J.: Lattice sieving via quantum random walks, pp. 63–91 (2021)
53. Albrecht, M.R.: On dual lattice attacks against small-secret LWE and parameter choices in HElib and SEAL. In: Coron, J.-S., Nielsen, J.B. (eds.) EUROCRYPT 2017. LNCS, vol. 10211, pp. 103–129. Springer, Cham (2017). https://doi.org/10.1007/978-3-319-56614-6_4
54. Guo, Q., Johansson, T.: Faster dual lattice attacks for solving LWE with applications to CRYSTALS, pp. 33–62 (2021)
55. MATZOV: Report on the security of LWE: improved dual lattice attack (2022)
56. Ducas, L., Pulles, L.N.: Does the dual-sieve attack on learning with errors even work? In: Annual International Cryptology Conference, pp. 37–69. Springer (2023)
57. Bi, L., Xianhui, L., Luo, J., Wang, K., Zhang, Z.: Hybrid dual attack on LWE with arbitrary secrets. Cybersecurity 5(1), 15 (2022)
58. Cheon, J.H., Hhan, M., Hong, S., Son, Y.: A hybrid of dual and meet-in-the-middle attack on sparse and ternary secret LWE. IEEE Access 7, 89497–89506 (2019)
59. May, A.: How to meet Ternary LWE keys. In: Malkin, T., Peikert, C. (eds.) CRYPTO 2021. LNCS, vol. 12826, pp. 701–731. Springer, Cham (2021). https://doi.org/10.1007/978-3-030-84245-1_24
60. Bi, L., Lu, X., Luo, J., Wang, K.: Hybrid dual and meet-LWE attack. In: Australasian Conference on Information Security and Privacy, pp. 168–188. Springer (2022)
61. Optimized Implementation of FrodoKEM (2023). https://github.com/microsoft/pqcrypto-lweke

Transitioning to Quantum-Secure Encryption Schemes

Shao Huang©, Songsong Li©, Ying Ouyang©, and Yanhong Xu$^{(\boxtimes)}$©

Shanghai Jiao Tong University, 800 Dongchuan Road, Shanghai 200240, China
{shaohuang,songsli,ouyang_ying,yanhong.xu}@sjtu.edu.cn

Abstract. To deal with the potential threat of quantum computers, both industry and academia have started to deploy schemes that are composition of classically secure and quantum-secure constructions. In particular, the IETF has proposed three composite encryption modes that establish a shared key using a combination of public key encryption, key encapsulation, and key exchange primitives. However, no security proofs are provided.

As a complement to their proposals, this work first defines various quantum CPA-security that capture the capability of adversary during the transition to the fully quantum world. Towards this goal, we follow the footprint by Bindel et al. (PQCrypto 2017, PQCrypto 2019) to categorize the adversaries according to whether the adversaries have a quantum computer and whether they have quantum access to the challenge queries. We then observe that our security definitions coincide with those defined by Gagliardoni (Thesis 2017), which could be of independent interest. Finally, we prove the quantum CPA-security of the first two composite encryption modes in the IETF draft. The results show that the composite schemes are secure as long as at least one of its components is secure.

Keywords: Composite encryption schemes · quantum security · security stabilization

1 Introduction

To prepare for the advent of quantum computers, it is imperative to begin planning the transition to post-quantum cryptography. In 2017, NIST initiated the standardization process of post-quantum cryptography [1] and received great attention from both the industry and academia. As pointed out in [1], transition to post-quantum cryptography may not be as simple as it appears. One reason is that there is unlikely to be a drop-in replacement for the current cryptographic algorithms. Another reason is that the trustworthiness of post-quantum algorithms is at question [10].

A common solution accepted by the community is to transit to a hybrid world, where a hybrid (or composite) algorithm consists of both classically secure algorithms and quantum-secure ones such that the hybrid algorithm is secure as long as at least one component is secure. Bindel et al. [5] first investigated

X. Lu and C. J. Mitchell (Eds.): SSR 2024, LNCS 15559, pp. 175–186, 2025.
https://doi.org/10.1007/978-3-031-87541-0_8

the use of composite signatures. In particular, they provided a novel security hierarchy based on how quantum the attack is, and several methods to combine signatures. Finally, they proved the quantum security of the proposed composite signatures. Following the same path, Bindel et al. [4] initiated the modeling of hybrid key encapsulation mechanism (KEM) and hybrid authenticated key exchange. Crockett et al. [11] then examined various considerations for integrating post quantum and hybrid key exchange and authentication into communication protocols such as TLS and SSH, and reported several implementations of hybrid schemes.

Giacon et al. [13] introduced KEM combiners as a way to enable trust from different KEM constructions. In particular, they proved that applying a split-key pseudorandom function to the concatenation of n secret keys obtained from n KEM constructions retains CCA-security if one of the KEM constructions is CCA-secure. Ounsworth et al. [17] explicitly defined eleven specific pairwise combinations, namely, ML-KEM composite schemes that mix ML-KEM with traditional schemes such as RSA-OAEP, ECDH, X25519, and X448. The critical part in these combinations is a core key derivative function KDF that combines multiple shared secrets into a single one. In a different document [15], Ounsworth et al. recommended using Keccak as the underlying KDF. Recently, Barbosa et al. [3] proposed a hybrid KEM named X-Wing, combined from X25519 Diffie-Hellman key exchange and ML-KEM-768 KEM [2], and proved its CCA-security. The three followup works [3,15,17] can be thought of instantiations of [13].

In addition, the internet engineering task force (IETF) has spent great efforts in designing/formalizing/summarizing various composite schemes, including composite encryption [14], composite signatures [16], hybrid key encapsulation [15,17], hybrid key exchange protocols in TLS 1.2 [9,18] and TLS 1.3 [19,20]. However, to the best of our knowledge, no formal security analysis had been provided for the three composite encryption modes [14]. In this work, we aim to provide a formal analysis for the first two composite encryption schemes presented in [14]. We remark that the third composite encryption scheme contains arbitrary mixture of encryption, key encapsulation mechanism, and key agreement component algorithms. It then applies a KDF to the concatenation of all the secrets of component algorithms and outputs the result. Therefore, security of this construction would rely on that of KDF, which is quite different from the first two constructions. Therefore, we consider proving the security of the third construction as future works.

Quantum Security. Boneh et al. [6] initiated the study of security of public key primitives in the quantum random oracle model, where the adversary has access to random oracle in superposition. A line of subsequent works by Boneh and Zhandry [7,8,21] extended the security of various cryptographic primitives to capture the capability of fully quantum adversary, where oracles accessible by the adversary are in superposition. Bindel et al. [4,5] and Gagliardoni [12] pointed out that Boneh and Zhandry's definition might be overly strong and it does not capture the capability changes of adversaries during the transition process. Instead, Bindel et al. [4,5] categorized the security notions depending on how quantum the adversary could be, and obtain a hierarchy of security notions. In contrast, Gagliardoni [12] employed what they call **Q0, Q1, Q2, Q3** principles to classify the quantum security.

Our Contributions. Following the blueprint of Bindel et al. [4,5], we describe several CPA-security notions for public key encryption depending on whether the adversaries have a quantum computer and whether they have quantum access to the encryption queries. In particular, this leads to three (meaningful) types of adversaries: fully classical adversaries (CC), post-quantum adversaries (QC) where the adversaries have a quantum computer but have only classical access to the encryption queries, fully quantum adversaries (QQ) where the adversaries and the honest participants are all quantum. We then define CC-CPA (the traditional IND-CPA), QC-CPA, and QQ-CPA notions using the corresponding type of adversaries.

Next, we observe that these three notions coincide with the CPA notions in **Q0, Q1**[1], **Q3** classes defined by Gagliardoni [12], which could be of independent interest.

Finally, we prove the quantum CPA-security of the first two composite encryption schemes presented in [14]. In particular, our results show that the two composite schemes are QC-CPA secure if at least one of their components is QC-CPA secure.

Comparisons with Some Existing Works. Note that [3,13,15,17] proposed composite KEM schemes and proved the CCA-security of the resulting composite schemes. However, they did not consider the capability changes of the adversaries during the transition process. More specifically, they only allowed fully classical adversaries, and did not consider the quantum random oracle queries that QC adversaries could have made[2]. In contrast, we prove the QC-CPA security of the two composite encryption schemes [14]. To be fair, the differences lie in the facts that they [3,13,15,17] proved CCA-security while we only prove CPA security. It is an intriguing open problem to prove QC-CCA security for the composite encryption schemes [14], and to extend their results to QC-CCA security.

Organizations. In Sect. 2, we first recall definitions of public key encryption, key encapsulation mechanism, and the quantum CPA-security definitions according to [12]. In Sect. 3, we then provide our new quantum CPA-security according to the footprint by Bindel et al. [4,5]. Section 4 then provides the quantum CPA-security of the first two composite encryption schemes presented in [14]. Finally, we conclude the paper in Sect. 5.

---

[1] **Q1=Q2** when we consider the CPA security of PKE.

[2] This argument does not apply to the constructions proposed in [13] that do not use hash functions or random oracles.

2   Preliminaries

Public Key Encryption Schemes. A public key encryption scheme PKE consists of the following three polynomial-time algorithms.

Keygen(1^λ). Given the security parameter λ, this algorithm outputs encryption-
    decryption key pair (pk, sk). Note that pk also specifies the message space
    $\mathcal{M} = \{0, 1\}^\ell$ and ciphertext space $\mathcal{C} = \{0, 1\}^{\ell_c}$ for two positive integers ℓ, ℓ_c.
Enc(pk, m). Given the public key pk and a message m from the message space
    $\mathcal{M}$, this algorithm outputs a ciphertext c.
Dec(sk, c). Given the secret key sk and a ciphertext c, this decryption algorithm
    returns a message m' or $\perp$ indicating decryption failure.

Correctness. A PKE scheme is said to be correct if for any $\lambda \in \mathbb{N}$, for any
m, any (pk, sk) $\leftarrow$ Keygen(1^λ), we have Dec(sk, Enc(pk, m)) $= m$ with all but
negligible probability.

Definition 1 (IND-CPA security of PKE). *Let* PKE *be a public key encryption scheme, and* $\mathcal{A}$ *be any PPT adversary. Then* PKE *is said to be IND-CPA secure if the advantage of* $\mathcal{A}$, *defined as* $\mathbf{Adv}_{\text{PKE},\mathcal{A}}^{\text{CPA}}(1^\lambda) = |\Pr[\mathbf{Exp}_{\text{PKE},\mathcal{A}}^{\text{CPA}}(1^\lambda) = 1] - \frac{1}{2}| = \mathsf{negl}(\lambda)$.
    $\mathbf{Exp}_{\text{PKE},\mathcal{A}}^{\text{CPA}}(1^\lambda)$.
    (pk, sk) $\leftarrow$ Keygen(1^λ).
    $b \leftarrow \{0, 1\}$.
    $(m_0, m_1) \leftarrow \mathcal{A}(\text{pk})$ *with* $m_0, m_1 \in \mathcal{M}$.
    $c = \text{Enc}(\text{pk}, m_b)$.
    $b' \leftarrow \mathcal{A}(\text{pk}, c)$
    Return $(b' = b)$.

We now recall the syntax of key encapsulation mechanism (KEM) and its IND-CPA definition.

Let KEM be a KEM scheme that consists of three polynomial-time algorithms.

Keygen(1^λ). Given the security parameter λ, this algorithm outputs encryption-
    decryption key pair (pk, sk). This algorithm also specifies the key space $\mathcal{K} = \{0, 1\}^\ell$ and ciphertext space $\mathcal{C} = \{0, 1\}^{\ell_c}$ for two positive integers ℓ, ℓ_c.
Encap(pk). Given the public key pk, this algorithm outputs a ciphertext c and
    a key $k \in \mathcal{K}$.
Decap(sk, c). Given the secret key sk and a ciphertext c, this decryption algo-
    rithm returns a key k' or $\perp$ indicating decapsulation failure.

Correctness. A KEM is said to be correct if for any $\lambda \in \mathbb{N}$, any (pk, sk) $\leftarrow$
Keygen(1^λ), and any $(c, k) \leftarrow$ Encap(pk), we have that Decap(sk, c) $= k$ with
overwhelming probability .

Definition 2 (IND-CPA security of KEM). *Let* KEM *be a key encapsulation mechanism, and* $\mathcal{A}$ *be any PPT adversary. Then* KEM *is said to be IND-CPA secure if the advantage of* $\mathcal{A}$*, defined as* $\mathbf{Adv}_{\mathsf{KEM},\mathcal{A}}^{\mathsf{CPA}}(1^\lambda) = |\Pr[\mathbf{Exp}_{\mathsf{KEM},\mathcal{A}}^{\mathsf{CPA}}(1^\lambda) = 1] - \frac{1}{2}|$*, is negligible.*

$\mathbf{Exp}_{\mathsf{KEM},\mathcal{A}}^{\mathsf{CPA}}(1^\lambda)$
$(\mathsf{pk}, \mathsf{sk}) \leftarrow \mathsf{Keygen}(1^\lambda).$
$b \leftarrow \{0, 1\}.$
$(c, k_0) \leftarrow \mathsf{Encap}(\mathsf{pk}).$
$k_1 \leftarrow \mathcal{K}.$
$b' \leftarrow \mathcal{A}(\mathsf{pk}, k_b, c).$
Return $(b' = b).$

2.1 Quantum CPA-Security of PKE

Gagliardoni [12] in his thesis defined quantum security in several categories to encompass different types of scenarios in the presence of quantum devices. Post quantum security, captured by the so-called **Q1** principle, allows the adversary to have quantum access whenever the security model implies that the adversary computes the function on his local device. Superposition-based quantum security, depicted by the **Q2** principle, allows an oracle to be accessible by the adversary in a quantum way if such oracle is accessible in the classical way. They also considered the fully quantum world **Q3**. In [12], they formulated the post quantum security and fully quantum security of PKE, which we recall below. It is worth noting that the post-quantum security **Q1** and superposition-based **Q2** quantum security notion coincide regarding the CPA-security of PKE (Fig. 1).

Definition 3 (quantum IND-CPA security of PKE). *Let* PKE *be a public key encryption scheme, and* $\mathcal{A}$ *be any quantum PPT adversary. Then* PKE *is said to be post quantum IND-CPA secure if the advantage of* $\mathcal{A}$*, defined as* $\mathbf{Adv}_{\mathsf{PKE},\mathcal{A}}^{\mathsf{pq\text{-}CPA}}(1^\lambda) = |\Pr[\mathbf{Exp}_{\mathsf{PKE},\mathcal{A}}^{\mathsf{pq\text{-}CPA}}(1^\lambda) = 1] - \frac{1}{2}|$ *is negligible. Then* PKE *is said to be fully quantum IND-CPA secure if the advantage of* $\mathcal{A}$*,* $\mathbf{Adv}_{\mathsf{PKE},\mathcal{A}}^{\mathsf{fq\text{-}CPA}}(1^\lambda) = |\Pr[\mathbf{Exp}_{\mathsf{PKE},\mathcal{A}}^{\mathsf{fq\text{-}CPA}}(1^\lambda) = 1] - \frac{1}{2}|$*, is negligible. Note that we let* $\mathcal{A}$ *output* $|\mathsf{state}\rangle$*, indicating that* $\mathcal{A}$ *is quantum.*

$\mathbf{Exp}_{\mathsf{PKE},\mathcal{A}}^{\mathsf{pq\text{-}CPA}}(1^\lambda).$	$\mathbf{Exp}_{\mathsf{PKE},\mathcal{A}}^{\mathsf{fq\text{-}CPA}}(1^\lambda).$
$(\mathsf{pk}, \mathsf{sk}) \leftarrow \mathsf{Keygen}(1^\lambda).$	$(\mathsf{pk}, \mathsf{sk}) \leftarrow \mathsf{Keygen}(1^\lambda).$
$b \leftarrow \{0, 1\}.$	$b \leftarrow \{0, 1\}.$
$(m_0, m_1, |\mathsf{state}\rangle) \leftarrow \mathcal{A}(\mathsf{pk}).$	$(|m_0\rangle, |m_1\rangle, |\mathsf{state}\rangle) \leftarrow \mathcal{A}(\mathsf{pk}).$
$c = \mathsf{Enc}(\mathsf{pk}, m_b).$	$|c\rangle = \mathsf{Enc}(\mathsf{pk}, |m_b\rangle).$
$b' \leftarrow \mathcal{A}(\mathsf{pk}, c, |\mathsf{state}\rangle).$	$b' \leftarrow \mathcal{A}(\mathsf{pk}, |c\rangle, |\mathsf{state}\rangle).$
Return $(b' = b).$	Return $(b' = b).$

Fig. 1. Experiments $\mathbf{Exp}_{\mathsf{PKE},\mathcal{A}}^{\mathsf{pq\text{-}CPA}}(1^\lambda)$ and $\mathbf{Exp}_{\mathsf{PKE},\mathcal{A}}^{\mathsf{fq\text{-}CPA}}(1^\lambda).$

3   New Quantum CPA-Security of PKE and KEM

We have just seen the classical and quantum definitions of PKE following the **Q0**, **Q1**, **Q3** principles. Here, we follow the footprint by Bindel et al. [5] to define a hierarchy of intermediate notions, distinguishing between whether honest parties are encrypting classical or quantum messages (i.e., does the adversary have access to classical or quantum challenge queries?), and whether the adversary is classical or quantum. Our hierarchy is as follows.

1. Fully classical adversary (CC): the adversary at all times uses only a classical computer and computer ciphertext for classical messages. This corresponds to the traditional IND-CPA security notion.
2. Quantum adversary, classical queries (QC): the adversary at all times can use a quantum computer. However, the honest participants in the system only use encryption keys on classical computers, so the challenge queries are always accessed classically.
3. Fully quantum (QQ): The adversary at all times can use a quantum computer, obtains challenge ciphertexts from a quantum encryption oracle.

Note that CQ is not considered, where the adversary has a classical computer while the honest users have a quantum computer.

We then define CC-CPA, QC-CPA, QQ-CPA security of PKE by letting the adversary be of CC, QC, and QQ type. It is then not hard to see that the notion of QC-CPA of PKE coincides with that of post quantum CPA, and QQ-CPA coincides with that of fully quantum CPA. We, however, will use the terms QC-CPA and QQ-CPA instead of pq-CPA and fq-CPA in this manuscript.

Regarding the QC-CPA and QQ-CPA security of KEM, we propose the following Definition 4 according to the different types of adversaries.

Definition 4 (quantum IND-CPA security of KEM). *Let* KEM *be a key encapsulation mechanism, and* $\mathcal{A}$ *be any quantum PPT adversary. Then* KEM *is said to be QC-CPA secure if the advantage of* $\mathcal{A}$*, defined as* $\mathbf{Adv}_{\mathsf{KEM},\mathcal{A}}^{\mathsf{QC\text{-}CPA}}(1^{\lambda}) = |\Pr[\mathbf{Exp}_{\mathsf{KEM},\mathcal{A}}^{\mathsf{QC\text{-}CPA}}(1^{\lambda}) = 1] - \frac{1}{2}|$ *is negligible. Then* KEM *is said to be QQ-CPA secure if the advantage of* $\mathcal{A}$*,* $\mathbf{Adv}_{\mathsf{KEM},\mathcal{A}}^{\mathsf{QQ\text{-}CPA}}(1^{\lambda}) = |\Pr[\mathbf{Exp}_{\mathsf{KEM},\mathcal{A}}^{\mathsf{QQ\text{-}CPA}}(1^{\lambda}) = 1] - \frac{1}{2}|$*, is negligible.*

4   Composite Encryption Schemes

To deal with the advent of quantum computer, the internet engineering task force (IETF) [14] had explicitly defined three composite encryption modes. In this work, we will focus on the first two modes. The first mode utilizes N different PKE schemes and the second is a generalization of the first one that supports a mixture of PKE and KEM. However, they did not consider the security of those composite encryption schemes. Therefore, we will first describe the two schemes and then prove their security (Fig. 2).

$\mathbf{Exp}_{\mathsf{KEM},\mathcal{A}}^{\mathsf{QC\text{-}CPA}}(1^\lambda)$	$\mathbf{Exp}_{\mathsf{KEM},\mathcal{A}}^{\mathsf{QQ\text{-}CPA}}(1^\lambda).$
$(\mathsf{pk},\mathsf{sk}) \leftarrow \mathsf{Keygen}(1^\lambda).$	$(\mathsf{pk},\mathsf{sk}) \leftarrow \mathsf{Keygen}(1^\lambda).$
$b \leftarrow \{0,1\}.$	$b \leftarrow \{0,1\}.$
$(c,k_0) \leftarrow \mathsf{Encap}(\mathsf{pk}).$	$(|c\rangle, |k_0\rangle) \leftarrow \mathsf{Encap}(\mathsf{pk}).$
$k_1 \leftarrow \mathcal{K}.$	$|k_1\rangle \leftarrow \mathcal{K}.$
$b' \leftarrow \mathcal{A}(\mathsf{pk}, k_b, c).$	$b' \leftarrow \mathcal{A}(\mathsf{pk}, |k_b\rangle, |c\rangle).$
Return $(b' = b).$	Return $(b' = b).$

Fig. 2. Experiments $\mathbf{Exp}_{\mathsf{KEM},\mathcal{A}}^{\mathsf{QC\text{-}CPA}}(1^\lambda)$ and $\mathbf{Exp}_{\mathsf{KEM},\mathcal{A}}^{\mathsf{QQ\text{-}CPA}}(1^\lambda).$

4.1 Composite Key Transport Using Encryption

Let $E_1, \ldots, E_N$ be $N \geq 2$ public key encryption schemes. We now describe the first composite key transport scheme by combining these N schemes.

$\mathsf{CKT1.Kg}(1^\lambda).$ For each $i \in [1, N]$, run $(\mathsf{pk}_i, \mathsf{sk}_i) \leftarrow E_i.\mathsf{Kg}(1^\lambda).$ Return $\mathsf{pk} := (\mathsf{pk}_1, \ldots, \mathsf{pk}_N)$ and $\mathsf{sk} := (\mathsf{sk}_1, \ldots, \mathsf{sk}_N).$

$\mathsf{CKT1.Enc}(\mathsf{pk}, \mathsf{CEK}).$ To encrypt a binary message CEK of length ℓ, this algorithm performs the following steps.

1. Sample $S_1, \ldots, S_{N-1} \overset{\$}{\leftarrow} \{0,1\}^\ell.$
2. For $i \in [1, N-1]$, compute $C_i = E_i.\mathsf{Enc}(\mathsf{pk}_i, S_i).$
3. Compute $S_N = \mathsf{CEK} \oplus S_1 \ldots \oplus S_{N-1}$ and $C_N = E_N.\mathsf{Enc}(\mathsf{pk}_N, S_N).$
4. Return $\mathsf{CT} := (C_1, \ldots, C_N).$

$\mathsf{CKT1.Dec}(\mathsf{sk}, \mathsf{CT}).$ Parse $\mathsf{CT} := (C_1, \ldots, C_N).$ This algorithm performs the following steps.

1. For each $i \in [1, N]$, compute $S_i' \leftarrow E_i.\mathsf{Dec}(\mathsf{sk}_i, C_i).$
2. Compute $\mathsf{CEK}' = S_1' \oplus \ldots \oplus S_N'.$
3. Return $\mathsf{CEK}'.$

Correctness. The above composite key transport scheme is correct as long as the underlying N encryption schemes are correct.

CPA-security. We prove the CPA-security of the above composite key transport scheme in Theorem 1. It implies that as long as one of the underlying encryption scheme is QC-CPA secure, then the resulting composite key transport scheme is QC-CPA secure.

Theorem 1. *For $i \in [1, N]$, let E_i be X_iY_i-CPA secure encryption scheme. Here $X_iY_i \in \{\emptyset, CC, QC\}$, where $X_iY_i = \emptyset$ means that the scheme is not even IND-CPA secure. Then the above composite key transport scheme CKT1 is $\max\{X_iY_i\}_{i\in[1,N]}$-CPA secure.*

Proof. First of all, let us consider the case where at least one of the schemes is QC-CPA secure. Without loss of generality, assume E_1 is QC-CPA secure. We would like to prove that the above composite scheme CKT1 is QC-CPA secure.

Our idea is to reduce the QC-CPA of E_1 to the QC-CPA of the composite scheme. In particular, assume that $\mathcal{A}$ is an adversary that wins the experiment $\mathbf{Exp}_{\mathsf{CKT1},\mathcal{A}}^{\mathsf{QC\text{-}CPA}}(1^\lambda)^3$ with non-negligible advantage ϵ, we now construct an adversary $\mathcal{B}$ that wins $\mathbf{Exp}_{\mathsf{E1},\mathcal{B}[\mathcal{A}]}^{\mathsf{QC\text{-}CPA}}(1^\lambda)$ with non-negligible advantage $\epsilon' \geq \epsilon$, by running $\mathcal{A}$ as a subroutine.

Let $\mathcal{C}$ be a challenger that interacts with $\mathcal{B}$ in $\mathbf{Exp}_{\mathsf{E1},\mathcal{A}}^{\mathsf{QC\text{-}CPA}}(1^\lambda)$. To begin with, $\mathcal{C}$ runs $(\mathsf{pk}_1, \mathsf{sk}_1) \leftarrow \mathsf{E}_1.\mathsf{Kg}(1^\lambda)$ and sends pk_1 to $\mathcal{B}$. Upon receiving pk_1, $\mathcal{B}$ also generates $(\mathsf{pk}_i, \mathsf{sk}_i) \leftarrow \mathsf{E}_i.\mathsf{Kg}(1^\lambda)$. Set $\mathsf{pk} := (\mathsf{pk}_1, \ldots, \mathsf{pk}_N)$ and $\mathsf{sk} := (*, \mathsf{sk}_2, \ldots, \mathsf{sk}_N)$. Next, $\mathcal{B}$ invokes $\mathcal{A}$ by sending pk to $\mathcal{A}$.

At some point, $\mathcal{A}$ outputs two messages $\mathsf{CEK}_0, \mathsf{CEK}_1$ to $\mathcal{B}$. The latter then samples $S_2, \ldots, S_N \xleftarrow{\$} \{0,1\}^\ell$ independently and defines $S_{1,0} = S_2 \oplus \ldots \oplus S_N \oplus \mathsf{CEK}_0$ and $S_{1,1} = S_2 \oplus \cdots \oplus S_N \oplus \mathsf{CEK}_1$. Next, $\mathcal{B}$ sends $S_{1,0}$ and $S_{1,1}$ to $\mathcal{C}$ and receives back a ciphertext $C_1 = \mathsf{E}_1.\mathsf{Enc}(\mathsf{pk}_1, S_{1,b})$ for a randomly chosen bit b. Also, $\mathcal{B}$ computes $C_i = \mathsf{E}_i.\mathsf{Enc}(\mathsf{pk}_i, S_i)$ for $i \in [2, N]$. Finally, $\mathcal{B}$ sends $(C_1, \ldots, C_N)$ to $\mathcal{A}$ and receives back a bit b'. Then $\mathcal{B}$ relays b' to $\mathcal{C}$.

First, we argue that $\mathcal{A}$ could not tell the difference of the above simulated view from $\mathcal{B}$ and a real view from an authentic challenger involved in $\mathbf{Exp}_{\mathsf{CKT},\mathcal{A}}^{\mathsf{QC\text{-}CPA}}(1^\lambda)$. Note that in the simulation,

$$(S_1, S_2, \ldots, S_N) = (S_2 \oplus \cdots \oplus S_N \oplus \mathsf{CEK}_b, S_2, \ldots, S_N), \tag{1}$$

where $S_2, \ldots, S_N$ are chosen independently and uniformly from $\{0,1\}^\ell$. In the real experiment,

$$(S_1, S_2, \ldots, S_N) = (S_1, S_2, \ldots, S_{N-1}, S_1 \oplus \cdots \oplus S_{N-1} \oplus \mathsf{CEK}_b), \tag{2}$$

where $S_1, \ldots, S_{N-1}$ are chosen independently and uniformly from $\{0,1\}^\ell$. It is not hard to verify that two distributions of (1) and (2) are the same, therefore $\mathcal{B}$ perfectly simulates the view of the adversary $\mathcal{A}$.

Therefore, if $\mathcal{A}$ could be able to tell the difference of a ciphertext of CEK_0 from that of CEK_1, then (1) implies that $\mathcal{A}$ could tell the difference of a ciphertext of $S_{1,0}$ from that of $S_{1,1}$. As a result, $\mathcal{B}$ can use $\mathcal{A}$ to win the experiment $\mathbf{Exp}_{\mathsf{E1},\mathcal{B}[\mathcal{A}]}^{\mathsf{QC\text{-}CPA}}$. Therefore, the advantage of $\mathcal{B}$ is no less than that of $\mathcal{A}$, i.e., $\epsilon' \geq \epsilon$.

Next, let us consider the case where all schemes are just CC-CPA secure or not secure at all. It is then straightforward to prove that the composite key transport scheme is $\max\{X_i Y_i\}_{i \in [1,N]}$-CPA secure. Due to high similarities with the first case, we omit the details.

$\square$

4.2   Composite Key Transport Using Encryption and KEM

Let $E_1, \ldots, E_N$ be $N \geq 2$ public key encryption schemes or key encapsulation mechanism. The second composite key transport scheme works as follows. It is worth mentioning that E_N in this composite scheme must be an encryption scheme due to the design.

---

[3] Note this experiment is the same as $\mathbf{Exp}_{\mathsf{CKT1},\mathcal{A}}^{\mathsf{pq\text{-}CPA}}(1^\lambda)$.

CKT2.Kg(1^λ). For each $i \in [1, N]$, run $(\mathsf{pk}_i, \mathsf{sk}_i) \leftarrow \mathsf{E}_i.\mathsf{Kg}(1^\lambda)$. Return pk : $(\mathsf{pk}_1, \ldots, \mathsf{pk}_N)$ and sk := $(\mathsf{sk}_1, \ldots, \mathsf{sk}_N)$.

CKT2.Enc(pk, CEK). To encrypt a binary message CEK of length ℓ, this algorithm performs the following steps.

Let st =: 1.

  1. If $\mathsf{st} < N$ and E_i is a PKE, then sample a random $S_i \stackrel{\$}{\leftarrow} \{0,1\}^\ell$ and compute $C_i = \mathsf{E}_i.\mathsf{Enc}(\mathsf{pk}_i, S_i)$. st =: st + 1.

  2. If $\mathsf{st} < N$ and E_i is a KEM, then compute $(C_i, S_i) = \mathsf{E}_i.\mathsf{Encap}(\mathsf{pk}_i)$. st =: st + 1.

  3. $\mathsf{st} = N$. Compute $S_N = \mathsf{CEK} \oplus S_1 \ldots \oplus S_{N-1}$ and $C_N = \mathsf{E}_N.\mathsf{Enc}(\mathsf{pk}_N, S_N)$.

  4. Return CT := $(C_1, \ldots, C_N)$.

CKT2.Dec(sk, CT). Parse CT := $(C_1, \ldots, C_N)$. this algorithm performs the following steps.

  1. For each $i \in [1, N]$, compute $S_i' \leftarrow \mathsf{E}_i.\mathsf{Dec}(\mathsf{sk}_i, C_i)$ or $S_i' \leftarrow \mathsf{E}_i.\mathsf{Decap}(\mathsf{sk}_i, C_i)$.

  2. Compute $\mathsf{CEK}' = S_1' \oplus \ldots \oplus S_N'$.

  3. Return CEK'.

Correctness. The above composite key transport scheme is correct if the employed encryption and KEM are all correct.

CPA-security. We observe that it suffices to consider the CPA-security of the second composite key transport scheme that employs a single KEM as E_1 and a single encryption scheme E_2. This is because that the proof for the general case could be easily adapted from that for the simplified case where a single KEM and a single encryption scheme are used. We now prove the CPA-security of this simplified case in Theorem 2. As in Theorem 1, it implies that the second composite key transport scheme is QC-CPA secure if one of the employed schemes is QC-CPA secure.

Theorem 2. *Let E_1 be a X_1Y_1-CPA secure KEM and E_2 be a X_2Y_2-CPA secure encryption scheme. Here $X_iY_i \in \{\emptyset, CC, QC\}$. Then the composite key transport scheme* CKT2 *constructed from E_1, E_2 is* $\max\{X_1Y_1, X_2Y_2\}$-*CPA secure.*

Proof. We prove this theorem via two reductions. For $i \in \{1, 2\}$, if there exists an adversary $\mathcal{A}$ that breaks the $\max\{X_1Y_1, X_2Y_2\}$-CPA security of CKT2, then we build $\mathcal{B}_i$ to break the $\max\{X_1Y_1, X_2Y_2\}$-CPA security of E_i. Here $X_iY_i \in \{\emptyset, CC, QC\}$. Let $\max\{X_1Y_1, X_2Y_2\} = QC$ since the other case $\max\{X_1Y_1, X_2Y_2\} = CC$ would then be straightforward.

Reduction 1. Let $\mathcal{A}$ be the adversary involved in experiment $\mathbf{Exp}^{\mathsf{QC\text{-}CPA}}_{\mathsf{CKT2}, \mathcal{A}}(1^\lambda)$ with non-negligible advantage ϵ, we now construct $\mathcal{B}_1$ that wins the experiment $\mathbf{Exp}^{\mathsf{QC\text{-}CPA}}_{\mathsf{KEM}, \mathcal{B}_1[\mathcal{A}]}(1^\lambda)$ with non-negligible advantage.

Let $\mathcal{C}_1$ be the challenger that interacts with $\mathcal{B}_1$ in $\mathbf{Exp}^{\mathsf{QC\text{-}CPA}}_{\mathsf{KEM}, \mathcal{B}_1[\mathcal{A}]}(1^\lambda)$. First, $\mathcal{C}_1$ runs $(\mathsf{pk}_1, \mathsf{sk}_1) \leftarrow \mathsf{KEM.Kg}(1^\lambda)$, samples a random bit c and a random key $S_{1,1}$, computes $(C_1, S_{1,0}) \leftarrow \mathsf{KEM.Encap}(\mathsf{pk})$, and sends $(\mathsf{pk}_1, C_1, S_{1,c})$ to $\mathcal{B}_1$. Upon receiving the tuple from $\mathcal{C}_1$, $\mathcal{B}$ also generates $(\mathsf{pk}_2, \mathsf{sk}_2) \leftarrow \mathsf{PKE.Kg}(1^\lambda)$ and sends $(\mathsf{pk}_1, \mathsf{pk}_2)$ to $\mathcal{A}$.

$\mathcal{A}$ then sends two keys $\mathsf{CEK}_0, \mathsf{CEK}_1$ to $\mathcal{B}_1$. Afterwards, $\mathcal{B}_1$ samples a random bit b and computes $C_2 \leftarrow \mathsf{PKE.Enc}(\mathsf{pk}_2, \mathsf{CEK}_b \oplus S_{1,c})$. $\mathcal{B}_1$ then sends (C_1, C_2) to $\mathcal{A}$. Upon receiving a bit b' from $\mathcal{A}$, $\mathcal{B}_1$ outputs $c' = 0$ guessing that $S_{1,c}$ is encapsulated in C_1 if $b' = b$ and $c' = 1$ otherwise. The challenger $\mathcal{C}_1$ then outputs 1 if $c' = c$.

We now calculate the advantage of $\mathcal{B}_1$, denoted by ϵ'. Consider the following two cases.

Case 1 $c = 0$: In this situation, $\mathcal{B}_1$ perfectly simulates the view of $\mathcal{A}$. Thus $\mathcal{A}$ outputs $b' = b$ with proability $1/2 \pm \mathbf{Adv}_{\mathsf{CKT2},\mathcal{A}}^{\mathsf{QC\text{-}CPA}}(1^\lambda)$. Thus $\mathcal{A}$ outputs $b' = b$ with probability $1/2$. Thus, $\mathcal{B}_1$ outputs $c' = 0$ with probability $1/2 \pm \mathbf{Adv}_{\mathsf{CKT2},\mathcal{A}}^{\mathsf{QC\text{-}CPA}}(1^\lambda)$.

Case 2 $c = 1$: In this situation, both C_1 and C_2 have no information about b. Particularly, $S_{1,c}$ perfectly hides CEK_b. Thus $\mathcal{A}$ outputs $b' = b$ with probability $1/2$. Thus, $\mathcal{B}_1$ outputs $c' = 0$ with probability $1/2$.

Let us now compute the advantage of $\mathcal{B}_1$, denoted as ϵ'.

$$\epsilon' = \mathbf{Adv}_{\mathsf{KEM},\mathcal{B}_1[\mathcal{A}]}^{\mathsf{QC\text{-}CPA}}(1^\lambda) = \left| \Pr[\mathbf{Exp}_{\mathsf{KEM},\mathcal{B}_1[\mathcal{A}]}^{\mathsf{QC\text{-}CPA}}(1^\lambda) = 1] - \frac{1}{2} \right|$$

$$= \frac{1}{2} \left| \Pr[c' = 0 | c = 0] - \Pr[c' = 0 | c = 1] \right|$$

$$= \frac{1}{2} \left| 1/2 \pm \mathbf{Adv}_{\mathsf{CKT2},\mathcal{A}}^{\mathsf{QC\text{-}CPA}}(1^\lambda) - \frac{1}{2} \right|$$

$$= \frac{1}{2} \mathbf{Adv}_{\mathsf{CKT2},\mathcal{A}}^{\mathsf{QC\text{-}CPA}}(1^\lambda).$$

Reduction 2. Let $\mathcal{A}$ be the adversary involved in experiment $\mathbf{Exp}_{\mathsf{CKT2},\mathcal{A}}^{\mathsf{QC\text{-}CPA}}(1^\lambda)$ with non-negligible advantage ϵ, we now construct $\mathcal{B}_2$ that wins the experiment $\mathbf{Exp}_{\mathsf{PKE},\mathcal{B}_2[\mathcal{A}]}^{\mathsf{QC\text{-}CPA}}(1^\lambda)$ with non-negligible advantage.

Let $\mathcal{C}_2$ be the challenger that interacts with $\mathcal{B}_2$ in $\mathbf{Exp}_{\mathsf{PKE},\mathcal{B}_2[\mathcal{A}]}^{\mathsf{QC\text{-}CPA}}(1^\lambda)$. First, $\mathcal{C}_2$ runs $(\mathsf{pk}_2, \mathsf{sk}_2) \leftarrow \mathsf{PKE.Kg}(1^\lambda)$, and sends pk_2 to $\mathcal{B}_2$. Upon receiving pk_2 from $\mathcal{C}_2$, $\mathcal{B}_2$ also generates $(\mathsf{pk}_1, \mathsf{sk}_1) \leftarrow \mathsf{KEM.Kg}(1^\lambda)$ and sends $(\mathsf{pk}_1, \mathsf{pk}_2)$ to $\mathcal{A}$.

At some point, $\mathcal{A}$ outputs two keys $\mathsf{CEK}_0, \mathsf{CEK}_1$ and sends them to $\mathcal{B}_2$. Afterwards, $\mathcal{B}_2$ computes $(C_1, S_1) \leftarrow \mathsf{KEM.Encap}(\mathsf{pk}_1)$, and sends $\mathsf{CEK}_0 \oplus S_1$ and $\mathsf{CEK}_1 \oplus S_1$ to its challenger $\mathcal{C}_2$. The challenger will encrypt $\mathsf{CEK}_c \oplus S_1$ for a randomly chosen bit c, and sends the resulting ciphertext C_2 back to $\mathcal{B}_2$. $\mathcal{B}_2$ then sends (C_1, C_2) to $\mathcal{A}$. Upon receiving a bit b' from $\mathcal{A}$, $\mathcal{B}_2$ sets $c' = b'$ and then outputs c' to $\mathcal{C}_2$. Finally, $\mathcal{C}_2$ outputs 1 if $c' = c$. It is straightforward to see that the advantage of $\mathcal{B}_2$ is the same as ϵ.

To summarize, if ϵ is non-negligible, then ϵ' is also non-negligible. This concludes the proof. □

5   Conclusion and Open Questions

In this work, we propose quantum security for both PKE and KEM, following the footprint of Bindel et al. [5]. It then turns out that QC-CPA and QQ-CPA security of PKE coincide with pq-CPA and fq-CPA defined by Gagliardoni [12], which is of independent interest. With the formal definitions, we then provide security proofs for two composite key transport schemes by the IETF draft [14]. Our results show that the resultant composite schemes are QC-CPA secure if at least one of the employed building blocks is QC-CPA secure. This then offers us confidence of employing these composite schemes during the process of transiting to the fully quantum world.

A number of questions arise following this work. A first question is to formally prove the QQ-CPA security of the composite schemes. It is also interesting to provide formal proofs for the third composite scheme considered in [14]. In addition, it is quite intriguing to construct composite encryption schemes that are CCA secure and also to prove its quantum security. This is challenging as it allows quantum random oracle queries to the adversaries. Last but not the least, it would be beneficial to instantiate the above composite modes with concrete CC-CPA and QC-CPA schemes, and even further employ them in real-life scenarios.

Acknowledgments. This work is partially supported by the National Natural Science Foundation of China under Grant number 12101404, and by Huawei Technologies Co., Ltd.

References

1. National institute of standards and technology (NIST): Post-quantum cryptography: call for proposals (2017). https://csrc.nist.gov/Projects/post-quantum-cryptography/post-quantum-cryptography-standardization/Call-for-Proposals
2. Module-lattice-based key-encapsulation mechanism standard (2024). https://csrc.nist.gov/pubs/fips/203/final
3. Barbosa, M., et al.: X-wing. IACR Commun. Cryptology **1**(1) (2024). https://doi.org/10.62056/a3qj89n4e
4. Bindel, N., Brendel, J., Fischlin, M., Goncalves, B., Stebila, D.: Hybrid key encapsulation mechanisms and authenticated key exchange. In: Ding, J., Steinwandt, R. (eds.) PQCrypto 2019. LNCS, vol. 11505, pp. 206–226. Springer (2019). https://doi.org/10.1007/978-3-030-25510-7_12
5. Bindel, N., Herath, U., McKague, M., Stebila, D.: Transitioning to a quantum-resistant public key infrastructure. In: PQCrypto 2017. LNCS, vol. 10346, pp. 384–405. Springer (2017). https://doi.org/10.1007/978-3-319-59879-6_22
6. Boneh, D., Dagdelen, Ö., Fischlin, M., Lehmann, A., Schaffner, C., Zhandry, M.: Random oracles in a quantum world. In: ASIACRYPT 2011. LNCS, vol. 7073, pp. 41–69. Springer (2011). https://doi.org/10.1007/978-3-642-25385-0_3
7. Boneh, D., Zhandry, M.: Quantum-secure message authentication codes. In: EUROCRYPT 2013. LNCS, vol. 7881, pp. 592–608. Springer (2013). https://doi.org/10.1007/978-3-642-38348-9_35
8. Boneh, D., Zhandry, M.: Secure signatures and chosen ciphertext security in a quantum computing world. In: Canetti, R., Garay, J.A. (eds.) CRYPTO 2013. LNCS, vol. 8043, pp. 361–379. Springer (2013). https://doi.org/10.1007/978-3-642-40084-1_21

9. Campagna, M., Crockett, E.: Hybrid Post-Quantum Key Encapsulation Methods (PQ KEM) for Transport Layer Security 1.2 (TLS). Internet-Draft draft-campagna-tls-bike-sike-hybrid-07, Internet Engineering Task Force (2021). https://datatracker.ietf.org/doc/draft-campagna-tls-bike-sike-hybrid/07/, work in Progress

10. Castryck, W., Decru, T.: An efficient key recovery attack on SIDH. In: Hazay, C., Stam, M. (eds.) EUROCRYPT 2023. LNCS, vol. 14008, pp. 423–447. Springer (2023). https://doi.org/10.1007/978-3-031-30589-4_15

11. Crockett, E., Paquin, C., Stebila, D.: Prototyping post-quantum and hybrid key exchange and authentication in TLS and SSH. IACR Cryptol. ePrint Arch. p. 858 (2019)

12. Gagliardoni, T.: Quantum security of cryptographic primitives. CoRR abs/1705.02417 (2017). http://arxiv.org/abs/1705.02417

13. Giacon, F., Heuer, F., Poettering, B.: KEM combiners. In: PKC 2018. LNCS, vol. 10769, pp. 190–218. Springer (2018). https://doi.org/10.1007/978-3-319-76578-5_7

14. Ounsworth, M., Gray, J., Mister, S.: Composite Encryption For Use In Internet PKI. Internet-Draft draft-ounsworth-pq-composite-encryption-01, Internet Engineering Task Force (2022). https://datatracker.ietf.org/doc/draft-ounsworth-pq-composite-encryption/01/, work in Progress

15. Ounsworth, M., Gray, J., Pala, M., , Klaußner, J., Fluhrer, S.: Composite ml-kem for use in the internet x.509 public key infrastructure and CMS. Tech. rep., Internet-Draft draft-ietf-lamps-pq-composite-kem-04, Internet Engineering Task Force (2024)

16. Ounsworth, M., Pala, M.: Composite signatures for use in internet PKI. Internet-Draft Internet-Draft draft-ounsworth-pq-composite-sigs-06, Internet Engineering Task Force (2022). https://www.ietf.org/archive/id/draft-ounsworth-pq-composite-sigs-06.html

17. Ounsworth, M., Wussler, A., Kousidis, S.: Combiner function for hybrid key encapsulation mechanisms (hybrid KEMs). Tech. rep., Internet-Draft draft-ounsworth-cfrg-kem-combiners-05, Internet Engineering Task Force (2024)

18. Schanck, J.M., Whyte, W., Zhang, Z.: Quantum-Safe Hybrid (QSH) Ciphersuite for Transport Layer Security (TLS) version 1.2. Internet-Draft draft-whyte-qsh-tls12-02, Internet Engineering Task Force (2016), work in Progress

19. Stebila, D., Fluhrer, S., Gueron, S.: Hybrid key exchange in TLS 1.3. Internet-Draft draft-ietf-tls-hybrid-design-11, Internet Engineering Task Force (2024). https://datatracker.ietf.org/doc/draft-ietf-tls-hybrid-design/11/, work in Progress

20. Whyte, W., Zhang, Z., Fluhrer, S., Garcia-Morchon, O.: Quantum-Safe Hybrid (QSH) Key Exchange for Transport Layer Security (TLS) version 1.3. Internet-Draft draft-whyte-qsh-tls13-06, Internet Engineering Task Force (Oct 2017), work in Progress

21. Zhandry, M.: How to construct quantum random functions. J. ACM **68**(5), 33:1–33:43 (2021). https://doi.org/10.1145/3450745

Author Index

© The Editor(s) (if applicable) and The Author(s), under exclusive license
to Springer Nature Switzerland AG 2025
X. Lu and C. J. Mitchell (Eds.): SSR 2024, LNCS 15559, p. 187, 2025.
https://doi.org/10.1007/978-3-031-87541-0